Me. And Me Now

A 1970s' Kiwi Hippie Trail Adventure

Alan Samson

Writers Ink
Apt 5317, Meadowbank Village
148 Meadowbank Rd
Auckland 1072, New Zealand
alanmsamson@gmail.com

ISBN 978-0-473-53140-9

Design and typesetting by Ann Howarth

Cover photo: an uneasy calm in Bangkok
at the end of Thailand's 1973 10-day war.
Title page photo: author Alan Samson, 1973.
Back cover photo: courtesy Kleoe Aoki.

Every effort has been made to trace the copyright holders and obtain permission to reproduce photos. Please get in touch with any enquiries or any information relating to images or the rights holder.

Dedication

This memoir of self-exploration along the "hippie trail" in the early seventies is for Alastair. I dearly hope that its expression of his father's flaws, mistakes, idiocies and recklessness will provide him – and any other reader – with some insights into the trail, the times, and the author's eccentricities. I hope too that it gives readers enjoyment. At the very least it was a rollicking good adventure.

[The hippie trail] … youthful travellers whose motivations and hopes seem incredibly naïve from today's perspective, but who, nevertheless, often displayed a fearless attitude to travel and an optimistic expectation that their journeys would be transformational (S. Gemie & B. Ireland, *The Hippie Trail: A History*).

Acknowledgements

A very special thanks is owed to my friend Ann Howarth who helped me hugely with every aspect of the confusing publishing process and whose enthusiasm, unbeknown to her, on several occasions kept me from giving up. Thanks too to the close friends and relatives I have incessantly peppered for support over several years who could not be blamed for doubting a published work would ever see the light of day: alphabetically, Karen Goodger, Ken Samson, Greg Stutchbury, Ali Tocker and Alastair Tye Samson.

Contents

Introduction

The following is the story of a young New Zealander's travels through Southeast Asia, India, Pakistan and Afghanistan in the early 1970s. The trek itself might not have been unique, but the times certainly were. These were the days of heightened idealism among many of the world's youth as the Vietnam War escalated before the inconceivable defeat of the mighty power that was the United States of America. These were also the days of a mass migration of young travellers, many styling themselves as "hippies" or "freaks", wandering the so-called "hippie trail", beginning from the southern hemisphere or the northern, but invariably landing in Asia.

Along the way, these travellers invariably saw and did many of the same things. Their's was a commonality of interest spurred on by an internationally burgeoning anti-war movement, fuelled further by a healthy dollop of idealism and experimentation – the last an odd mix of drugs and the great eastern religions. Some of their adventures were extraordinary. Like thousands of others, I dabbled in all of the above. Part of a madding crowd, my experiences might hardly be worth a second look, except for the fact – perhaps as a latent journalist – I kept an extensive diary of not only my dabblings, but an eye on the smouldering background of the South and Southeast Asian region.

These were truly historic times for South and Southeast Asia: wars continuing, wars ending, wars looming, not to mention coups and insurgencies. Through all, the hippie trail wound its inexorable way, largely oblivious to its political surroundings. Unfortunately, on the relatively few occasions its story has been told, it has been overly romanticised – or trivialised. But it, too, is part of the history. If for that reason alone, this one man's experience of the tide bears telling. I hope it is of interest.

Footnote

The "Me. And Me Now" title for my retrospective is not my invention, but I hope it captures something of the metamorphoses forged out of the life-forming journeys of the thousands of young men and women who for decades have embarked on lengthy travels and, upon their inevitable and expected return, steered their ensuing lives and philosophies from a base of their experiences. Even though his reference was to something else entirely ("All yielding she tossed my hair. Kissed, she kissed me. Me. And me now"), I thank the rollicking James Joyce (*Ulysses*) for his inventiveness.

For authenticity, I have adhered to the names of places as they were at the times of my travel. Ceylon was newly renamed Sri Lanka, East Pakistan had recently become Bangladesh, but Myanmar was still Burma, Yangon still Rangoon, Mumbai still Bombay etc. For reasons of courtesy and privacy, I refer to my numerous travelling companions by their first names only, reserving surnames for officials or otherwise significant characters, confident that even the most indiscreet of their stories will not put them in harm's way after a nearly 50-year hiatus.

Alan Samson

Me

By the time I reached my twenties, I had done the not-uncommon, in fact expected Kiwi thing of lurching through numerous, disparate jobs, played sport with little skill but great enthusiasm, as well as the similarly young Kiwi thing of over-drinking and partying. I grew up with New Zealand's notorious 6 o'clock swill. I did not do drugs, though not from any purity of spirit – they simply were not a part of my or my friends' repertoire. I had no clear idea of what I wanted to do with my life.

Then, nearly 50 years ago, I had an OE (overseas experience) that changed my outlook on different cultures, religions, philosophies, and aspirations. It was an OE born out of others' as well as self-expectations – what else was a Kiwi supposed to do in his early 20s? Notably, it was also an OE that unexpectedly plunged me into the early 1970s' maelstrom of a Vietnam War-era "hippie trail", marked by drugs, spiritual seeking, and a healthy dollop of idealism. And when I returned home, miraculously, I found my way into journalism, that imperfect but rich profession that, to this day, encourages the pursuit of truth and fairness.

The "hippie trail" I stumbled into is difficult to quantify. The concept comes with no clear boundaries let alone definition. It cannot be explained according to where its travellers departed from, or the precise routes that they took. But for thousands of young travellers heading to the heart of the Middle East and South and Southeast Asia in the 1960s and 1970s – typically to Nepal, India and Afghanistan and, for some, on to North Africa – it was a powerful magnet.

In their *The Hippie Trail: A History*, Gemie and Ireland assert the trail had no official existence. "No flag identified its territory; no organisation directed its travellers; no leader wrote its manifesto; no prominent philosophers attempted to make sense of it; no major novelists have written about it; and no archive has been created to preserve its memory." The researchers found two "reasonably articulate" arguments used to justify doing the trail: a search for cheaper, better or more easily available drugs, and a spiritual quest. "Many travellers found that there was another, equally important, dimension to their experience: their inner journey. In other words, travelling along the trail affected them."

Significant to the trail was the opening up of cheap overland travel from the late 1950s and the commercial coach tours that proliferated not too much later, with promises of destinations that "ordinary tourists" could not experience. With these, evolved the partly snobbish distinction between "tourist" and "traveller", the former suggestive of being guided to holiday or sightseeing destinations, the latter of an unstructured wander involving somehow more profoundly experiencing a region. Of course, at the start of my travels, none of this had meaning for me. I was simply setting off on an OE.

When Gemie and Ireland asked interviewees if they had thought of themselves as hippies, only a few said yes. They quite sensibly therefore adopt the term "hippie-trailers", rather than "hippies". These days, of course, the key overland routes of these travellers, whether from Asia to Europe or vice versa, are closed. It is no longer possible for anyone, let alone "drug-smoking hippies", to wander aimlessly through Afghanistan or Iran. Add to this the tighter economic times young New Zealanders are increasingly finding themselves caught up in, and the practice of OE, at least in its long-form, meandering nature, sadly, seems to be on the decline. Kiwis are still great travellers, but the practice typically now requires putting down roots abroad and a lot of working and saving along the way. Add a pandemic to the mix and the whole world is off-limits for free-style travel!

OE is, of course, jargon for "overseas experience", a rite of passage in which the young – not just Kiwis – head off abroad before settling down. In the Kiwi version, however, the departure has been typically not for a wimpish month or two, but years. The Downunder practice emanated from the reality of growing up in a small country far from the heavily populated rest-of-the-world, and a correlating expectation that travel anywhere was only worthwhile if the trip was a long one. The distance from New Zealand to Europe is nigh on 20,000kms. Even reaching fellow Downunder-ers across the ditch requires navigating roughly 2500kms of vast, sparse Pacific Ocean; by comparison, London to Stockholm is a scant 1500kms jaunt through countrysides of heavily populated wayfarers' cornucopia. Small wonder that OEs out of New Zealand have been known to last decades!

Looking back now over my hippie trail/OE memory snapshots, I will try to live up to the Joycean inspiration, even though the emphasis is necessarily on *intent*, not ability. But before my story gets underway it is probably sensible to offer an opinion – right at the start – what makes this "hippie trail" OE in any way noteworthy. Why bother?

One could argue just putting to paper one Kiwi's adventures – and his inevitable return home – is in a small way the story of generations of New Zealanders, telling a story that to some degree is revealing of the essence of them all. But it is also interesting, I think, for its timing. The early 1970s were, after all, the years or the coat tails of momentous events like the Vietnam War, India's conflicts with China and Pakistan, the secession of Bangladesh from Pakistan, Thailand's remarkable "10-day war", and the "Yom Kippur" assault on Israel by Egypt and Syria, not to mention a flourishing Asian traffic in American draft dodgers – all claiming to be Canadians – and the momentum given in consequence for what amorphously became known as the trail. It was a time of changing attitudes, a questioning of authority, and a widespread rejection of many of society's traditional norms.

A window can be cast on these changing attitudes by exploring the reading material favoured by these mostly young travellers. The Gemie and Ireland survey reveals a remarkable commonality of books read. Setting aside times of bookshop famine when choice was dictated by what was available, almost everyone they polled had read Jack Kerouac's *On the Road*, Hermann Hesse's *Siddhartha* and, slightly after my travel time, Robert Pirsig's *Zen and the Art of Motor Cycle Maintenance*. To this list, one could add Alan Watts' *The Book: On the Taboo Against Knowing Who You Are*, his earlier *The Way of Zen*, Carlos Castaneda's *The Teachings of Don Juan: A Yaqui Way of Knowledge*, and many others.

Gemie and Ireland refer too to the commonality of the music listened to – The Beatles, the Rolling Stones, Jimi Hendrix, Cream, and various authors of the psychedelic. One could easily add to the list Bob Dylan and Joan Baez. But it might be a stretch to use these bands/singers as exemplars of any one section of society. Among the young, their reach was simply too universal. One could however highlight a typical determination among such travellers to explore the history, religions and culture of the societies encountered along their journeys.

What hasn't changed over the years is the enduring pull of home. This is not just true of Kiwi travel. Pasternak shows a clear understanding of the homing urge when he says of his character Yuri Andreyevich, returning to his beloved Moscow after years of war and revolution: "The first real event since the long interruption was this vertiginous home-coming ... in the knowledge that his home was still safe, still existing somewhere, with every smallest stone in it dear to him. This was the point of life, this was experience, this was the quest of the adventure seekers and what artists had in mind – this coming home to your family, to yourself, this renewal of life (*Doctor Zhivago*)."

Camus too captures the essence of the return in his essay *Between Yes and No*: "If it is true that the only paradises are those that we have lost, I can find a name for this tender and inhuman feeling which inhabits me today. An emigrant is returning to his country. And I am remembering. The irony and tension fade away and I am back at home ... we have only one detail to recreate all this love, but this is enough: the smell of a room that has been shut up for too long, the particular sound of a footstep on the road ..." (*Selected essays and notebooks*).

My favourite account, however, comes from Kiwi icon Janet Frame, about to end her troubled sojourn abroad. "When I was about to go home to New Zealand I did not need reasons for returning; but others needed to know why, to have explanations," she wrote. "I could have said that, sitting at my sewing machine table looking out at the fields of East Suffolk, I had known a sensation of falseness, of surface-skimming ... the feeling, perhaps, when after writing a letter and sealing it and writing the address on the envelope one might find that the stamp won't hold ... whatever my reasons for returning to New Zealand, I knew I would try to make them sound as elevated as possible; but I did experience this unease in Suffolk, knowing that thousands of miles away there was a cabbage tree or a clump of snowgrass or a sweep of sky ..." (*The Envoy from Mirror City*).

Many Kiwi OEs have been exciting, some remarkable, some shrouded in mystery. An example of all three may be that of home-grown "spy", civil servant Bill Sutch who in the early 1930s travelled extensively through the United States, Europe, Scandinavia, Afghanistan and the then Soviet Union, though some of his experiences may have been exaggerated. In his book *Bill & Shirley: A memoir*, his son-in-law Keith Ovenden calls his claim of an epic walk from the Arctic Circle to India via the Caucasus and Afghanistan, "hokum"; 1997 research by former New Zealand ambassador to Moscow Jim Weir, similarly concludes that at least part of his journey was little more than a tourist visit. Nevertheless, various reports have him sleeping rough on his travels ("to see how the poor of other countries had to live") and contracting malaria in India. His detractors would claim the Soviet leg, just before the worst of the Stalinist purges, was where he was "turned" and became a traitor.

The travel of this Kay One Double-U One had prosaic origins, ensuing from an inexplicable decision, in the very first couple of days, to walk out on a paid return ticket to Tel Aviv to begin a two-year meander from Bangkok – with a few side turns – to Kabul. There was nothing prosaic, however, about the outcomes. With a casual, thoughtless wander into the shining offices of a Singaporean airline office, perhaps seeking air conditioning, I changed the course of my odyssey and who I would become. For a green young man barely turned 20 it was a life-changing decision, with much of that metamorphosis owing to the new freedoms of the trail – explorations with drugs and religion, and the heady highs to be gleaned from just wandering, doing what one wanted, when one wanted.

My life growing up in Christchurch had been closeted, though not always easy. I and my older brother Ken lost our engineer father to a wasting illness (the rare auto-immune disease pemphigus vulgaris) when I was 10, Ken 14, brought up subsequently by a loving mum who tried hard but did not always manage to control her sons or cope well with what life threw at her. She was a prominent feminist of her time, working hard for and leading numerous causes, most notably the making of jury service compulsory for women (a step towards gender equality), and in persuading a requirement for common drugs such as aspirin and panadol to be only available in foil tabs (an anti-suicide measure). Paradoxically, one of her favourite aphorisms was, "whenever times get really hard, splash out on yourself" – invariably meaning a bottle of good Scotch.

The sudden loss of income saw the family uprooted, moving from comfortable Bryndwr suburbia to an un-insulated fibrolite house, unconnected to sewerage or water, in the seaside village of Brooklands. During our time there, thanks to mum's persistence, we progressed from night cart collection to long drop to septic tank. I vividly remember the excitement of our first-ever fridge and our first-ever, flickering, black and white television. We had a well that delivered brackish water. Every winter our pipes froze – and cracked – and we'd huddle for warmth around an ineffective fireplace. But with a nearby lagoon and river we had idyllic access to water sports and fishing and endless outdoor play. In summer, life was great.

Older brother Ken confidently threw his teenage self at his sport almost as a metaphor for life. By the time of my travel, after having briefly hung his work-life flag to a couple of international companies, he was already enjoying adventures that took him and his then wife to South Africa from where they crewed a trimaran to the US Virgin Islands. There they settled for a while, both finding paid work with the American Peace Corps.

By contrast, I followed a somewhat tortuous path without any sort of clarity about what I wanted to do or be, leading me through a tangle of jobs: police cadet, housemaster at a boys' welfare home, more of the same at a local school for the deaf, a stint clearing sports fields of stones at a nearby army camp, hotel steward, cocktail barman, trainee hotel manager, culminating in a lively two years as a flight steward with home airline, Air New Zealand. The last dangled a carrot to its employees of a 90 per cent discount on international flights, a carrot extended – as a one-off – to anyone resigning after having worked fulltime there for a minimum of two years. The deal only applied for a return ticket. I chose Tel Aviv, Israel – there and back – for NZ$40!

It is the first days of January 1973. My airline background has paid off. Former colleagues on this first leg to Singapore have plied me with free champagne and, on landing, the chief steward has graciously allowed me to share the cabin crew bus into town. But that's where the honeymoon has ended. There is no way I can afford the four and five-star luxury of the hotels the stewards will be – that I once was – staying in. So when I'm dumped on the side of, though familiar, affluent streets near Orchard Road I feel abruptly alone. I am hopelessly underprepared, overdressed, clueless about how to find cheap accommodation, and struggling under a massive pack insanely bought a week earlier in a Cashel St, Christchurch sale.

In my first half-hour on the road, I am offered drugs.

PART A: TRAIL ADVENTURES

The author's forged press card – essential
for access to many forbidden locations.

The author's forged student card – the key to
accommodation and other discounts.

Singapore joined the Federation of Malaysia in 1963, ending 144 years of British rule broken only by Japan's WWII occupation. In 1965, amid growing ethnic tensions, it seceded as an independent republic. The last British forces withdrew in 1971, though a token presence remained a couple of years more (New Zealand maintained a presence till 1989). 1973: iron-fisted, founding prime minister Lee Kuan Yew, is still in power. He is unsympathetic to the "flower-power", "hippie" infestation that has descended upon Southeast Asia.

I

Singapore sting

Singapore to Thailand: in which a young traveller learns how to be wary – and how to take chances; embracing serendipity; and the peculiar joys of youth hostelry.

There is a glorious rainbow that beckons those with the spirit of adventure ... look at the horizon, find that rainbow, go ride it. Not all will be rich; quite a few will find a vein of gold; but all who pursue that rainbow will have a joyous and exhilarating ride (Lee Kuan Yew).

I don't do drugs, officer

Under warm, late-afternoon sky shroud, breathing heavily in the mildly cloying atmosphere of the tropics, I try to put the affluent behind me, walking quickly from the grandeur of Singaporean shopping malls into a sudden web of grey plaster housing, faded and stained.

I'm 23 years old, without guidebook or useful preparation, and haven't a clue how I'm going to find an affordable hotel. I'm in new-country daze and it's starting to get dark. I know I stand out like a sore thumb, dressed in clean-cut clothes and my pack bright orange and big enough to dwarf Mt Kilimanjaro. I'm feeling nervous.

And that's when I'm approached by a group of four men, comically, even more well-dressed than I am. They're wearing dark grey office-work pants and smart jackets. "Would you like to buy some drugs?" Really, it was that stilted. There is no mention of what type of drugs they are offering, nor any flavour of street talk. They are serious, polite and well spoken. There's no mucking round, no street language. Even to a newbie, they are out of place and I squint at them my uncertainty. The instant decision I make is a good one.

"Sorry, I don't do drugs," I mutter. Which at the time is true. "Are you sure? Good price." They stare at me for what seems an eternity before turning with almost military precision and disappearing down a side alley. I sense their disappointment.

I find out what is going on later after one of those inevitable discussions travellers get into. But I have already guessed: ramrod Prime Minister Lee Kuan Yew is firmly entrenched in power and even beginning travellers like myself are imbued with stories of forced haircuts for the untidy and the birch for the misbehaving. It is neither the place nor the time to take risks. Was it an Australian who was caned recently for scratching a car? In this instance – much more dangerous – there is a crackdown going on against drug use among backpackers. Entrapment is par for the Singaporean course. It's a sting.

This is January 1973, post-60s' flower-power idealism but the culture lingers among dreamy-eyed European, Australasian and American travellers. And the authorities in conservative Asia are not always impressed.

Soon after, I am heartened by two young boys who corral me, peppering me with friendly questions. "Have you been to America? How about England? Have you seen Manchester United play?" Thanks to Air New Zealand largesse I can nod the affirmative for the first two, failing at the third hurdle, but I assume heroic stature when I am able to gush along with them about the magic of George Best.

This is an odd feeling for a newbie, walking an old part of town with no clear destination. The boys lead me to a drab Bencoolen St hotel – NZ$2.50 per night. It has only the bare essentials, but it's comfortable. Showers and toilets are on the floor below, the former comprising a tap and a bucket, the latter my first squat. There is no hot water. Remembering advice given me by my much-travelled brother, I thump-wash my sweat-laden clothes on the floor of the shower, as I shower.

On my first night, truly alone on the edge of Asia, I have plenty of time to think. The attempted sting had shaken me a little. A prison cell on the first day might have been a disastrous if storybook start to my OE and, in a sense, it was my inexperience that had saved me. Buy drugs? Even if I had the inclination, I lacked the courage or any sense of procedure that might have encouraged me to barter. And in the unlikely event I had been given any, I would have had no idea what to do with them.

Sitting on my bed in my unadorned hotel cell, my mind was spinning. An initial moment of self-doubt – could I cope with this sort of solo travel malarkey – soon passed. But was Israel important to me? With just the remnant of NZ$40 at risk from a change of plans, I could do anything I wanted. It was just a thought, without substance but consuming. Back in my room after a jaunt to a nearby street mee (noodle) stall, I fell asleep alone, reflecting on a philosophy expounded randomly by the driver of the airline cabin crew bus into town. "A man without money," he had told me after hearing of my underfunded, unstructured travel plans, "is a man without soul." On that basis, I thought with a flash of panic, I might be just about to lose mine.

Hitting the suburbs the next morning, I investigated the first romantic idea that popped into my head: replacing Israel as a destination with the Soviet Union via the trans-Siberian railway. But my vague new plans were soon dashed. Few of the travel agencies I spoke to had heard of the trans-Siberian, let alone of Vladivostok, the eastern starting point. The Soviet embassy politely suggested I seek out Soviet Shipping. *If* I managed to book a ticket, they told me, there would be no trouble with a visa. Soviet Shipping – of course on the other side of town – was less helpful. "Sorry, we take no passengers on our boats." Air India gave me an address for an Indian shipping company that it said definitely visited Vladivostok – but could only be boarded from Bombay.

Another long walk took me to the shipping company's small offices near celebrated Raffles Place where I was politely advised: "Sorry we take no passengers on that run." Clearly the Soviet Union – at this stage of my travels – was not going to happen. Walked-out and exhausted, I treated myself to a lonely Malay meal at a corner stall, consoling myself that one day I would make that journey.

But the next few days changed everything. Biting the bullet, I confirmed my onward flight to Bangkok – still part of my $40 extravaganza – but not before bravely taking a huge punt and cancelling the next leg to Israel. To this day, I am unsure why, though I remember feeling dizzy from the heat and revelling in the air conditioning of the airline office in question.

From then on, in the way of all free-style travel, all manner of possibilities began to pop into my life. A travelling companion would later philosophise: "Adventures aren't just available to a fortunate few. The trick isn't just to recognise the opportunities but to act on them, which very few have the courage to do." I didn't have to wait long.

Good companions

At Bangkok's Don Mueang airport, an announcement was made about a significant delay to the on-going flight, which, given my cancellation, obviously no longer applied to me. But it included an airline offer of a room in which to freshen, plus free lunch and dinner at the comfortable Mandarin Hotel. Rationalising that such serendipity rarely befell me, I cheekily tested the airline's efficiency. No one checked my entitlement and, learning fast, I gratefully accepted a wad of gratis coupons – and a free tourist bus into town.

Asia had not yet sunk in. I had walked a few busy streets in Singapore and now travelled a flash bus to a flash hotel looking just like every other flash hotel I had stayed in during my airline tenure, without ever absorbing anything. I had arrived in downtown Bangkok, without a glimpse of the city through tinted glass bus windows.

Probably because of my unkempt appearance – I had changed into jeans and was unshaven – I was given haughty treatment by hotel staff, but a beautiful hot shower made the indignity worthwhile. Then it registered: I had nowhere to stay and no plans. Sitting nervously amid the luxury, I went through my things, unearthing a youth hostel guide that indicated nearby premises, repacked my giant pack, and headed out into town. The hostel was difficult to find but after a few wrong turns I tracked it down in the grounds of a large school parked on the edge of a university. It was decrepit and dusty, but adequate. For someone under 24, the cost was 13 baht a night – about NZ60c.

This was the start of my adventure. There was a diverse group of travellers here, all of them looking at ease and at home. Sue, from Portland, Oregon talked tantalisingly of having hiked South America, Europe and much of Asia. As the sun went down, I slept fitfully on a hard bed barely cushioned by a thin mattress, sharing the pleasure with what seemed like a million mosquitos. The hostel had provided mosquito nets but my inexperience at putting such a thing up left a gaping door for the midnight visitors.

The next day, a Saturday, people gravitated to the hostel dining area, and not only hostellers. During the afternoon, we were surprised by the visit of an Australian soldier, a Captain Paul Jackson of SEATO (South East Asia Treaty Organisation), a United States-led body set up "to halt the spread of communism". Why he felt the need to drop in on a group of suspect-looking youth hostellers, I had no idea, but he was pleasant enough and we heard him out politely as he spoke persuasively of "non-military" activities, of the "educational" work being done among the Thais.

This was new ground for me but – despite the on-going Vietnam conflict – I was sceptical as he continued to assert a looming communist threat to greater Asia and beyond, the much talked of "domino effect". To vigorous questioning, he conceded the threat was "less than before", but would not accept that this was due to a shift in public thinking from outdated cold war mentalities. His generation's "yellow peril" was still very real for him. SEATO, of which New Zealand was a member, remained extant till 1975, after the end of the war.

After he left, I talked about the conflict with Sue, an Australian from Sydney, and a Japanese man from Stockholm. All of us were fierce Vietnam War opposers, with home memories of watching incredible pictures of death and violent protests on our televisions. It was the first time any war had entered living rooms in such a way and, as a consequence, it was hardly surprising that each of us was emotional in our opposition. I had vivid memories of my mother and me standing in silence around our black and white set at news times. Caught up in my travels, I had mentally parked the war to one side, even though I was at this moment just a few hundred kilometres from conflict.

The talk became gentler as we switched topics to travel, perhaps because the Japanese man pulled out a chillum, patiently leading me through the process of smoking it. I cloaked my inexperience by claiming it was the use of a pipe that was new to me. By the end of the session, I had ambitiously decided to fly to Calcutta, to then hike on through Europe with, for some reason, Athens as an end point. But first, the others persuaded me, I should join them in a jaunt to the northern town of Chiang Mai, a town reportedly awash with wonderful food – and good weed.

And so it proved. After first exploring Bangkok by crook and cranny, the four of us, dreamily tackled Chiang Mai and its abundant pleasures. But when Sue suggested we move on to try to enter still-at-war Laos, only I jumped. This was new for me, an of-the-moment decision leading to a monumental change of plan. But I was an easy apostle and, a few weeks later, Sue and I were on a bus headed for the northern town of Fang.

Unbeknownst to us, three days earlier, United States president Richard Nixon had called a halt to bombing in North Vietnam, but the larger region, including in Laos and Cambodia, was still very much at war. Unbeknownst to almost everyone, under the inoffensive catch-title "Operation Freedom Deal", large-scale bombing had been stepped up in Cambodia.

Laos did not yet pan out for us – we were barred from crossing the Mekong by the Thai authorities. Cambodia did.

> With victory in Vietnam elusive, the US in 1969 began bombing North
> Vietnamese forces in Cambodia; in 1970, Cambodian army head Lon
> Nol ousted Prime Minister Sihanouk, proclaimed a Khmer Republic,
> and sent his army to root out North Vietnamese forces in his country.
> 1973: Phnom Penh is effectively under siege, the US steps up bombing,
> and the Vietnam "peace" pact is signed. Lon Nol suspends offensive
> operations in vain hope of a cease-fire – and the U.S embarks on more
> than 150,000 further bombing missions.

II

A tiger ready to pounce

Cambodia: joining a military convoy to besieged Phnom Penh;
shepherded away from gunfire by loyalist soldiers; shuddering
under the drone of B52 bombers; and an abortive attempt
to reach occupied Angkor Wat.

*In 1970 a military coup ... overthrew the government of Prince Sihanouk
and American and South Vietnamese troops entered Cambodia. One estimate
is that 600,000 people, nearly 10 per cent of the Cambodian population
were killed in this extension of the war* (J. Glover, *Humanity:
A Moral History of the 20th Century*).

Peace please, but not the Viet Cong

You could visit Cambodia in 1973. But the stern-faced embassy official
in Bangkok wanted some assurances before he would issue us with visas.
"Will you give an undertaking you will fly to Phnom Penh? That you will
visit only Phnom Penh? And that you will leave the same way?"

Cambodia – in 1973 known as the Khmer Republic – was a mess.
Nominal leader was vice-fisted Marechal Lon Nol. But by 1973, the
vice-fist was corroding. Despite devastating, and continuing, American
bombing, it was a country very much out of the marshal's control.

The southern capital, Phnom Penh was deemed "safe", as was Battambang, the northern administrative outpost near the Thai border. Pailin, the lawless, western mining town, was deemed marginally so. Much of the land between, however, belonged to whoever's soldiers happened to be passing through at any particular moment of time. Asian wonder of the world Angkor Wat was in the hands of the Khmer Rouge. And according to US Airforce records declassified by US President Bill Clinton in 2000, B52 bombing raids would continue over wide areas of the country till August 1973. I arrived in the last week of January.

Still travelling with Sue, I discovered at the Khmer embassy in Bangkok how travel-smart she was. In response to his questions and without lying, she asked the embassy man politely about flights into Phnom Penh and, reassured, he stamped our passports. The next day we caught a train to Thai border town Aranya Prathet, then took a short bus trip to Poipet, the last Thai outpost. Here our papers were cleared by a surprised official torn between the knowledge that no "tourists" were allowed to cross at this border and the indisputable fact our visas were in order. "I don't know," Sue replied to his questioning. "We just applied and got it."

From Poipet, there were two kilometres – and numerous competing taxis – to the border. We walked it. At the final stage of the crossing, was a 200m strip of no-man's land, a sombre walk between flags and gun posts. On the Cambodian side was a train, a glorious steam antique about to depart for Battambang. It was awash. People were falling out of windows, clinging to carriage roofs. This was our style! We rushed to the ticket office, ordered third class tickets, and immediately banged heads with Khmer inscrutability. The ticket man nodded politely – and relieved us of a first-class fare. A brisk gesture, and a guard materialised to escort us to a first-class cabin reserved for just four people. We could not complain: the 150km trip cost us about 80c.

In our carriage, we introduced ourselves to a friendly Cambodian couple who shared with us their mangostine and sugar cane, while the outside of our cabin throbbed under the weight of literally hundreds of outriders, all clinging precariously to anything it was possible to keep a grip on. The task of the latter was made more difficult by the enormous amount of baggage they were desperately clinging to. As the train chugged into motion, there was a flurry of excitement as a man leapt from rooftop to the ground in a vain attempt to avoid armed police.

The train shunted laboriously. It stopped frequently. And at each fathomless stop, there was a surge of excitement as the outriders dived into bushes, retrieving carefully wrapped packages to add to their already voluminous stores. There had to be a thriving black market and we wondered just what goods were held in such high regard. Already it was evident the war had caused prices to rise astronomically.

At Battambang, we found a local wat (Buddhist temple) where we asked if we might spend the night. As was to happen frequently on my travels, we were welcomed graciously, with charm and kindness. The only clue to the war was the head monk's insistence I accompany him to the police station to have my passport number noted. For some reason, they just needed documentation from the man.

The monk had a clear intellect and calm that I would forever associate with the Khmer. He spoke Khmer, of course, but also French, English, more than one Chinese dialect, and was learning German. Not for the last time, I shrank at the exposure of my own monolingualism. At night we were paraded in front of a classroom of young, aspiring monks and questioned about our lives and our home countries. The head monk treated the occasion as a teaching exercise. They were not reluctant to discuss the war. "We want peace," one told us, "but not the Viet Cong."

There was a 6am bus for Phnom Penh. By 9am, the last of the passengers had boarded and the bus started. But it immediately stopped and emptied. "Sorry," a passenger translated for the driver. "It is now too late for the bus to make Phnom Penh before curfew." Taxi! Battambang had what they called "collective taxis", meaning they essentially served as buses, cramming in whoever had the coin. The 291km journey cost us 500 riel ($2.50) and the travel was less than luxurious. After we were squeezed into a section of the back seat, the cab moved sluggishly into the middle of a military convoy – truck after truck of uniformed soldiers, all with guns slung casually about their bodies.

Our cab was jammed between towering khaki buckboards. Avenues of trucks. We moved. We stopped. Every few kilometres, we stopped. At strange military outposts, boy scout barrier arms, and more soldiers. At each of these outposts, our driver slipped a banknote to the soldier on duty. Sometimes, he rolled the note and dropped it on the road and a soldier sauntered across to retrieve it.

Middle Cambodia unravelled for us as a green, attractive country, tropicana. Only, the houses along our route belied the image. Their walls were burnt and blasted. And the road itself was shell-shattered and furrowed. In fact, the road was so bad our trip lasted a full eight hours. Avenues of trucks flowed each way and jams and congestions were numerous and monotonous. I frequently had time to get up and walk around. The soldiers were surprised, some openly amused, by my presence. I was given gifts of fruit. Nobody talked about the war. Or the blasted, deserted houses.

First sign of Phnom Penh was the stark Sangkum Bridge, known locally as the Japanese bridge. It was in utter despair. Its middle pillar had been obliterated and the girders beside were collapsed, sunk in Mekong tributary, the Tonle Sap. How safe was Phnom Penh? Soldiers outnumbered ants. Every street was lined with barbed wire barricades, ready to be swung across the road at the 10 o'clock curfew. Along Moha Vithei 9 Tola, one of the main streets, the guard posts eyed the civilian population warily from vantage points in front of infinite government ministries and, a little further along, from outside the Chamcar Mon, the offices of the President of the Republic of Khmer.

Boys seemingly hardly passed 10 and girls little older, wore the army green with the ease of old soldiers. Only the occasional impish grin betrayed youth. All inner roads in Phnom Penh were protected by wire. Finding reasonably priced accommodation was not easy. We had to argue before being accepted as guests at an "unauthorised" hotel but, thankfully, were successful. The differences in price were spectacular.

Paris Accord

The next day we walked the gauntlet of barbed wire to the American Embassy where we were told a peace treaty, the Paris Peace Accord, was due to be signed the next day – tomorrow – Saturday, January 27, 1973!

The agreement, I was told candidly by an official, required the Americans to withdraw all its troops. Other terms included: All prisoners, including those of Laos and Khmer, were to be returned to their respective nations of origin within 60 days; the Viet Cong were not to infiltrate Laos or Khmer; earlier Geneva agreements were to be abided by; US was to help South Vietnam economically; South Vietnam was to retain its autonomous government; and North Vietnam must recognise the sovereignty of South Vietnam. I wondered how effective all this would be.

"Ho! Ho!" An Australian journalist parked at the embassy gave us his terse take on the possibility of actual peace. He told us the Khmer Rouge had strategically buried secret caches of weapons for later retrieval. "Even if they agree to leave, what's to stop them returning," he asked. He was adamant local insurgents Khmer Rouge, would continue their fight. "You can't blame [North Vietnam leaders] Ho Chi Minh and Le Duan for this state of affairs. On the contrary. The [1954] Geneva Conference agreed to a temporary division for Vietnam before elections that would choose a president and reunite the country. It's the Americans who are responsible for the war's persistence. It's the Americans who have ignored the terms of the accord."

He was disturbed by our travelling overland to Phnom Penh. Some of the areas we had covered were still under the control of the Khmer Rouge. "You must have encountered Khmer Rouge without realising it." He was unsurprised when we mentioned the payments required en route. Needless to say, he thought us fools and we did not argue.

Sue and I walked to the post office, a building outside the city centre. As we reached it, gunfire echoed about us. Abruptly, soldiers surrounded us, herding us back towards the town centre. The firing was close, though from the other side of the Mekong, perhaps a kilometre from where we had been standing. As we returned to the centre, the screams of urban living – notably the ubiquitous pinball alleys – drowned out the gunfire. The locals seemed unaware. Then it was 10 o'clock and the strictly enforced curfew clamped all townsfolk to their beds. It was deathly quiet.

Strangely, the city did not seem frightened, nor overly depressed. Only the barbed wire and those youthful eyes peeping inquisitively from under their too-large American army helmets seemed to herald war. And the gunfire. The next morning we were told that US Embassy staff were forbidden under any circumstances to leave inner city limits. Perhaps that was not surprising considering our previous night's experience. This day, as we ventured across the Tonle Sap, soldiers were indiscriminately firing off practice rounds into the river from a moored vessel named "Ally", at angles defying common sense.

We had a glimmer of more peaceful times when we sneaked in to the Royal Palace to watch the once renowned Royal Cambodian Ballet at rehearsal. No one hindered us. But it was a surreal interlude to watch young women and men leaping and swaying for an hour of non-stop grace. The operation of the company had been suspended since the advent of war. I was told this was a rare – closed – practice.

By the Monday, news of the "peace" accord had reached all of Phnom Penh. Huge posters were stretched across the streets liberally daubed in Khmer lettering. But there was no elation. A townsman keen to practise his English translated for us. "The Khmer will not fall for the talk of peace," he said. "The Vietcong will not withdraw, regardless of what's been signed. They will simply become Khmer Rouge. Before, the Khmer Rouge were very small. Now they will become very large and powerful."

The posters warned against complacency. They likened the Vietcong to the tiger – dangerous, unpredictable, and ready to pounce. Flags flew from every shop frontage. Broadcasts of peace emanated from infinite transistors. But the Khmer citizenry remained impassive. One had the feeling that life would continue as it had yesterday and would again tomorrow. The cries of peace seemed an anachronism, the tiger of the flags a good analogy. From then on, we stayed close to the city centre.

I've come to shoot the enemy

A few days later, Sue and I boarded a landrover taxi bound for Psa Tmo Puok, the final stopping place before the Banteay Chhmar ruins, a last safe point before the site of the fabled Angkor Wat temple complex. We had been told Angkor Wat could not be reached because it was in the hands of the Khmer Rouge. Naïvely, we thought we would give it a try.

The ride was, as usual, rough with dust, smothering scenery that in other circumstances might have been attractive. Wizened water buffalo treading their centuries-old paths paid scant attention to the youths at their helm, let alone a pair of strange-looking Westerners. We might have forgotten the war, if not for the deep growls of unseen aircraft overhead. "B52s," muttered a fellow passenger authoritatively. We arrived at Psa Tmo Puok shortly after midday where we were straightway accosted by a Lieutenant Colonel Suo Hnel, second in charge to the governor of the local military base. Taking firm control, he drove us to the base and delivered us to a private bedroom.

He spoke no English. But from somewhere emerged an interpreter named Kol Thuom and, with his help, we managed fine. "This is no place for tourists," Kol told us, before proceeding to overwhelm us with his welcome. Through Kol, Suo stressed he wanted us to have happy memories of Khmer. Anything, but anything we wanted, we were to see him.

At 7am we left in an army jeep with Kol and a Swiss archaeologist who had arrived with a personal guide and a substantial army entourage. It was clear by now we had no chance of reaching Angkor Wat, but thanks to the timely visit of the important Swiss visitor, we had access to other relics from the 12th century era of famed Khmer ruler and temple builder, Jayavarman VII. We drove fast to Banteay Teap ("Time of the Army"), a haughty remnant of a temple of crumbling rock. A scramble among leftover towers, then a protective call from our army guides had us promptly back aboard the jeep and, not long after, we were safely at Banteay Chhmar ("Time of the Cat").

Banteay Chhmar, Kol told us, was a place for prayer and peace, notable for its Buddhist origins. With 39 decaying towers it was an imposing edifice and, as our eyes grew accustomed to the gloom of the encircling forest, we were subsumed in awe for a culture long past. Sitting under the shade of banyan trees, courtesy of camp commander Major Chieng Veng we were entertained by classical Khmer music, python-skinned drums, xylophones and gourd-shaped lyres providing eerie background as lunch was laid before us. As we dined on curried chicken served up with beer and Scotch, a 16-year-old boy we were told had been to battle three times sang mournfully about a soldier who, on his return home, had discovered his wife had left him for another.

Kol Thuom shared with us the basics of his Theravada Buddhism faith. As he emphasised the importance of good living, he was as aware as we of the irony, considering the times and what his country was going through. He sounded imponderably sad as he switched to speak of Angkor Wat, wonder of the ancient world, now a stronghold of the communists. "I believe it has been pillaged beyond recognition," he told us. It was hard to take in that Angkor Wat was a relatively short drive away from where we sat.

As he spoke, I began to sense what he had been through, the courage, the determination, expressed so softly yet firmly. He had been 16 years a monk, three years a staffer with the American Embassy in Phnom Penh, two years a guide at Angkor Wat, and was now a soldier. "I want peace. I have come to shoot the enemy," he said. Strange words. Yet perhaps not so strange.

Of the Vietcong, he was forthright: the Cong had little respect for the saffron robe and even a peaceful Buddhist would fight to protect his own. "One week ago, a cowherd reported 50 Vietcong in the jungles above Tmo Puok," he told us. "We went to our homes and armed ourselves, then sought out the enemy. We are no longer afraid. We are brave men. But we are also kindly men. You must report this to the people of your country."

Kol was convinced the war was lost for the Americans. "When the French ruled, we were frightened of the European," he said. "Then we learned not to be afraid – a little man can easily find his target from dense bush, and the European is large in size and easy to hit." Many were now revelling in their new-won confidence, he said. But the next stage should be peace.

The Scotch polished off, we washed away our meal with smar, a potent rice spirit, the Major proudly promising, "no hangovers". He elicited my impressions of Banteay Chhmar, and bade me keep in touch. But it was Kol Thuom I would remember: the double-handed handshake, his vast smile, and cocker spaniel eyes, totally expressive. In parting, he begged me to write him and told me I was a "gentle man", a compliment I treasured.

Years later I made a concerted effort from New Zealand to track him down, eliciting the help of Amnesty International. Amnesty tried hard, but was unsuccessful. It is history that the *peace* I had witnessed collapsed cruelly and it seemed improbable that this soldier and holy man, so close to the front line, had survived a lost war and the subsequent brutal rule of a man called Pol Pot.

Nixon, Number One!

It wasn't quite the end of our Khmer adventure. After returning to Battambang near the Thai border, Sue and I on whim caught another convoy, this time to the western ("wild west") town of Pailin, famous for its rubies and sapphires – and its bandits. As seal rapidly gave way to what was little more than dirt track, we began to see why an 83km journey should take seven hours.

The journey was even more animated than the ride to Phnom Penh. Guards with guns seemingly bigger than themselves leapt on and off the bus, some of them shooting rapid fire at fruit, birds and anything that looked remotely as if it had or could move. When we came to areas of vegetation, they started bush fires, ostensibly to smoke out Khmer Rouge or – more likely for this region – bandits. The previous weekend the convoy had been attacked and pitched battles had lengthened the trip to 13 hours. Gunfire was common, but we could not discern if any guerrilla activity had taken place – the convoy was of an awesome length.

We crossed sabotaged bridges at regular intervals. One collapsed behind us as we drove across and, in some areas, it was evident that trees had been felled to block the road and only recently been cleared. When we eventually reached Pailin, we carefully avoided the hotel, requesting accommodation instead at the local wat. The monks welcomed us, but with the proviso we first register at the local police station for a "letter of approval".

There, elegant-looking commissioner Inspector Loeung Chhom Phon told us in rapid-fire French, "je ne parle pas Anglais". Concentrating with school-day ears, we gathered he was concerned about our safety. Out of the blue discovering some English, he insisted we reside with him rather than at the wat. It was an uncomfortable moment. His underlings directed us to a food stall where we ate well before being massively overcharged. Fortunately, our hosts stepped in and paid for us. The Commissioner was obviously well off: he had modern stereo equipment and lived well. Later that evening he went nightclubbing in clothes even a former flight steward might envy.

These were not peaceful times. In town we looked on aghast as a man with a bloody bayonet at his side and a bleeding hand was thrust roughly into the back of a truck and driven away. We saw another man clasping a partially severed arm. Signs at the city limits screamed "Dangereux" and other such warnings. We adhered closely to a 6pm curfew.

Over the next week, we explored, starting with the Burmese-style Wat Phnom Yat, high on the hillside overlooking the town. It was a steep climb, but well worth the effort. Barely visible along the narrow road to Battambang we could see a silvery convoy, its roar out of all proportion to its size. An elderly man pointing excitedly at my beard pulled me to a lower level of the pagoda to show me a rare Buddha image – resplendent with a beard like mine. Such a revelation! We parted with 12-inch smiles. We also visited the prospecting areas where men panned streams with baskets, shaking and swirling and sifting with fingers. Alongside, in huge chasms, generators belched water and workers threw pans of sludge skywards, catching them adroitly. The scene reeked of an earlier century.

Meantime, I modified my views of the inspector: despite his pretence he knew no English, he was kindly and, at times, almost shy. One night, his brother dropped by and talked freely to us about the war, notably of the "abduction" by China of Prime Minister Prince Sihanouk on March 18, 1970. In fact, after he was toppled from power that year, Sihanouk had fled to China to form a government in exile. When the time came for us to leave, the brother carefully wrote his personal details in my notebook – before abruptly having second thoughts and insisting I tear out anything that might lead back to him!

Back in Battambang, Sue and I were invited to join a Khmer family for a hotel meal. We drank Negrita rum which, we were informed – along with President Nixon – was "Number One"! Our host repeatedly toasted Nixon for ending the war. Of course, none of us predicted the continued bombing, nor the rise of Pol Pot who, in three years, would stamp his brutal mark as Prime Minister of Democratic Kampuchea. Khmer suffering was far from at an end.

Singapore was the only member state to quit the Malaysian federation, and all that remained resented the economic successes of their ethnic Chinese populations. In 1968, coinciding with the Vietnam War, the Malayan National Liberation Army (Chinese armed wing of the Malayan Communist Party) ambushed security forces in the northern Peninsular Malaysia. 1973: spearheaded by the Liberation Army, communist factions continue a campaign of bombings and assassinations that extends into East Malaysia.

III

Hitching and headhunting

West to East Malaysia: the vagaries and joys of hitchhiking; a cave sleepover on an island for two; a longhouse encounter with dried heads; and plotting a path across the jungles of Borneo.

A successful war-party returning home makes no secret of its success …
as the villagers come out to gaze on them, those who have taken heads
stand up in the boats. The heads, slightly roasted, are wrapped up in
palm leaves and placed in baskets in the stern of the boat
(Hose and McDougall, *The Pagan Tribes of Borneo, Vol. 1*).

Moon spirits

Sitting at a Georgetown, Penang stall, Sue and I struck up a conversation with a middle-aged Chinaman named Mr Ong. I had him help me with some Malay translations, which somehow segued into a torrid lecture on the plight of the Chinese. His fervour took me by surprise. I was aware of the insurgency that had erupted on the peninsula in 1968, and of the parallel insurgency in Eastern Malaysia, but knew little beyond that. I was unaware that rebellion persisted.

Though clearly neither rebel nor terrorist, Mr Ong asserted communism was a "very desirable thing". Wary of being overheard, he praised

China's "great technical strides", pointing to its claimed eradication of venereal disease. The foreign press had simplistically labelled the uprising as "communist", he said. "At a certain level of subsistence, only the belly is important. It is only when we are fat and well fed that politics has meaning."

There was, he continued, a racist bias against the Chinese. A recent diktat required Malay to be the language of all public enterprise. In schools, this meant that all textbooks had to be in Malay, which severely limited learning. "Bahasa is simply not comprehensive enough, especially for technical subjects," he said. "Emphasis on the home language is all very well, but when it stunts educational attainment, only harm can come of it."

Tao by upbringing, Mr Ong told us he had had visions, in fact had visited the heavens, where he had been schooled by the spirits. At times he seemed like a soft-spoken Billy Graham, his visions crystal clear and his eyes shining as he spoke of them. He had been to the moon. It had at first been difficult for him to reconcile the Americans' 1969 moon walk but he now understood that lunar beings were spiritually on a different plane, invisible to unexpected visitors. "The Americans weren't first," he digressed. "When Neil Armstrong took his first step on the moon, he found a Chinese coffee shop already there waiting for them." It was a good joke.

Days later we were to hear a very different view of the communist inroads. After hitching deep into the Cameron Highlands, we came across Czech "refugee" Marlim. Well over six-feet tall, with big blond beard and a bounteous smile, he told us that before the 1968 Soviet-led Warsaw Pact invasion of his country he had been a writer though, at the time of the invasion, had been in the army.

"When they invaded, Czech people turned round all the street signs, causing the tank convoys to travel hundreds of miles off route. And when they began witch-hunts for certain individuals, free radio broadcast a plea for all Czechs to destroy the signs and all town maps. It became impossible for them to locate their targets." The Soviets were stupid, he said.

Marlim had left behind a wife and a child, divorcing his partner before fleeing. "Divorce was the only way to keep my family safe," he said. "I only live to fight communism." He had written to the South Vietnam government offering help in their struggle, but been declined. "Communists only respect the fist," he said. "Anything less is regarded as weakness." His was not the usual stance along the trail.

A few weeks later Sue and I parted company, she headed for Australia and New Zealand, I intent on seeing more of Malaysia and Indonesia. In things travel, Sue was a master and a mentor, sniffing out cheap fares like a doberman pinscher. If not for her, my adventure might never have eventuated.

Island for two

Hitching down the eastern coast to Kuan Tan, I broke my journey after spotting an appealing, seemingly uninhabited, island offshore. Though reluctant to ferry a lone person, a boatman agreed to take me for M$6, with the proviso, should he have passengers the next day, my return would be for free; should there be none, he would collect me a few days later for an additional $10. The island was Pulau Kapas.

Halfway across, he stopped to dive for exotic shells and I borrowed goggles and a snorkel to admire multi-coloured fish darting nervously. His haul was impressive. Cone shells and large spitting clams were thrown aboard while his three naked children dived seawards again and again. Eventually dropped off, I swam until the sun deserted me then walked along the beach to find I shared real estate with an elderly Malay. Living in a small shack, he had a net permanently laid to sea for his sustenance. More importantly, he had a yard full of coconuts that beckoned me hungrily. It took few signs to indicate my desires and I wandered away with a large coconut clasped firmly under my arm.

Setting up camp in a small cave at the edge of the shore I fell asleep with but ants and mosquitos for company. Sleep was at first fitful but crashing waves on reef and the lapping of surf, nudged me gently towards the new day. The sun had not yet appeared but it was already light and a delicate half-mist played games with the sea's reflections. Shortly after midday, a cacophonous roar jolted my solitude – my gamble had paid off. I jumped aboard and was taken on a further diving tour. I took no part in the fishing but happily floated.

It was mid-afternoon before I was on the road again, but I had hardly waved goodbye before a car stopped for me, going all the way to the state's capital, Kuan Tan. The Chinese driver inevitably slipped into dissatisfactions with Malay rule. The Sino-Malay riots of 1969, he said, were "an expression of strength" in response to Chinese electoral gains. Guns had been turned on the Chinese, and the foreign press had raised the spectre of communist insurgents. "We learned a bitter lesson," he said. "The Malays are 40 per cent of the population, but 90 per cent of the armed forces. To fight on would have been to invite massacre."

The White Rajah and a plan hatched

The slow-moving *Rajah Brooke* creaked with the weariness of old age. Even its name belonged to another era. The human Rajah Brooke was an Englishman, famous as the so-called "White Rajah of Sarawak" in the mid-1800s' days of imperialism when all Englishmen stood 10ft tall. Crossing the South China Sea from Singapore to Sarawakian capital Kuching, I had an assigned sleeping spot below decks in an area of wooden benches suspended by chains, propped on all sides by loosely tethered cargo. It was almost comfortable.

As the sun descended in brilliant red vestments, we passed the *Kitty Hawk*, the huge US aircraft carrier carrying planes in far greater numbers than I considered possible. A couple of months earlier, parked off the Vietnam coast, its sailors had instigated an anti-war "riot" that would later spark a Congressional inquiry into naval discipline. It would be retired to San Diego soon after.

As breakfast merged with lunch and dinner, I devoured Part 2 of Dostoevsky's *Brothers Karamazov*. I had not read Part 1 but had learned the wisdom of seizing hold of any reading material as it became available. Part 2 had come courtesy of a swap at the Singapore Youth Hostel. When my eyes tired, I befriended a young Chinese from Jahore. He could not comprehend my travelling alone. To him it seemed extraordinarily brave, and more than a little foolhardy. If he could have foreseen my next couple of months, he might have suffered an apoplexy!

Thanks to a timely semester break, I found free accommodation at Kuching's theological school, sharing a room with English Stephen and his French girlfriend, Martine. While they set out to explore, Anglican minister Father Michael shouted me a restaurant meal of sweet and sour fish and memories of the *Rajah Brooke* quickly faded.

The next day, I sat in at the local teachers' college as the priest led a discussion on the Corinthian lesson of "love". When he told his students those who loved Christ were better off than followers of other religions, I couldn't resist challenging him, albeit weakly. After, I followed him on his hospital rounds where he was more impressive. When a woman waiting for an operation told him she was afraid of dying, he told her, "That can't happen. No one would have you in the other world. You have been far too wicked!"

On the walk home, a young man accosted us, offering "nice girls". When we declined, he jumped on Father Mike, begging to be allowed to feel the size of his testicles. The Father tried to calm the man, saying rather oddly, "come with us to the house". A few other similarly inclined men encircled us, one of them putting his arms around me. My response, "piss off or I'll clock you", had the desired effect – and, I think, impressed Father Mike.

A couple of days later, clutching a letter of introduction from the father, I hitched 85km to coastal Sebangan where I presented myself at the St Luke's Anglican Church. Here I was reunited with Stephen and Martine and, with time on our hands, the three of us hatched an ambitious plan. What a great adventure it would be, one of us concocted, if we could cross the dense Bornean jungle that bisected Sarawak! We didn't have a clue how this could be achieved, though the Sri Lankan priest helpfully told us we would have to traverse ferocious rapids before crossing the rugged Dulit Range that separated this side of Sarawak from its northernmost reaches. We would also have to rely on the hospitality of the local Dyak tribespeople and their famous network of communal "longhouses".

"The Dyak tribes were once headhunters," he said matter-of-factly. "Manage all that and you should have easy access to Brunei." It was a plan! We talked long and it was close to midnight before I bedded down in the vicarage next door. Later I learned the Father had asked Stephen and Martine if he might watch while they had sex. They had declined.

Hitching solo to Betong, next town on the line, I walked for hours without sight of a vehicle before a solitary bus stopped. The driver, amused by my determination to keep walking rather than pay, took me for free, right to the door of the local St Augustine's church, for which I had another letter of introduction. Filipino Father Gaweli insisted I ate, which I did, watched with wide eyes by his adopted Iban son, Malacca. Iban was one of a complex network of Dyak tribes and sub-tribes: the boy had been rejected after his birth father dreamed his presence would bring death to the family. Father Gaweli averted the tragedy by manufacturing his own "dream": that he was to become the father of an Iban boy. And Malacca was handed over!

Dried heads on the ruai

Good deeds were the order of the day. When we told Father Gaweli of our vague plans, he arranged for us a sleepover at a nearby Iban longhouse to familiarise us with what might lie ahead. Rumah Panggi was built spectacularly on a long platform spread-eagled on stilts on a high slope above a river. We cautiously climbed a rain-slippery staircase carved from an angled log to be greeted warmly by the Tuai Rumah (headman), a loud snorting of pigs below, a screeching of tethered fighting cocks within, and a yelping of canines. Taking the Father's advice, we presented him with some tinned pork and a package of rice. These were not rich people.

The main length of the living platform – the ruai – had no dividing walls, providing sleeping space for the single men, and a working area for all. Along the edges were a few individual rooms where married couples and single women had a *semblance* of privacy. Whole families crammed into these rooms and space was at a premium. At front was a porch, where one could wash from barrels, or urinate over the side, without having to make the long hike to ground level.

The headman and his English-speaking son took us on a guided tour and, for a while, we enjoyed watching a game of Sepak Takraw, a volleyball-like game played with the feet. Back on the ruai, we were fed on huge platefuls of rice with side dishes of the pork we had brought. Harvest was just beginning, which for now spelt hardship; after, there would be festivities. Both rice and pepper were commanding good prices this year but, for the moment, belts were necessarily tightened.

In a pool off the ruai alongside bare-breasted young mothers washing clothes we lathered ourselves enthusiastically, instant entertainment for ogle-eyed children as we jumped and splashed as if at the seaside. Afterwards we returned to the main living area where we sat cross-legged for talk that, per tradition, penetrated the long hours and lilted to the sounds of bottles clanking.

Shown a copy of the Dyak Law and Adat (custom and traditional law), I buried myself in its pages of offences and penalties. If an unmarried woman became pregnant and did not claim the father, he would be fined 40 cati (a crop measure of about 1⅓ lbs, worth about M$1) and plasi menoa (redistribution of an offender's share of the common property); whoever told lies or passed false news so as to cause disturbance might be fined a pickul (100 cati); diving contests and other ordeals such as enduring boiling water or fire, were forbidden (in "diving", the guilty party was he who surfaced first). In earlier days, those who committed an undefined "major" incest were impaled together!

The term "longhouse" had nothing to do with length. From the Malay, "long" meant the mouth of a river, though might also refer to a small kampong or community. The houses originated as a collective defence against warring neighbours in days when headhunting was commonplace. In fact, six or seven proud examples wrapped in palm leaves were on display in this house, though their wrapping precluded clear identification. It was sobering to hear "Jepun" spat back at my questioning, reference to the brutal WWII occupation of Sarawak by the Japanese. Thankfully the practice had fallen from grace but I was conscious of many well-sharpened "parangs" (machetes) hanging from the walls.

We were offered "chap lang khow", a rice spirit "authorities" had declared illegal because of high incidences of tribal drunkenness. The law was clearly not taken seriously: Russian-style, we demolished each glass at one gulp. Guests were usually offered "tuak", a less potent wine, and we deemed it a privilege to have been given the stronger concoction. Approaching midnight, we made a move towards bed, knowing full well our hosts would otherwise entertain us all night out of courtesy, despite facing heavy harvesting tasks at dawn.

Waking at dawn to the cries of the cocks, we were summoned to the room of the headman's son for tea, biscuits and chat. He told us this longhouse was divided on religious grounds, the majority being Baha'i, converted from Christianity by promises of free rides into town and superior prices for crops. One group stayed at one end of the ruai, the other, in the centre. The Tuai Rumah remained "neutral", though both his son and grandchildren were Christian.

The son was pessimistic about the future. "Our communal life will disappear as the young get better educated and towns become more attractive to them," he said. A growing fascination with Western culture, "pop music and dancing", did not augur well. "The end will come when living becomes too expensive," he said. "Everybody will move to the towns and look for safe government jobs."

Base camp Belaga

It was time for our real trip to begin – crossing the Dulit Range, the steep jungle spine bisecting central Sarawak and Indonesian Borneo (Kalimantan). Straddling the border of the Kapit and Miri divisions of interior Sarawak, it promised to be a steep climb, in parts reaching 1500m, with difficult rivers with rapids to traverse in both divisions, both sides of the Dulit.

By now, we had a rough plan. Our starting point would be "base camp" settlement Belaga, the last river port accessible by regular river traffic. From there we would have to find our way up rivers we did not yet know the name of, stop at longhouses we were not sure existed, then cross over the range on foot to a river network that would somehow lead us to the seaport of Miri. From there, with more conventional means of travel at our disposal, it would surely be easy to reach the royal principality of Brunei.

And the first part was. We hitched to Sarikei on the edge of the Rajang where it spilled into the South China Sea, and boarded an express boat for Sibu. We sped up the Sungai Sarikei into the widening Batang Rajang, reaching Sibu late in the afternoon. Scoring free board at a Methodist church, we hid from a sudden downpour and got to know each other. Steven, bespectacled and earnest, was an Oxford University arts' graduate; Martine, jovial and outgoing, had studied at the Sorbonne in Paris. They were both just 22 years old yet had travelled remarkably: they had once bought a camel to be part of a month-long caravan train through the Sahara Desert! I took notes.

In the morning, we boarded another express boat and headed further up the Rajang. Amid far too many passengers, we squeezed into seats, settling awkwardly in undersized frames. Thankfully, at the first stop many disembarked. Our progress henceforth was overseen by several longhouses from which curious onlookers waved us cheerfully onwards.

At Kapit, which we reached before midday, the tribesmen were straight out of the jungle, earlobes extended like macabre flesh earrings, loincloths, long flowing black hair, and tattoos etched across arms, torsos and necks. If not for the smiles that were always evident, it might have been terrifying. It was unclear which tribes they represented. We slept, again for free, in a Methodist guesthouse.

Another early start. We scrambled under rain to catch a launch already leaving shore. Stephen and I leapt on board magnificently while Martine collapsed in mud, yards behind, only to learn this was the express back to Sibu. In sodden, mud-caked clothes, we found the Belaga-bound boat a hundred metres upstream, and joined a rush of competing tribesmen, all in loincloths. Most sported flowing locks across their shoulders, though a few had Friar Tuck roundheads or small pigtails drawn neatly at the back.

We were heading into Kayan tribe territory, at last approaching the remoteness we sought. While our craft struggled against a series of strong rapids, we basked under golden sun. There was jungle on both sides now. As night fell, a barely noticeable moon illuminated clouds, with glimpses of white tiers of gnarled woodland peering over encroaching hill shoulders.

We reached Belaga at 9pm, finding by now-expected free accommodation in a community hall. Belaga was fantastic, its heart a river platform lined by a rickety row of stalls, with a long walkway that also served as town gathering point, to talk, or just sit. At every corner there was something new: baskets with crafted black and ochre designs; public stools carved as grotesque spirits; a tearfully caged honey bear suddenly visible in a corner; partially cured beaks of the rare and sacred hornbill; peahens, dogs, children, fighting cocks, geese, ducks, jungle screams, bustle, squalor – atmosphere!

Having to frequently explain the purpose of our visit, we practised the narration, in part to make it clear in our own heads: river trip up the Koyan tributary, a footslog climb over the Dulit Range to the Tinjar river on the other side, thence upstream to any point where the intersecting Baram river might be crossed by foot. All were disparaging. Tribesmen crossed to the Tinjar, but foreigners?

Adding to our difficulty was the fact we weren't really sure ourselves. We had a destination but even that was unclear. Our "plan" was to trust others – including former headhunters – and hope. The local administrative officer was "officially discouraging"; the missionary, however, reinvigorated our hopes, promising to investigate on our behalf. All we could do now was wait.

The last river port before the interior, a government outstation and a busy trading post, Belaga was a gathering point for diverse Dyak tribes. Even with the missionary's help, there were far too many sub-tribes to get to grips with. Among the Kajangs were Kejemans, Sekapans, Punan Ba, Punan Biau, Punan Lisama, Laharans and Tanjongs; among the Kenyahs, were Badangs, Uma Kalits, Uma Bakas, Uma Kelaps, Uma Sambops, and Long Banyans. Not to mention the Shans, the Ukits, the Sepings, and the many sub-tribes of the Kayans and the Ibans ... I gave up!

At the missionary's bungalow, we met a Kejeman replete with pigtail, tattoos, and rows of brass bangles on wrists and ankles. He had come for advice after a death. Should the departed be left for two weeks on the ruai, or for one? It had been the custom for corpses to decompose in the living quarters for weeks while celebrations exhausted the finances of the relatives. The priest recommended two nights maximum!

As we plotted our travel on the missionary's map, inquisitive eyes peered at us through cracks in the door. We were forever watched and followed, our every shift measured and dissected. Each morning we were woken by bangs on doors, windows flung open, shouts and eyes everywhere, most of it friendly. One night, however, beer was slopped through our hall shutters and a torch shone into our eyes. I managed to surprise the culprits, two drunken policemen and, with a few stern words, achieved peace.

It rained intermittently, but merely to sit in this literary trading post was a pleasure. When the sun finally shone, word reached us that a guide had been found who would take us to a longhouse on the other side of the Dulit Range, to Long Nibong, almost on the Batang Tingar, the start of the main river network to coastal Miri. The trip would cost us M$77 each, but no departure date was given us. We would be "advised". Fine by us – we had been on the verge of despair.

In the evening, we indulged heavily in the local brew, borak. Martine in particular succumbed, vomiting ingloriously outside our hall before falling asleep outside in Stephen's arms. We rationalised one instance of revelry was hardly out of place at a trading post where every night bored tribesmen did the same. The larger concern for me was the very public affections shared by Stephen and Martine, often interpreted as "loose" or "hippie". I was sure that much of the children's interest in our activities was aimed at *catching* Stephen and Martine.

We filled in our hours bathing. Dotted along the waterfront were rafts used for storing petrol, berthing boats, washing clothes, or any other activity connected with water. To wash, one had to dive in, climb out, then soap oneself. The women washed over their sarongs, once clean, donning a dry garment over the top and demurely easing off the first garment. Martine swam topless.

A breakthrough! After another day of doing nothing, word came through that our expedition would begin in the morning. It was time.

Sarawak's insurgency began in the 1960s; 1970 saw a number of ambushes, notably in Sibu, one resulting in 12 border scouts slain. "Rebels are young and ideologically motivated. They are recruited wholly among the Chinese, who constitute more than a third of Sarawak's population" (*NY Times*, 7.10.1970). 1973: Peace is signed between the government and the North Kalimantan Communist Party, though the guerrillas aren't to formally lay down arms for another 17 years; Malaysian press reports "about 500 terrorists operating in the lower, upper and mid-Rajang area".

IV

Nomads and leeches

Borneo: crossing the interior with the nomadic Punans; learning to live with leeches; no sex on the longhouse, please; and an offer of marriage.

[Punans] never indulged in headhunting, have a more Mongolian cast to their features and are content to live in the interior jungle. They neither build permanent homes nor cultivate crops, but live off wild fruits and sago, hunting game with blow pipes (J. Barclay, *A Stroll Through Borneo*).

Engine failure

Barely half an hour passed before our motor broke down in strong rapids, forcing us to continue "jalan kakan" (on foot), while a boat hand returned to Belaga for a new engine.

Our hike was not an easy one. The tracks were clear but slippery in a way that only a 100–150-inch annual rainfall could create, most of that in the monsoon period that was only now abating. The jungle was dank and everything creaked or crunched as collapsing rotten wood. My shirt became part of my body, and leeches swayed from their leaf tops in the effort to do the same. Occasionally, they succeeded, one end gripping horribly but painlessly to flesh, the other swaying for better hold as if to say, "look at me"! Clothes were no barrier, their claspers easily piercing such slight hindrances as wool or cotton. We began a count to see who suffered the most by the end of our travail.

Every so often it was necessary to mount narrow log bridges, some high above gullies, some partially immersed in river crossings. Once I slipped, drenching my pack, body and camera. The nine men accompanying us managed amazing feats of strength. Each had charge of a four-gallon petrol tank and I shuddered at the thought of the effort they expended.

We came to a halt at a rough shelter where a new motor was found for our use. This engine too, failed. Hours passed while the leader of our party, Erang Opai, sweated over the machinery. He got it going, but barely. Fortunately, we stumbled upon another Dyak party who lent us their engine for rapids ahead. Those navigated, a boat was sent back with the borrowed motor, while ours was reaffixed for a hoped-for more placid journey ahead. And so it proved – except for one frightening moment when we were caught in rapids with our engine out of commission, and again, when we were swamped, leaving the helmsman clinging perilously to a vine overhang midstream.

Despite all, we arrived safely at Kut, a Kayan transit hut. Skilled bushmen, the Kayan had erected a series of rough cabins across the divide. We were fed rice flavoured with the tinned stewed pork we had provided. Stephen and Martine again provided entertainment with their not-so-tacit embraces, but I was too tired to be even remotely judgemental.

The morning's trek proved just as hard as the previous day's. By mid-morning, we had run the gauntlet of vines, rotten logs, hidden gullies, sunken tracks, and every other conceivable form of torture the jungle could mete out. But we made it safely and early to Umah, a hut above stilts where Erang decided the motor was no longer up to it. We made our camp while two men were dispatched to find a replacement.

Because of our willingness to pitch in, our three remaining guides, Erang, Saging Supan and Lenjau Ingan, warmed to us. Saging had a poisoned finger from a millipede bite but had been unable to get proper treatment at Belaga, which added urgency to our passage. Thankfully no more rapids manifested and we reached the Kenyah settlement, Sambop, by mid-afternoon. Sambop was a large longhouse, something to be grateful for after it became evident we would be stuck here for some time. Our guides had decided to take a long break, ostensibly for rest and equipment recovery. We were given a room – to be shared with Erang, his wife, and his six children.

Things took an unpleasant turn when a man demanded a place on our expedition. I told him we had spent much money and could only afford three guides. "We hired Erang. Ikut Erang [we obey Erang]." Nevertheless, he became a member of our party, Lenjau dropping from the reckoning. Meanwhile, a rummage through our bags by Erang family members relieved me of my antiseptic cream, Martine's lint bandages, and sparked anguished pleas for medicine for a long list of minor ailments. Erang had medicines of his own, including a bottle of Chinese pills with a label promising to cure indigestion, sexual importence (sic), sexual exhaustion, lumbago and headaches.

When night fell, we were led to one end of the ruai to enjoy traditional Kenyah dance – the "Ngajt" – in which the women tied black and white feathers to their wrists, and swayed rhythmically with graceful hand and arm movements. When the local talent had been exhausted, the feathers were tied to Martine's hands and her awkward actions evoked howls of laughter. My borak-fuelled effort was equally foolish.

Our days fell into an idle pattern. I watched on for hours as the women pounded raw padi, flicking the rice back into place with their feet without ever losing rhythm: one, two, three, lift, flick, pound. The young children ran naked or barely saronged, forever shouting and laughing. They were never punished, but one word from an elder brought strict obedience, not necessarily without a cheeky salvo in return. The older children were unfailingly polite.

Everyone smoked. Girls barely into their teens sucked on custom-built cheroots, betel nut teeth crying out for dental intervention. It was tantamount to an insult to refuse a cigarette and I learned the art of taking one puff then allowing it to slowly extinguish, thus always having a crumpled but harmless butt hanging from the side of my mouth.

One morning it was announced we would leave later in the day but Erang's youngest child became ill. Or so he said. The previous evening he had requested payment for the entire trip, which we had refused, instead offering M$50 now, with the balance to be settled at our destination. He had sullenly agreed. "Bagus [good]?" "Bagus." But we did not travel.

On the Sunday, the tribespeople gathered for a church service and I joined them, while Steve and Martine bathed. When religious niceties were done, Erang led me to the far end of the ruai where I was sat in a corner and served borak. And the smiles returned.

Marriage proposal

A line of smartly dressed young women filtered into the room. Erang, smiling broadly, told me to pick one "to take back to your country as your wife". "You are young and strong," an interpreter translated. "I am too young to support a wife," I protested. "Besides, Kenyah girls do not like beards!" They laughed at this and the subject was thankfully dropped. The women filed out.

Later, the three of us joined a queue for "Badi", the dance of farewell. "Kon Tak, Kon Tak" was chanted in a kind of drone as we followed our leader in a conga line around the ruai. A first verse welcomed us to the longhouse; a second pretended it was the Kenyah, not us, who were leaving. Intoned mournfully, it was clear that the departure of guests was a sorrowful occasion.

Not woken in the morning with cries of "besok" ("tomorrow"), it took some time to absorb the reality that the trip was on again. And we started promisingly. Belaga river levels had dropped and the rapids we encountered were navigable. Hereon too, the river narrowed and jungle could be closely experienced. We stopped for breakfast at a small hut where we drank Chap Lang Khow. There was a still in the hut.

But soon after, rapids snapped a propeller blade and our engine died midstream. At a command from Erang that required no translation, we leapt overboard and began desperately hauling it to calm waters. Further rapids, and a submerged rock broke yet another propeller blade. While brightly coloured kingfishers skimmed the water alongside, we took turns with a paddle before reaching Long Ru under late afternoon shadow, a solitary Punan hut where we were greeted with astonishment.

Hunting with blowpipes

There could surely be few places as primitive as this: no walls, just a leaf roof over pole supports, a single room that was barely 4m by 3m. As night fell, we were fed on monkey – which had no discernible taste – then fell asleep under sudden, torrential rain that pierced our roof and drenched our clothing.

The Punans were alarmingly friendly. When I sat on the sleeping platform, they gathered around me. When I wrote, they took the pen from my hands and scribbled, lifted the diary and thumbed through its pages. Each measured himself against me, laughingly standing on tiptoe to seem taller. Most came only to my shoulder. They liked my watch, my passport, my pen, and presumably my raincoat – it disappeared during the night!

Below our platform, two men fashioned parangs from molten steel using crude bamboo bellows. They knocked and tapped with a home-made hammer, but the finished blade was razor sharp. When I pointed at some long blowpipes hanging from the roof, a Punan aimed one at a tree about 100 metres distant, blew mightily, then grunted with satisfaction, though we could not discern whether he had found his target. The blowpipes were about two metres in length with perfectly smooth inners. For hunting, darts were dipped in a poison apparently effective enough to kill pigs. I was glad we were on friendly terms.

That night Erang informed us he had to return home and the Punans would take us the rest of the way to Long Nibong. Our party now comprised three Punans, three Orang Putih (white people) and one very small boat. We set off in the morning, nervously, our Plimsoll line close to the top of the boat's side.

I developed diarrhoea but the Punans regularly stopped to fish and my "saya mau berak" ("I need to crap!") was not always necessary. While they dangled nets (always successfully), I dived hurriedly ashore. For me, the day was hell, though Martine and Stephen assured me they were enjoying themselves. We stopped at a small langkow where I watched on as the others gorged themselves on fish and rice.

The next day I strengthened. The Punans fished enthusiastically, emitting loud shrieks as they heaved their backs through rapids, splashing happily as they de-snagged their nets. But when impossible rapids forced us to walk with our packs, our exertions were in excess of anything beforehand. We left the Punans to wrestle the boat overland to calm waters.

When we stopped at yet another unexpected hut, I enjoyed sitting alone by the river, entranced by the sounds of the insects and the birds and the fireflies making love. The river glowed. We dined, as always, on fish and rice, the fish offered copiously and with some attempt at variety: for breakfast it was boiled; for dinner, it was fried, but in such vast quantities of oil and splashed water that the effect was of boiling.

We paddled hard in the morning until mid-morning when we glided into a tributary called Taupin where our guides tethered the boat, hiding net and paddles for their later return. It was time to walk.

"I love you"

By midday I was inwardly screaming and it was only seeing Martine also struggling that kept me going. With sweat pouring across our faces, it was impossible to appreciate jungle scenery. No longer did the kingfishers dart cheerfully about us, and sounds that were previously music, now jarred. We peppered our guides with the question, "jau" [far]? "Jau," they would reply and we would respond with sickly grins and plod on.

In late afternoon, the answer changed to "tedak jau" (little far) and Martine, who was on the point of giving up, found new wind. We were following a small mountain stream that freshened us and it was fitting that the langkow we were aiming for was at the crossroads of a bubbling brook and a new river, the Lubang. Luxuriously, we had fresh drinking water and a chance to bathe.

As night dropped, a pale yellow enveloped the sky, tinting the bush and the mile-high timber so that we looked upwards eerily through a kind of funnel. Rain, of course, spoiled the performance. And Lujau. As I tried to sleep he tried to mount me, whispering, "I love you" as he splayed across me. Moving fast, I spent the night outside with bare timber poles for my mattress, and sleeping little. My "tedak bagus" and "saya tedak permimpuan" ("not good" and "I am not a girl"), shouted loudly for all to hear, did the trick and I was not molested again.

Our morning task was to cross the swift-flowing Lubang. We stripped to our underwear, entrusting our packs to the Punans who, after a titanic struggle, deposited them dry and safe on the other side. I began my crossing alone, but retreated when I realised the river was too swift for me. The Punans returned to haul us bodily to safety on the far shore where we sat gasping as if we had just tackled Everest. No time for rest, however, and hard slog was again the order of the day – till we met a group of Punans from Nibong. Tobacco and gossip were exchanged, a meeting of old friends miles from home.

The next day's walk was the hardest yet. Following small hill streams, the path was always slippery and small sand pebbles soon filled our shoes. Once I tumbled from a steep ridge, falling five or six metres before managing to halt my fall on a fern clump. My cumbersome pack was fair game for creepers to trip or knock me sideways. Our guides slipped into a chant to aid our rhythm.

As an encouragement, we checked our leech scores. With 25 so far, Martine was the tastiest. Stephen had had 15, I, just 12. Kiwi was clearly not a favoured leech diet! We stopped for wild fruit, enjoying two types of mangostine, one rounded (lauing daun), the other with star ridges (pendau), but both with definite revival qualities! Apart from some massive centipedes and large ants, we saw little life, though did glimpse a millipede with brilliant red skirting which Udau comfortingly assured us could kill a man.

Then, one sudden hillside slide down, and we were arrived at the Nibong river, within smelling distance of civilisation. We had crossed the Dulit! We had crossed the divide! And immediately, from nowhere, a boat hailed us. News of us had travelled. Guided now and cruising along easy waters, we were soon at our next longhouse stopover, Long Nibong, where we shook hands with a long welcoming line before quickly falling asleep in a private room off the ruai.

Morning was the usual longhouse busy: the women crushing tapioca, the men mending nets, the pigs chasing other pigs, the hens, other hens, and the dogs fighting loudly. There was a flurry of excitement when Catholic Father Guido emerged from his own jungle trek. His boat was berthed here and we were about to ask for a ride – until we saw how big his party and how small his craft. But he kindly helped us arrange passage to the next longhouse, Long Attong, on the Tinjaar, the final leg of our traverse.

When departure time came, thunderous rain evoked the ritual lament, "besok", and we settled on our mats with a placid acceptance that would have made a Punan proud. Our hosts were as generous as they could be: mealtime provided no variety from rice and a spinach-like vegetable alongside a few grains of salt and a lukewarm pot of water for us to make our own tea – on which occasions, companies of our hosts manifested magically.

The day started with a flourish. Someone's pig had eaten someone else's chicken and warring factions loudly berated all and sundry. The conflict worsened at feeding time when the animals were patrolled vigorously, any intruders beaten away with rather more vigour than necessary. A pet hornbill, its wings clipped, hopped untethered about the ruai. With hawk-like talons and a long, rose-red beak in contrast to its flat tail of black and white horizontal stripes, it was remarkably whole: hornbill tail feathers were highly prized for ceremonial hats and as decorations for the Ngajt dances.

When the time came to leave, a group of men requested M$10 payment for accommodation and makan, which we knew was against the rules of the "Adat". We gave them $5. For once not expected to paddle, we lay back for an armchair ride. We stopped once, at a small rumah high above the river, stilts splayed precariously into the hillside, necessitating a steep climb up a log stairway. The indoors moved shakily while the thin bamboo-slatted floor sagged. Far below, the Nibong etched its meandering path through gullies of rock and jungle, while this little langkow, defied gravity in utopian solitude.

After we had shaken hands with each of our host's family, he offered us rice, apologising for the lack of vegetables or meat. At parting, we again shook hands all round. "Selamat Jalan!" "Selamat Tinggal (both meaning "goodbye")!" Changing queues, I pretended to farewell Stephen and Martine, which evoked laughter, but in truth I would very much have liked to stay.

Remembering our earlier struggles, we crossed the mouth of the Lubang with relief, gliding into the broad Tinjaar at precisely 3pm. We had crossed safely from the 3rd to the 4th division – "jalan kakki" – and were now cruising towards the sea. Our hardships were over! It remained only to somehow reach Marudi where the Tinjaar joined the Baram, and our adventure would be done.

After more than seven hours on the river, we arrived at Long Atton, a Kenyah longhouse, where it was abundantly clear that wilderness was behind us. The headman's teenage daughter had her own room, plastered with pictures of Cliff Richards and various film stars, while her own record player incessantly blared dated Western pop. We dined on rice and dried babi (pork) then retired to the living area where I was asked about the 1969 moon landing. "Is it true?"

News of our having been charged for accommodation at Long Liau had reached Atton, and our hosts were scathing of Punan hospitality. No guest of the Kenyah ever paid, we were told forthrightly. With no boats scheduled to travel anywhere near to our Marudi target, we found a man willing to take us to the next longhouse, just two hours down-stream, for the cost of the petrol, M$10. When we learned his engine was broken, we renegotiated the fee – to $5.

At Long Dunin, reached before midday, the local teacher offered to paddle us to Long Luyang, a larger settlement that promised regular river traffic ahead. So, after a short interlude with the headman and his ample supplies of Chap Lang Khow, we stumbled back to the river. The forbidding Dulit Range was now but a distant reminder of aching tendons and blistered feet. As the teacher and a companion paddled, we leapt from the boat for our mandi, allowing the current to sweep us downstream beside the craft.

Long Luyang was a majestic (Kenyah sub-tribe) Sibop longhouse with 48 doors, its length far in excess of anything I had seen. It had a "rumah sakit" (hospital) and a priest's quarters, and its own generated electricity. Our hardships were surely over! The priest was Father Guido, met earlier at Liau, and we were greeted warmly. He helped us retrace our route on his wall map while an English nurse did her best to tend our various injuries. My ankles had swollen painfully, which she put down to a mix of heavy walking and a lack of vitamins.

To hire a boat to Marudi, we were told, would cost several hundred dollars. A local "jaja" (iron hawker) would cost just $10 each, but would not be travelling for several days. Worryingly, my entry permit expired in two days' time. But another day and there were still no boats, and activity on the ruai was minimal. We played chess using a set borrowed from Father Guido, practised our Malay, and slept. No boats the next day either! The jaja was now expected in the "near future".

Stop sleeping together!

Another morning dawned, and a serious-looking Father Guido addressed me. "Ah," he said. "The headman has – ah –asked me to ask that those two – ah – stop sleeping together." I gestured him towards Stephen. The Father started again, this time addressing the players. "If you don't stop sleeping together, the headman says you will not be allowed to remain." He gathered momentum. "Really, it's against every rule of the Adat."

On the Sunday, the Father conducted a service on the ruai, which I attended, while Stephen and Martine made themselves scarce. My arrival was greeted with broad smiles, which enlarged when I purposely took my place among the women. A uniformed Father Guido, looking impressive in purple and white, spoke passionately and the menfolk listened closely, though the women were distracted with babies.

After the usual alcohol-fuelled post-service gathering, I was informed the jaja had arrived. We were given a rousing farewell. As we left we were chased and pinioned by a group of teenage girls, who good-naturedly smeared blackening over our faces till we resembled tar babies, and were forced to drink borak till we doubted our ability to find the river, let alone a large iron boat.

The *Ching Huat* was a real old river tramp. It chugged awkwardly but with a well-oiled power that meant business. Its captain Ah Hoon was also an excellent cook – which endeared him to us very quickly. After brief stops at various camps and longhouses, we clanked to berth for the night at Long Terun, a small Kayan community where the older men remembered the English Rajahs and called us "young tuan", an almost subservient title. An enthusiastic Ngajt followed, borak flowed and at some point the three of us fell asleep on the ruai floor.

Six o'clock was a terrible hour to be awakened when not yet sober! The boat left at 6.15am, but, miraculously, we made it. I stripped to the waist and deposited myself at the prow where I fell asleep with the water spraying over me. Five hours later we nudged into a settlement slightly upstream of Long Teru, from where boats, we were promised, left regularly for Marudi.

Long Teru had a bazaar! This was the first market we had seen since Belaga and I wandered up and down the stilted veranda breathing in the smells. I lingered over rows of canned food, fresh cakes and kopi (coffee), a wonderful precursor to the civilisation we now craved so greedily. Meanwhile, Stephen found a boat, the *Yong Hin No1*, which was travelling early the next day.

Our afternoon passed in discussion with a Baha'i missionary. I was wary of missionary activity in Borneo: of so much more worth would be doctors and nurses but, because East Malaysia was mainly Christian, the government was seemingly reluctant to expel white missionaries. The Malaysian constitution defined the Malay citizen as Muslim but that faith had made few inroads in the Borneo interior. As a tribesman put it: "If I become a Muslim, I must stop smoking. If I become a Muslim, I must stop drinking. If I become a Muslim, I must stop eating babi. If I become a Muslim, I must stop living." Meanwhile, young children smoked cheroots with a practised air, and church services closed with colossal consumptions of borak. Islam hadn't a chance!

After stopping at several longhouses *Yong Hin No1* slipped into a long uninterrupted motorway of Tinjaar expanse. Two Kenyah shared their meal with us, a timely kindness as we were out of Malay funds. We could not even afford to pay our fare without first visiting a bank in Marudi, which we reached, with a flat feeling of finality, shortly before 6pm. This was a real town, with shops, restaurants – and roads! Our expedition was indeed over. We slept once more on board, partly because, not having yet paid, we had to, but also to cling to a way of a life that had become integral. Part of us did not want to move on.

As the morning sun emerged slowly from behind palm trees and a brilliantly crimson Baram River, Stephen interrupted my reverie with the news he had found another boat going all the way to Kuala Baram, the seaport preceding Brunei. The *Dusun* would carry us for M$5 each.

And after seven more hours, we reached the sea, by when, perched on the bridge for the duration, I knew intimate details of the boatswain's drinking problem, the mate's sexual frustrations, and a 19-year-old hand's aspirations to captaincy. When we tried to pay, a smiling captain assured us our company had been sufficient payment.

Racism and communism

Several times during the trek I had attempted to get people to open up about the insurgency, which I now knew for sure was not over. But it was not till Brunei that a young, educated tribesman talked freely to me. An employee of American engineering company Costain, Matthew told me all of Sarawak had been "infiltrated" by communism, with Sibu the hub.

The insurgency had more to do with dissatisfactions than ideology, he said, though the guerrillas carried membership cards that earned them free food at many Chinese shops. At election times, government officials descended on the longhouses, advising, "when you see this flag, it represents the government, so tick it; when you see this flag, it represents communism, so strike it out!" They also handed out posters reading, "Stamp out Communism".

Matthew said he would not return home to live under a "racist" Malay rule in which Dyaks were treated as an underclass. For one ethnicity there were job vacancies, for another, signs saying, "position filled". One's race also determined vastly different salaries. "Sarawakians resent having to pay ever-increasing taxes," he said. "They see their money disappearing into bottomless coffers at Kuala Lumpur."

A Punan once told me, "white is good, black not so good", and all the wonderful things I carried with me must have reinforced this silliness, though I argued the point vehemently. I had money, a magnificent pack, smart clothing, and was able to travel the world. Perhaps I was the worst thing to happen to Borneo.

Bringing Sabah into its federation enabled Malaysia to dismiss an 1878 Philippines' claim on the state with the argument its residents had "exercised their right to self-determination". Plotting to make Sabah an Islamic state, chief minister Mustapha from 1967 welcomed swathes of refugees from the Islamic Mindanao region of the Philippines and helped train its freedom fighters. He also secretly plotted to secede from Malaysia. 1973: Philippines continues to claim Sabah; Mustapha continues to accept large numbers of Mindanaon refugees.

V

300 yards off the beaten track

Brunei to Sabah: a mountaintop meeting with a hero; a brutal cockfight; a refugee crisis behind closed doors; communist rebels retreating; and an early glimpse of hardwood timber disappearing.

Kinabalu ... the glancing rays of the rising sun struck the tips of the pinnacles and moved slowly downwards until they streaked across the wet flanks of the plateau making them glisten like mercury. If I had ever any doubts about abandoning a career that would keep me sitting behind a desk in London, I lost them there (David Attenborough, *Life on Air: Memoirs of a Broadcaster*).

Steak from home

For an exhausted hiker, Brunei capital Bandar Seri Begawan was notable for the finding of a library with a copy of *Brothers Karamazov, Part I*. After farewelling Stephen and Martine, I felt a pang of loneliness, but was in no mood to hurry, especially as the library carried a series of the "Great Classics", a few of which I demolished sitting in the sun on the library steps.

My plan now to climb Mt Kinabalu in Sabah, I took a ferry to Labuan, an adjacent island state oddly set up as a distinct federal territory of Malaysia. I was hardly ashore before meeting a young volunteer student teacher from Brisbane who gave me a tour of his island on his motorbike. A tall, fair-headed science student, Ian introduced me to his flatmate Koh, and that night the three of us joined an amplified party held by a group of school pupils where marijuana was generously shared. It was rather incongruous hearing Ian addressed as "Sir" while the weed was passed.

I felt unwell in the morning, so Ian took me aboard an American oilrig to see its medic. The outside of the rig resembled a dirty barge, but below decks, all was immaculate. Each cabin had four bunks, a desk and a washbasin, electricity and air conditioning. The captain's cabin, other than being adorned with Playboy centrefolds, was no more grandiose. "I don't know why you eat this goddam local shite," the medic began his diagnosis. The Americans imported all their food, dining on steak and pork from New Zealand, sole from Dover, prawns from Singapore, and even the fruit was imported. "[Oil company] Brown & Root believes in the best for its employees," he said as he passed me vitamin pills and Alka-Seltzer. With the former, he struggled clumsily to extract sachets from a container, before impatiently spluttering, "Christ, take the whole box!"

Obeying the captain's injunction to "have a good feed", I joined a queue behind a man of football physique ladling three big beef steaks on to a plate along with thick French fries, but ignoring other offerings such as pork chops, spaghetti Bolognaise, cabbage and beans. A little overawed with my audacity, I chose a portion of each. Physically at a low ebb, I had stumbled on protein in inexhaustible quantities. All leftovers were thrown away, a grandiose gesture considering interior tribesmen were subsisting on rice.

Kinabalu or bust

A few days later found me sitting on the cabin roof of a prawn boat bound for Weston on the Sabah mainland, admiring the reflections of a brilliant moon over shadowed isles. But the jerking boat soon reduced shimmers to raucous coughs. I curled up in an uncluttered section of deck, the vibrations continuing till my moustache tickled and cramp permeated my legs. But suddenly it was light and we were edging through a maze of everglades where swamp birds glanced upwards from their breakfasts, shaking their beaks at us with annoyance.

I immediately began hitching the 30km to Beaufort where a train was reputedly available to Sabah capital, Kota Kinabalu. But reaching the town before midday, I decided to keep hitching on to the capital, 110km hence. I walked for nearly an hour before achieving Membakut, leaving more than 90km of substandard track ahead. But after four hours more in blazing sun, a tobacco salesman in a landrover rescued me, taking me all the way to the capital, albeit ploughing through potholes, his iron roof a none-too-gentle cushion for my bouncing head.

Reaching Kota Kinabalu just before nightfall, I wandered the main street, limping from exhaustion, when two young men stopped to talk and offered me a bed in their flat. Max was a design artist, Rahmin a seaman. Giving into my tiredness, I went straight to bed while my two hosts bizarrely doused house lights and began scaling neighbouring balconies, an act seemingly of voyeurism.

In the morning, the three of us made for town where Max had to work and Rahmin was to rejoin his ship. Still feeling ill, I visited the hospital, where a stool test confirmed I was suffering only from exhaustion, and vitamin pills were prescribed. Without further ado, I booked accommodation at the Mt Kinabalu National Park for the coming week.

Back at the flat, Max and Rahmin, with schoolgirls in tow, had launched an impromptu party. The flat was buzzing. At midnight, I was sitting in a corner with Solzhenitsyn's *Cancer Ward* while Rahmin, whose sailing had been delayed, topped my whisky faster than I could drink ("hey, drink up, man!"), a friend bellowed in my ear ("keep calm!"), and another vomited over the carpet.

Max had been a Colombo Plan student in Australia but been recalled when his studies gave way to other pleasures. But not before he had decided non-conformism was not a sin and that criticism of authority was a right. In Sabah, these realisations were monumental. Around him he had gathered a small group of mild reactionaries who enjoyed playing guitars and throwing off at the system. The biggest talking point, always, was the corruption of Tun Mustapha, Muslim Chief Minister of predominantly Christian Sabah.

Censorship was rife, Max said. When *Newsweek* reported on Philippines' "Islam question", referencing Mustapha corruption, that chapter had been removed from local issues. Corruption too, was rife. When any big project began, forewarned officials would invariably own adjacent land. Switching to Mustapha's "illegal" support of Islamic rebels in the southern Philippines, Max was adamant "Mussy" wanted to anoint himself Sultan.

Rocky mountain high

It took three well-timed rides, the last with a police van, to reach my planned nighttime stop at Kota Belud much earlier than expected so I pressed on for the National Park. Under ominous black clouds, it was only my "never go backwards" rule that prevented a hurried return. Thanks to a landrover taxi that declined to exact payment, I narrowly avoided a torrential downpour but was left bleakly alone, high on the Crocker Range, with the Kinabalu National Park – Taman Negeri – still 30km ahead.

My luck holding, I reached camp headquarters along with evening and another downpour that hastened my sprint to the front office. Inside, two smiling, familiar faces greeted me. Martine and Stephen had been delayed here for a week – the former unwell – and by coincidence, were booked for their climb the next day. We swapped tales like schoolchildren. For M$1 a night (student rate), we had generated electricity during the evening, gas stoves, a magnificent stone fireplace with ample supplies of firewood, flush toilets, and even mattresses on our beds! All this with views of thickly forested valley with a background of Mt Kinabalu rising steeply, like a leaping orca.

At 4095m a significantly higher, if less challenging, peak than Aoraki/Mt Cook, Kinabalu looked a formidable target, thick forest with a swirling tablecloth mist only occasionally revealing a ragged rock face that I was told was not even the peak. When four Australians arrived, we joined together to split a required guide cost – Peter, a pipe-smoking agriculture lecturer, John, a librarian, Jamal, a postgrad student, and Joan, a friend. They were all jovial, which augured well.

Beginning our ascent at 8am, a hierarchy of fitness was soon evident: Jamal lingered wearily at the rear with our guide; Martine, still unwell, also dragged early, with Stephen ever at her shoulder; one step forward, staggered John, continually cursing the mountain in vivid Australian vernacular; while Peter, Joan and myself took the lead.

When it began raining, those ahead hurried to make the first hut (Carson's), while those behind, plodded on resignedly. The first of us reached the camp shortly after 11am. Passed this point, the track inclined thoughtlessly. Our guide was nowhere to be seen, and it helped to make rude jokes about his fitness, though we hardly needed his services for this leg of the climb. We formulated plans for exacting payment for getting *him* to the summit.

We stopped for the night at the Panur Laban hut in the middle of an ever-worsening downpour, where I donned socks and jersey but was unsuccessful in banishing the cold. While our guide slept soundly, we lit kerosene stoves for makan, huddling together for the eating. As the food was spread out an army of rats scrambled over the bunks, unafraid of humans. We cleaned our dormitory thoroughly before settling in our sleeping bags, fully clothed.

Woken at 3am, we reacted slowly. Peter's well-organised group enjoyed hot soup while the rest of us dined meagrely on biscuits. The bad weather happily had dissipated, a casket of stars spilled higgledy-piggledy revealing a clear route to the summit. From here on, packs were not to be carried. The sole burden was the blackness of a moonless night. We dawdled over breakfast and it was not till 4.30 that our befuddled torsos eased into a line at last led by our guide swinging a single butane lamp. The stars had disappeared.

From here we had the benefit of pre-laid ropes. Initially, we could not see 10 metres in front of us, relying on the flickering butane beam to indicate a leftward step, or a rightward one. Our guide at last proved his worth. He knew from memory just where a rope lay, where a drop was hidden and even where the occasional piece of scrub or root could provide necessary foot or handhold.

The climb was deathly slow if not unduly exhausting. Inching up rock face by rope, sight unseen, was hard going. It may have taken half an hour, perhaps three quarters but, as light began to appear from natural sources, so too did the gradient, till we clambered beyond ropes to the Sayat Sayat hut, a last station for pause. Progress was easier now. A brilliant red sunrise had appeared about us and ropes were no longer necessary. Neither was the guide and I plunged ahead with the Australians while Stephen cajoled Martine, determined she achieve the summit.

"Hello, I'm head of the BBC"

We encountered a smiling Englishman, who in understated fashion introduced himself as "David, head of the BBC". His face could not be mistaken. David Attenborough had climbed the mountain two days earlier for filming; today's exercise was for pleasure. He still carried a Nikon, however, and we envied him the job that enabled such travel. He had recently been filming in New Guinea – with 110 porters! His latest projects had taken him through the Celebes and, most recently, to a small Punan settlement in Borneo. Even today, with no heavy equipment, he had three guides.

One of us complained to him of the growing numbers of tourists spoiling enjoyment of once out-of-the-way places. But Attenborough would have none of it, saying, "If you are prepared to walk 300 yards off the beaten track, even in the busiest of places, you can be alone." He invited me to look through his camera at the cloud swirling down the south face. I asked him when his filming would reach television. "The film might not turn out well," he replied with a grin. "[Pharmacists'] Boots are not always reliable." When Martine drooled over his camera he said matter-of-factly: "A couple of good photographs will pay for the trip – and a lot more."

Leaving the head of the BBC staring into space, we resumed our climb. Hands were no longer needed but we puffed and wheezed disproportionately so that later we were to wonder if oxygen shortage had affected our performance. Just below the final peak we paused for breathtaking views of rock and forest escalating under beautifully lit sky. The heavens were clear and we could clearly see small kampongs generations in the distance. Kinabalu National Park had dropped her misty veil for us, the privileged.

Joan was the first to the top. But none of us were hurrying, and I joined her at precisely quarter to seven. Clumps of flags were dotted there, limply signifying the successes of our predecessors. Predominant was a large red pennant inscribed, "Singer Sewing Machines". Delicate white clouds appeared, the sun daubing pastel colours on a firmament almost within touching distance. Far below, dwarf forest slipped into dense oak and conifers, and huge gullies tumbled drunkenly before rising anew, while waterfalls teased and a myriad birds whistled their appreciations.

By 7am, May 1, all had achieved the target, and John entertained us rousingly singing the *Workers' Flag* to celebrate, he said, the achievement, the day, and the "bloody great effort" involved in reaching the top. We signed a book the guide held as record of our success, then started down. In daylight, the descent was not difficult. We bumped into Attenborough again, stopping for another brief chat before hurrying on. As the rain began to bucket down, a thick mist setting in, we began walking slower, eventually entering the doors of our hostel soaked to the skin. The Australians shouted us dinner but it was bed that provided the best possible conclusion to a near-perfect day.

The next day all my companions moved on. The evening brought new guests, however, two Kiwis and an American who had joined together for the assault. One of the Kiwis had five years earlier done New Zealand's police cadet training course with me at Trentham, an amazing coincidence. People talked of "six degrees of separation" – for New Zealanders that surely should be amended to two!

Better to keep quiet

A week and a great deal of hitching later, I presented myself to Sandakan's immigration office, belatedly seeking an extension to my Malaysia visa, only to be told I must produce a sponsor, show all my money, detail my education and my work history, and list every country I had visited in the last eight years! With a minimum of lies, my visa was extended, but for two weeks only.

Barely had I reached the centre of this bustling town, when a thin Chinese with a camera slung over his shoulder accosted me, introducing himself as Anthony Lai Kui Siong, reporter of the *Sandakan Daily News* and correspondent for the *Brunei Borneo Bulletin News*. Like every good local reporter, he was interested in strangers and questioned me exhaustively. Everyone knew him. The policeman waved, the stall owner came to our table to talk, the pedestrian called to us from the middle of the street. And in each case, inquiring nods towards me were answered patiently.

Offering me board, Anthony paraded me incessantly, to his family, business acquaintances, workmates, and shopkeepers. Invariably, discussion turned to dissatisfactions with Mustapha. Mustapha, though Muslim, was not Malay but a Sulu Islander, islands under the jurisdiction of the Philippines. He actively supported the southern (Muslim) rebels in the Philippines, currently under the (Christian) rule of President Ferdinand Marcos. "Mustapha is the richest man in Sabah, easily a multi-millionaire," Anthony said. "Muslims are offered land and housing. They do better in employment and promotion. Ah, it's good to be Muslim." Anthony was Christian.

At the last elections, Anthony was forbidden to print anything questioning the government. Police had searched his office and colleagues been arrested. "It's reached the stage where we're hesitant to discuss anything controversial." Repeated to me often, the grievances rang true. "No Chinese will speak out in opposition," Anthony said. "All mail is censored and there would be much trouble. Better to keep quiet."

In Sandakan, where both newspapers were Chinese, groups of Malay would gather with a translator to explain the news. On television, however, it was the Malay voice that prevailed. Forty per cent of the population were Chinese, yet no Chinese programmes were broadcast. "Better to keep quiet," said Anthony.

A cockfight and a refugee camp

Anthony took me to a house in the suburbs to see a cock fight and, as his guest, I was welcomed, despite my odd reluctance to join in the betting. What betting! Hundreds of dollars passed from hand to hand, while voices rose alternately in anger and laughter. Betting was between individuals. If you wished to back a bird, you needed find someone who favoured another. The pitch of human competition grew steadily as a designated judge studied the avian combatants for signs of tampering.

The birds were sponged lightly and water was allowed to drip into eager beaks. Their extended rear talons were rubbed in spittle and dirt, while the creatures eyed each other hatefully and impatiently. Abruptly, each was dropped from handlers' grasp, leaping at each other's throats, talons flung harshly in thrust and defence. Three rest periods were allowed, called by either party, and within half an hour two of these had been used up, though the contest had been remarkably even. The older bird was a veteran. What was left of its plumage straggled; only its piercing eyes indicated spirit, but I picked it as a winner. It was, after all, still fighting. I silently approved as Lai placed M$10 on maturity.

It looked like being a long fight. Both circled each other warily, Bruce Lee feet flung viciously, beaks pecking sadistically at weak spots as they appeared. Suddenly, pandemonium! The older bird, up till now gaining a gradual ascendancy, started back in panic, blood streaming out of one eye, and the third rest period was hurriedly invoked. From then on, it was a cruel massacre and the contest was stopped.

In the morning, Anthony took me to outer suburb Labuk, where a story I had earlier heard but doubted was revealed to be true. A compound of barracks was surrounded by tall wire fences topped with barbed wire in the fashion of a prison camp. Washing hung from each window, but my interest lay with the faces behind, staring dully back at me. The complex was crammed with Filipinos, including numerous young children hanging boredly around the "protective" fences.

I wanted to question inmates, but Anthony would have none of this, driving off quickly to avoid being noticed. "Mustapha has encouraged a flood of southern Muslims seeking religious freedom," he said. "They have been six months behind barbed wire, just as the Jews were in

Cyprus." At least 30,000 refugees had entered Sabah, he said, the bulk of them now held on the nearby Bahala Island. The existence of these camps made for a sobering impression.

Paradoxically, on another day I watched vessels leaving for the Philippines loaded with returning refugees, apparently dissatisfied with the haven they had sought so eagerly. I stood with Anthony in silence, looking at their faces, and at the frail wooden "slum boats" that would return them. A Malay immigration official pounced on us. "Cameras are forbidden," he said.

We returned home where a reporter from opposition paper, *Merdeka* (freedom), interviewed me, with Anthony's blessing. All this attention was going to my head! The next edition, full-page article, included: "He hopes when he returns to New Zealand to look for a girlfriend and, after marriage, his wife can look after his mother." I didn't complain about inaccuracies. It brought me much friendly attention!

At night I visited Anthony's father, progenitor of four generations of Sandakan residents. At 70-plus, Lai Kim Fong had just returned from a hunting expedition. He proudly showed me a picture of himself with a fallen elephant – taken in 1934. He listened to my stories with genuine interest and approved of my living style, a rarity among Asians I had hitherto met. "I am disappointed with the lack of adventure shown by today's youth," he said. But when I told him of my plans to hitch with a fishing boat to Lahad Datu further around the coast, he tried hard to dissuade me. "Mr Alan, I would not appreciate fishing boat. It is very dangerous. There are monsoons and pirates." I did not tell him why I wanted to visit Lahad Datu, which was to find even more dubious passage across the Celebes Sea to Sulawesi in Indonesia.

Red rebels retreating

With a reporter as friend, I caught up on insurgency news. "New evidence of the reds losing battle", said a newspaper headline, referencing "more than 200 communists slain" in Sarawak. "There are now about 500 terrorists operating in the lower, upper and mid-Rajang area" – just where my Sarawakian jaunt through the interior had taken place! Terrorists were "intensifying attempts to lure children into their ranks", the report said.

In other news, a local had been "detained" for driving with an Australian flag on his aerial. A man had earlier been arrested for destroying worn-out Malaysian flags, even though he was replacing them with new versions. The winning song in a youth talent quest also made the news, its lyrics reading: "United youth, peaceful land/ Inspired by the new spirit/ Forever united, marching side by side/ Vowing solid unity/ The country develops in swift progress/ The people live in equal prosperity/ The steel-strong movement strides proudly forward/ To the gates of a golden future".

It was time to move on. I bought toys for Anthony's children and hoped they proved suitable. I had found cheap passage on a cargo boat bound for Lahad Datu and only the streamers were missing as encouraging shouts and waves sent the vessel trundling seawards. The *Kunak* was sister ship to the *Rajah Brooke*, its bill of fare identical: "Meal Before Preparation: Rice, 6oz; Fish, 3oz; Meat, 3oz; Vegetables, 3oz." I went to the Malay section but was refused service till my insistence brought the response, "Okay, but you can't switch afterwards to the Chinese section." It was a Pyrrhic victory. There was no fish on my plate.

Lahad Datu port was a good three miles from Lahad Datu itself, so I walked it. In a town that seemed like a smaller Sandakan, I drank tea, then registered with Immigration, and my way was now clear for what turned out to be a nightmare hitch to Tawau, the next port town on the line. This was timber country and, amid a confusing network of sideroads, sign posts were non-existent. Massive trucks rumbled their way through acres of billian (Bornean ironwood), merbau (kwila), and silangan batu, the famous hard woods of Sabah, their loads tethered tenuously. Past Silam, I saw massive silangan logs being loaded for export to Japan and, a little further on, was witness to miles of scorched pasture. Timber was everywhere receding.

At Tawau, a stall owner offered me free board at the local Chinese Association, "if you don't mind sleeping on a table". That problem solved, I dined at his stall, engaging in conversation with a man other patrons told me was "mad". They may have been right: he lectured me on Jesus Christ, occasionally rambling into Malay and Hakka, while I nodded politely.

I sat alone afterwards on the waterfront, reading Han Suyin's *The Morning Deluge* and was beginning to delight in China's communist successes, when three young Sulu Islanders, Filipino Muslims, stopped to talk. They had been a long time in Tawau but were unable to find work, and were desperate. As they talked, it became difficult to differentiate between Marcos and Mustapha, the former viewed as their Christian oppressor, the latter, a corrupt Muslim who had aided their escape but not delivered work. These islanders had found no glittering paradise. In Sabah they suffered no religious discrimination – just regular discrimination. "If Mustapha wants to encourage Filipino migration, he should provide work," they said.

Yet they felt safer here. The southern Philippines had become a breeding ground for rebellion. Uprisings were constant and everyone carried a gun. "Without a gun, one has no face. No one will give respect to a man that is unarmed," they said. Death was glamorous and ruthless killers lauded. Current popular figure was named Dante. My friends' descriptions made him sound like the Scarlet Pimpernel. "No one knows where he is or when he will strike!"

It was time to draw curtain on East Malaysia. I bought a boat ticket to Nunukan, on a small island just across the border in Indonesian Borneo. The time felt right.

A failed 1965 coup attempt by right wing army officers against Indonesian president Sukarno sparked a paradoxical purge of "leftists" by army head General Suharto that killed hundreds of thousands. In 1969, now President Suharto took over West Papua, a precursor to the later invasion and annexation of East Timor. 1973: Under Suharto's strong-armed "New Order" rule, tensions between Muslims and Christians simmer but are largely held in abeyance till after his (1998) resignation.

VI

Sailing with pirates

Sulawesi: setting sail with Bugis "pirates" before jumping ship for an unguided trek to who knew where; lavishly rescued by a Governor; a funeral marked by the ritual slaughter of hundreds of buffalo; ancient graves; and a malaria scare.

Bugis originated in Southern Celebes, around the area of Macassar. For years the Macassar Bugis resisted the monopoly the Dutch sought to impose on the clove trade ... their activities, of course, were termed piracy by the Dutch, the arch pirates (Sardar & Yassin-Kassab, *Critical Muslim 07: Muslim Archipelago*).

Magnificence and squalor

My boat slipped unobtrusively behind the half-Indonesian Sibatik island before docking at Nunukan town, which was wholly so. Nunukan rolled around a lightly inclined hill. Its few roads were dust tracks, but there was huge appeal in an azure-blue sea, glimmering at every angle.

A small boat was sailing this evening to Sulawesi but, knowing a passenger boat was sailing directly to capital Ujung Pandang (later renamed Makassar) in a few days' time, I was disinclined to check it out. But when I saw the craft, how rapidly my priorities altered! For this was a Bugis sailing boat, blue cloth wings flapping from half-hewn log mast, canvas tatters as roof above deck, and I knew such a chance would never eventuate again.

Being Saturday, the bank was closed, but I stalked the manager relentlessly, finding him at his home and, remarkably, not too displeased at being disturbed. US$20 changed, and I was on the wharf, gesticulating wildly. It took a while, but my persistence was rewarded and a small perahu ferried me to the *Lontara II*. Famed seafarers of southern Sulawesi, the Bugis were by legend pirates who profited from the colonial traffic of the Dutch, but were more likely farmers who turned to the sea only after the Dutch took control of Makassar port, stifling their ability to trade. Raiding may have been their only option.

Magnificence and squalor! *Lontara's* aft was a wooden cabin, half captain's quarters, half toilet and kitchen. At either side were large wood tillers, noosed to deck by rotan, below which the engine room spewed, a groaning Black Hole of Calcutta. A canvas ceiling hung loosely over propped log poles above decks provided cover for sleeping.

Boarding late, I slept fitfully on a metal roof above the captain's cabin under a shivering full moon. Throughout the night we etched slow, windless passage down the Kalimantan coast: pounding, each inch earned with engine sweat and toil. At 8am, land hove into view – Tarakan on Kalimantan (Indonesian Borneo) – but the sighting was but a shadow as we ploughed steadily on into deep ocean. Mid-morning, the sun forced the vessel's few passengers under canvas, and continued to do so till late afternoon. As cool breezes heralded evening, I struggled above the rear cabin to appreciate views as best I could. Our sails were high and full, and the steel sea rocked half-heartedly. Peace at last.

Crew members Elvis and Benny peppered me with questions which I did my best to answer with my dictionary as aid. Imperceptibly, my vocabulary improved. "Di-Indonesia, "bintung"," Benny would say pointing skyward. "Di-Inggeris, "star"," I would reply. I met the captain, Mohammed Ali, a slim, shy man who at first kept his distance. The days fell into a lazy pattern: each morning I would wake at six, hoist myself aft to take in the sunrise and the limpid oceans of ripples and flying fish, fresh breezes and pregnant sails; for breakfast, I would descend for one of Chef Odang's basic servings of rice and fish; from then, I had no recourse but exhausted sleep, more tiring than time awake.

Two nylon lines with hooks hung continually from our stern. When fish were caught, we ate well; when there were none, we subsisted on dried salt fish. A minute piece was tasty with a varied meal, but when that portion became the meal… The coffee occasionally offered was foul and the tea was little better. The fresh water carried, though boiled, had a strange musty taste.

I got to know the crew: Elvis, immaculately groomed; Benny, forever sick; and a youngster, undernourished, always dirty, clambering at bidding to engine room or to mast. My fellow passengers were a middle-aged Indonesian who spent his time polishing stones and dabbing perfume on his cigarettes, and a family of kids, one of whom was covered in scabs, another without toes. *All* Europeans carry medicine, so it was expedient to mention my only supplies were for malaria. Suddenly, Benny had malaria! I poked fun at him, emphasising the lack of it in Sulawesi. "Countries with malaria, bad. There is no malaria in Sulawesi. Sulawesi, bagus, number 1!" I was wrong.

Chef Odang, thin and wizened, prepared the food in the toilet. A large scar crawled across his back, but a smile of equal length negated any hint of ugliness. I made a point of always appreciating his cooking and my reward, inevitably, was the choice fish portion – the head! The kitchen and the toilet at rear were separated by a one-metre partition wall. The lavatory was a gap in the floor, requiring a squat with head visible from the kitchen and the deck. To wash after bowel movement, a bucket had to be lowered through the lavatory for sea water.

Late one afternoon, we eased passed land, Tanjung (cape) Bunganeer, but it was a distant presence and the daily routine continued. Makan was served between 3 and 5pm and, approaching 6, I would reoccupy my post above captain's cabin to enjoy sunset and the evening calm. Here I would be joined by various of the crew and my Indonesian lessons would continue.

Early one morning, Sulawesi Tengah (central) flopped into view, but the ship billowed on southwards. My reading material exhausted, I could only lie sluggishly, peering toward a coastline that was barely visible. As I settled another night for bed, rain attacked viciously, and I was directed to a small bunk in the engine room where I was dry, but had to endure an overbearing heat.

Sulawesi when it came, was an early morning drift into an idyllic setting of palms and black sand beaches. Our first stop, at Pusang Kayu, was brief. Captain Ali went ashore, but no trade eventuated and we were soon at sea again. Beaches and flaxen trees were always evident now and somehow the day was not quite so merciless. At early afternoon, we tethered off Sungei Lariang, a sparse desa (village) of a few thatched houses and a mosque. A small section of the mosque was in white stone with a wooden belfry or look-out post above and the inevitable Islamic dome, a green and silver skullcap glistening overhead.

I wanted to swim but was assured there were "buaja" (crocodiles) so ventured not. Instead, I stripped for mandi. We were anchored about 200 metres offshore and the water, amazingly, was fresh, the mouth of the Lariang river generating a considerable outwash. The crew renewed its supplies of fresh water simply by filling the tanks from the ocean. Soap lathered and, apart from the musty tea, makan was palatable. As I lathered, a crew member tipped buckets of magnificent water over me. When I washed my clothes, they dried instantly.

About noon the following day, we anchored off Sungei Sampaga. Again a tropical beauty prevailed, a few thatched rumah etched casually against palms, and I took the opportunity to go ashore where I was welcomed by the headman. As usual, I had to explain my trip and the headman delighted in telling me about some German travellers who had passed this way a year earlier. "Germany bagus, New Zealand bagus, Indonesia bagus," I was assured. "Bagus" was a much-overused term meaning anything from "good" to "magnificent".

Back on the boat, we barbecued pisang belimbing (banana starfruit), a welcome relief from rice and fish. It was not particularly tasty, but that day roast beef would not have been more appreciated. Evening makan was especially bagus, the rice mixed with a coconut grating and served with freshly caught sardine. For dessert, a glorious sunset: brilliant blues folded amid brilliant reds. Our sails were down, but the yellow log mast and mainstays were framed graphically against a background of palms and mountains. Water lapped around the foundations of houses and the ocean appeared as placid as if enreefed. We raised sail in pitch dark.

At 6am, well past the provincial border of Sulawesi Selatan (south), a very different scene unfolded. Still the palms clung to coast, but there were now heavily forested mountain jackets in velvet green, backdrop to pasture. Distant shimmers of silver indicated another mosque and another kampong. Above decks, Ramlin, a West Irian, pointed out landmarks. He looked more Aborigine than Indonesian and some of the crew went so far as to call him "monkey", which he laughed at. Once he pointed to a cloud-drenched mountain he called Sandana, telling me it had erupted in 1969. I was unable to verify this, though later identified a region with this name, far to the north.

I jump ship

Mid-afternoon, we broached Kampong Palipi (or Pelabuhan) and I was instantly in love. The water was a rich blue-green, enclaved within a harbour dotted with miniature islands. I went ashore and abruptly decided to end my voyage. I fed on bananas, then swam lazily and luxuriously, out to the *Lontara II* and back again. Bewitched, I soaked and sank in gentle sand and barely-lapping ocean.

When I told Muhammed Ali of my decision, he shared with me a glass of my first palatable coffee in a week and, before I left, passed me a piece of paper that must have taken him hours to compose: "Dear Sir, I have with to inform you, that I am the new student of New Zealand course and I want to try to write a letter to ask about new books International Labour Office, for I like of reading them and also I hope to write my name a subscribir of New Zealand. I to sit for exams. Don' you Samson, I'm afraid that to lost."

As the ship left, goodbyes waved till infinity and an echo returned from afar, "Bye, bye, Mr Samson", and I was sad. I consoled myself that I had enjoyed six days aboard a Bugis sailing ship, a rare feat.

A welcoming party organised a room for me with the family of Irma, a young woman who knew some English. As we walked together, we swapped words pidgin fashion. "In English, Mister? 'Lust', Mister? You are big, Mister. So big. I am so small." My vocabulary improved little. I started hitching at daybreak. The word "hitch-hike" did not exist in the Indonesian language and it was easy to see why. Horse-drawn buggies adorned with beautiful brass blinkers, overflowing with vegetables, fruit, coconuts and sugarcane, trotted between kampongs in parade ground symmetry. But not once did I see a vehicle with room enough for one large Orang Putteh with pack!

Only the sea provided respite from a merciless sun. I reached Somba at midday, a small desa with a single street where I was hurried to police headquarters. The local army commander was summoned. He interrogated me politely, but it was a timely reminder of the prominence of authority in Indonesia. At the village's outskirts a policeman offered me a ride to Magene, the first significant town ahead, but insisted on first taking me to his home where he rummaged through my things. Asking repeatedly for obat (medicine), he found my supplies deep inside my pack. I lied about the curative value of each medicine and gave him nothing. When by 3pm a promised vehicle had still not arrived I resumed my hike, relieved to be out of his grasp.

Kampong followed kampong till, in early evening, I wandered into Balombong, the largest village yet, where a horde of children crowded about me. Royally welcomed by the tua rumah, I followed him to his home. In I went, and in went the children. A table broke under the strain while more bodies poured through windows and doors. The next morning I found a beach in which to bathe, walked, stopped and talked, and walked again. Bliss and blisters. I discarded my shoes, hoping whoever found them would make good use of them. But this I doubted. I had big feet! The final kilometre into Magene, I rode on the back of a truck, crowded with people and produce. After 38km, it was my first Sulawesi ride.

At the Governor's pleasure

Led to a rest-house, I from habit requested cheaper accommodation and was redirected to a large house on the edge of the town belonging to the district governor, or Bupati, who insisted I stay with him. H.A. Rasjil Sulaiman was clearly a wealthy man: I dined sumptuously on flavoured rice, chicken, beef, fish, chillies, egg dishes, finger bowls attended the plates, and little silver platters were on hand for the bones.

Afterwards, I was taken to police offices where I was sternly told my visa entitled me to enter Indonesia, but I lacked police permission to travel within each province. My entrance had been "highly irregular". Things were straightened out, but not before I had filled in countless forms and promised to go directly to the state capital. When I asked permission to stay in Magene another four days to rest, however, this was granted. By good fortune, the governor would be visiting Ujung Padang at about that time and I would accompany him.

I was never alone. Groups of children attended me as a gathering storm. I had been followed before, but never like this: Hamlin feet pounded around me, and voices shrieked endlessly. Adult onlookers looked displeased but the tidal wave kept coming. I stopped. A thousand youths fell against me. Market fruit stands collapsed, rice baskets overturned, till, at last, adult voices were raised in anger. I escaped to a coffee shop, tiredly requesting that the children be kept out, and there met Syafrullah, son of the local junior school headmaster, who guided me safely back to the governor's.

I was fed again. At every meal a serving of bread was placed strategically next to my plate, which I pointedly ignored, tackling instead the huge platefuls of rice. My hosts asked me about eating habits in

New Zealand, and each answer I gave miraculously came alive at the dinner table. I stressed I wanted Indonesian food, saying bread was not a staple at home. Subsequently, afternoon tea would be served to me in my room – with four huge pieces of bread!

Listening that night to *Voice of America*, I caught the tail end of a report about a New Zealand protest over French nuclear testing off Mururoa Atoll. Mention was also made of an expedition setting out from Ecuador in a small log craft for Australia, hoping to prove an Aboriginal migration from South America. Thor Heyerdahl was mentioned.

One night, the Bupati summoned me to join him and his staff in the living room. As we supped tea, a translator addressed me: "Bupati asks me to tell you that you have behaved yourself well. You must not mind children crowding around you. They are just glad to see you. He finds you polite and courteous within the family. Not like other foreigners."

At each meal, Bupati's wife, the nyonya, explained my eating habits. "He doesn't eat bread! Yes, rice!" Amazement all round and I would smile, happy that they should be happy. The nyonya was a handsome woman with a smile that exuded the charm of the gentry. Bupati's progeny seemed to have infiltrated all Magene and his house was a gathering place for extended family. The man sweeping rooms was a cousin, the girl sewing in the kitchen was a niece, and the others all indelibly linked on a tentacled family tree.

Out of the blue, the policeman reappeared, wanting to re-examine my documentation. But when he began writing in my passport an explanation of why I did not carry proper authorisation, I protested vehemently. Belatedly accepting he was unauthorised to write in passports, he produced glue and paper to hide the offending paragraph. When I stopped him, he produced a rubber! We compromised: he could draw neat lines through his thesis but sign the mistake clearly so that I could not be blamed for desecrating a passport.

On May 31, there were celebrations recognising the anniversary of the founding of the local "kodom" (military). The day also acknowledged the resurrection of Christ (Kenaikan Isa Almashi). I dressed as well as I was able, shirt ironed (thanks to my hosts), and joined Bupati and his wife for a chauffeured ride to the local hall. Bupati outshone all. Medals swam around his chest while Nyonya, always a few paces behind, was quietly elegant in a gold-flecked sarong.

I was seated imposingly in the front row, the women on one side, the men on the other, with Bupati and other dignitaries at the front, among them, the Supreme Commander of Somewhere, with medals even more impressive than my host's. There were speeches, a prize giving for sporting finesse, and little sealed envelopes for the guests. My envelope contained rice, a biscuit and a sachet of peanuts. Then all sat back to watch performances of traditional dance.

I spent much of the following day, dreaming. I watched the ocean, a long, spiral alcove with a smattering of boats at rest. Occasionally, village women walked into view, poles across necks hauling vast amounts of produce; or groups of rag-tag urchins at play. At evening meal, a servant brushed flies away from my head with a fan and, I'm ashamed to say, the role of honoured guest suited me. After, I sat for a final time around my bed with the children of the household. I was sorry to be leaving. I fell asleep well after midnight, happy in the knowledge Indonesia was leading Denmark in the Thomas Cup (badminton) final.

We set off for Ujung Pandang at 8.30am, but not before an almost formal farewell from staff and family. I wrote my address several times then shook hands enthusiastically with everybody present, children included. Nyonya and I shared a joke about the size of European noses. I promised to cut mine off so that I might look Indonesian. Then I climbed into the leading of two landrovers, both mirror-shining, trying to relax as we gathered speed. We stopped once, for makan, where the Bupati's curt command had restaurant staff scurrying to hoist curtain dividers to ensure our privacy.

Reaching Ujung Pandang, Sulawesi's largest and capital city under late afternoon shadow, I was driven directly to the *Alaska Hotel*, which gave me a huge room with a private bathroom, two beds and a wardrobe, and I was left with a sneaking suspicion my bill was being subsidised. Early the next morning, the Bupati dropped in to say goodbye and I thanked him as profusely as I was able. When he bade me write in his diary I wrote a sincere eulogy of Indonesian kindness.

Help! I need chicken!

"Perhaps Mr Samson would do us the honour of saying grace?" Invited to a family dinner by a man I had met at a food stall, I tried. "For what we are about to receive, may God be truly grateful!" The meal, a goulash of rice and mixed vegetables looked delicious, but I had started to feel ill.

I had one must-do trip planned for Sulawesi, to Tator, a linguistic contraction for Tana Toraja, a site notable for its prow-shaped houses and its open "burials" high in hillside caves. The funerals for the latter were famously celebrated with mass killings of buffalo. But never had I felt so ill. Feeling lonely and having no one to share my self-pity with, I postponed my excursion. The next day was no better. A concerned reception clerk wanted to take me to hospital. When he asked me how he could help, I implored him, "ayam, ayam". I desperately needed water. Ayam? The word for "water" was "ayer"! In my confused state, I had begged him for chicken!

The manager later told me he had been summoned with the cry, "Quick, one of the guests is dying!" At the worst of my illness, I was unable to stand, but I hoped that at no stage was death a proposition. Along with my fever came a sharp migraine, which stabbed inconsiderately. I made one final, absurd exertion – to the bus station – rebooking my Tator ticket for the morrow.

With typical obstinacy, I boarded the bus for Rantepao, the stopover en route to the burial grounds, not knowing quite what to expect or, frankly, caring. The bus ploughed comfortably enough to Parepare, always in the shadow of a second bus, which punctured. Half an hour later it was our turn to lose a tyre. Our companion vehicle broke down. Not much later, we broke down again and it was clear we would not reach Rantepao till a very late hour. It was harrowing too, for the driver. He was usually safe in the Macale valley by 5pm but this night was spent negotiating steep mountain drops that elicited "ees" and "oohs" from the passengers. Reaching our destination after midnight, the driver knocked on a hotel door for me, explaining my dilemma to a startled innkeeper.

Feeling iller than ever in the morning, I confined myself to bed. Twenty-four hours later, I was desperate enough to haul myself to the hospital where, without any suggestion of a diagnosis, I was injected in the buttocks and laden with medicines. Fearing I had malaria, I raised the possibility with a nurse. Bristling, she told me the disease had been wiped out in Sulawesi, though her claim was nonsense.

Burials and mass sacrifices

Hearing of a funeral at nearby Tondon, but in no condition to walk, I was fortunate to meet Alex, the owner of a motorcycle, who offered to take me there, and afterwards, to the famed Tator graveyards.

Our path resembled a speedway track. There were long sections where we had to push the bike, mud sinkholes and hard ruts restricting our passage. Coming to a river crossing, we had to ditch the bike and continue on foot. Then, over a fragile bamboo bridge, up a hill and across, and we were at last at the collection of huts that was Tondon.

The roof of the deceased's home, or "Tongkonan", was arched like a ship prow, which was why some anthropologists presumed a seafaring origin for these inland people. It was an incredible construction. The frontage was decorated with buffalo horns, signifying those who had died; the woodwork below was equally elaborate with etchings of the cock (symbolising bravery), the moon (blessing), and the buffalo (prosperity). "He who has buffaloes is never poor," I was told. Buffaloes had the added distinction of being the bearers of the soul to the afterlife. The greater the bovine sacrifice, the easier the journey for the deceased.

The home was seething with guests who had brought with them large numbers of pigs and buffaloes as gifts. Pigs were slung casually from poles across visitor shoulders, to be dropped, shrieking, from a height; buffalo were delivered on all fours. As the yard became littered with livestock, it sunk in just how much was being given relative to life earnings. It was colossal. A buffalo had been slaughtered just before my arrival and, when makan arrived shortly after, it unsurprisingly featured buffalo. What else!

I was told that saving for an elaborate send-off was more important than any earthly aspirations. And it showed. Reciprocal obligations made it impossible not to gift buffalo to a bereaved family and, over centuries, vast communities were ensnared in debt. The gift of animals reinforced a family's reputation, strengthened ties, as well as displaying its own wealth propitiously. When every funeral required many months of feasting and offerings, the average Tator was perpetually poor. But he must give. The Adat demanded it.

Reclaiming the bike, Alex and I bumped over terrible roading to nearby Marante where an ancient graveyard was hewn into a limestone cliff, its base littered with bones, including several skulls that eyed me bitterly. These were centuries-old commoners' graves; the nobles were housed above, their clifftop sites marked with wooden effigies that peered down upon me haughtily. Further on, at the more famous gravesite of Londa, similar effigies could be seen at their lofty balconies. The effigies represented the nobles interred within; the network of caves at the base was bespattered with the bones of the commoners.

Alex had one more funeral to show me. Several months previously, his father-in-law had died and he had not yet been laid to rest – in some cases the deceased could be kept in the home for years before burial! Craftsmen at the family's Mendoe home were still at work, carefully chiselling symbols on the burial structures. I followed Alex up a ladder into the house where the embalmed body lay under a red robe. A wife (there were several) was knelt in grief, as was her duty for the many months before the ceremony. She was rarely permitted to leave his side. The ceremony of death began after the "tossing" of the corpse for the feet to fall to the south, towards Puya (heaven). A gong was sounded and a buffalo slaughtered. Then, and only then, was the corpse declared dead, and the celebrations could begin. Feeling suddenly very much the interloper, I did not linger.

My fever returned, I lay in my perspiring hotel bed for much of the following week. I had not had a proper meal for days and this was noted, for my host brought me a meal of rice and chicken. I managed one mouthful. My headaches were unbearable and I was depressed. The staff were superb, however, washing my clothes and keeping me supplied with tea, for no extra charge. I was surviving on "lasa", a small fruit with a sweet white flesh. If I had not discovered it, I would have been in a quandary, for I could manage nothing else. In desperation, I booked a ticket back to Ujung Pandang and a week later, *somewhat* recovered, was aboard an ocean-going ferry bound for Surabaya, Java.

Suharto's 1965 purge killed an estimated 80,000 Balinese. Paradoxically, a resurgence of Balinese culture ensued, largely owing to a growth in tourism that reinforced Balinese identity. On mainland Java, the 1970s saw the emergence of militant Muslim group Jemaah Islamiah and the creation of the al Mukmin Islamic boarding school in Ngruki, a school that would subsequently produce almost all of Indonesia's terrorists. 1973: in Bandung, mobs kill and rape Chinese residents and destroy their businesses; Jakarta is the scene of strident protests.

VII

Hanuman the star

Bali and Java: A near thing scaling a volcano; becoming immersed in the Ramayana epic: a backwoods puppet theatre, an open-air opera in temple ruins over four nights of a full moon, and watching a master puppeteer from back stage.

The Dalang (puppet master) … is obviously a superior person. Apart from his skills, he must have great endurance; traditionally a wayang kulit (puppet shadow play) performance starts after sundown and lasts without interruption until sunrise, with the Dalang as sole performer, never leaving his place (Claire Holt, *Art in Indonesia: Continuity and change*).

This guy's in deep trouble!

The plan was to climb active Bali volcano, Gunung Batur. I had hooked up with an American, Jim, and we figured we could traverse its two peaks then descend for R&R at some hot springs tucked on the side of its caldera lake. Easy. We noted, but ignored, that the volcano was 18km northwest of the oft-erupting Mount Agung. Of course, we required no guide!

Ahead on one side of us, was a patchwork-quilted valley of richly cultivated land, on the other, deeply etched fingers of hard lava falling just short of Lake Batur. It took nearly two hours to reach the valley, where we panted over tea in a small warung lying in wait at the mountain's feet.

The valley was easily crossed. But the ascent got progressively harder as jandals and sandals slipped and sharp lava bit painfully into our feet and legs. For a while, sparse scrub provided handholds, but this gave way to bare lava ridges and we soon began to appreciate how hard this climb was to be. As we followed the spurs, the sides dropped away to nothingness, and the absence of firm footing had us scrambling.

In a mad dash over some loose scree, Jim slipped, ending up crawling on his stomach to a small rock outcrop. As he struggled, his bag, containing passport and money, slipped from his shoulders. Coming up behind on a scree slide to his left, I shouted across that I would make a grab for it. "Leave it," he shouted back. But committed, I slid over, catching hold of the bag and slinging it over my shoulders as I ran uphill. I too slipped but, adrenalin-fuelled, refound my footing. "Throw it away," Jim cried, "it's too difficult." He had a point: if I had slowed, I might have fallen. But I made it.

From a solid rock vantage point, we reasoned it would be easier to go up than down, but the loose lava crumbled at our touch and nothing even vaguely solid appeared to aid us. To our right, spitting pieces of rock were accompanied by hisses; behind us, grand scenery went unappreciated. Slipping backwards nearly as much as we advanced, we reached a point almost in touch of the summit. Above us, a sharp cliff rose for a few metres, with a modicum of scrub for handholds. I tried. One metre higher, I became stuck, unable to go further, and was forced to drop back, eyes shut, with only Jim to halt my slide.

Obviously, we had chosen the wrong route to the summit. Defeated, we had to descend, which was no less terrifying. Not having footholds up meant not having footholds down, and at no time could we trust momentum to reach a point ahead. We followed a different spur down and unwittingly became trapped when it came to an abrupt end, steep drop to the left, crater ahead and to the right.

We sat, flummoxed, for an age. Eventually, I retreated uphill as far as I was able, then slid-jumped onto the next lava spur to my left. I made it, but immediately began sliding. Jim later told me I called out, "I'm in trouble, Jim, big trouble. This guy's in deep trouble!" Rolling desperately to my left I grabbed at a piece of scrub coming towards me from below and this was half uprooted before I came to a halt, arms and legs cut and bruised, but mind very relieved. From my new vantage point, I was able to direct Jim to a safer passage and the new spur provided access passed the danger zones.

Now after 5pm, it was too late to reach a town safely so we requested accommodation at the solitary warung where we shivered all night on a shared sack mattress on wood. But we were fed well. In the morning, our host asked payment of 500rp each. When I looked askance, he reduced his request to 400, still a too-high price, but we were powerless to argue after the event.

We left early, still high among the hills, joining a queue of villagers carrying huge loads on their daily walk to market. Once again, lava outflows could be admired and it was salutary reflecting how dangerous the previous day's assault had been. Paced by the villagers, we quickly reached a township, Kintamani, where we enjoyed a breakfast as break-fast had seldom been enjoyed before.

Surabaya Sue

With no destinations in mind, bar the tourist ones stumbled on, we walked the short distance to the Ulun Dan Batur temple, entering through one of the split entranceways common to Bali. We had been told it was "number two" in Bali, and the view from the top encouraged the assessment. From here, the volcano seemed gentle and dormant: our private valley was hidden, and the lake was resplendent, a pot of gold at the end of the rainbow.

Continuing our hike, we met Ken, an Englishman wandering equally aimlessly, and joined him on a crowded truck ride to Bangli. The ticket collector was a young girl with an effervescent personality. We traded names and she searched Ken's bag, howls of laughter ensuing when she found some perfume in one of the bag's pockets. When rain began to fall, we all huddled close under plastic sheeting, the women on board screaming with mock terror.

The three of us booked into the losmen Darma Putra where upon learning I was from New Zealand, the manager greeted me effusively. His youngest child had been mute, he told me, but miraculously found his voice after being blessed by a New Zealand priest. The manager was the nephew of the former rajah of the Kingdom of Bangli and, though royal privilege had long passed, a regal bearing pertained.

He told us a local legend. "In olden days, killing a mouse was forbidden: if one was killed, even accidentally, millions of its friends would angrily descend on the padi fields, eat everything, and all the villagers would starve." To this day, mouse cremation ceremonies were held once every 10 years and each kingdom (Bali had eight) maintained a mouse temple, inside of which lived a huge mouse god, "as big as a table". "Of course," he added, "not everyone is spiritually aware enough to see the mouse god!"

Our host was a cousin to K'Tut Tantri, famously known in earlier days as Surabaya Sue, an American broadcaster and authoress renowned for her broadcasts on behalf of the Indonesian republicans during the Indonesian National Revolution of 1945 to 1949. K'Tut had been adopted by the Rajah. Her Indonesian name signified "fourth born", or "youngest", which she qualified for, for being adopted – thus automatically deemed the youngest.

Our host had inherited 40 hectares of land but, under President Suharto's land "reforms", had lost everything. In the meantime, he had invested in four wives who had yielded 21 children. "I hadn't anticipated losing my wealth," he said wryly. Of the 21, 17 were still at school! Now he maintained this small losmen, relying on extra money from selling wood maps of Bali.

Wayang Kulit

Next door to the losmen, was a handsome brick house full of paintings by Ardhana – "royal painter of Bangli" – and, no surprise, brother-in-law of the losmen manager. The paintings were of epic proportion, to be marvelled at for their precision and scale. Their subject matter in almost every case, issued from the story of Hindu epic the *Ramayana*, a text that had intriguingly popped up in almost every religious practice, art, and dance, encountered on the trail.

Back on the road, Jim and I stopped to talk with a young schoolteacher, Nyoman, who invited us to a shadow puppet play – a Wayang Kulit – at his village of Metera that evening. The headman had just built a new house and the performance was to be part of the opening ceremonies. The performance, I was excited to hear, would be of the *Ramayana*. Wayang Kulits were performed regularly in Denpasar as tourist attractions, sometimes for exorbitant fees, but the authentic religious performance was not easily viewed. The performance not due to start till 10pm, we decided to try to first reach one more temple, at Besakih, referred to us as "the best in Bali". Easier said than done. Lost in back paths, it was quite a trek, including a scramble up a steep rock face and a traverse of a cascading waterway. Increasingly conscious of the imperative to return before dark, we walked with urgency.

Besakih, appearing as three distinct temples, was dedicated to the holy trinity of Brahma, Shiva and Vishnu. Sadly, a 1963 eruption of the neighbouring Gunung Agung volcano had badly damaged it and much that we now viewed was new or poorly restored. Behind, a lychee tree cast an eerie shadow as the heavens opened and a further deluge came. It was now 5 o'clock and, our chances of seeing the Wayang Kulit fast disappearing, we stuck out our thumbs.

We managed a lift part way, to Nongan, from where we sprinted to cross danger spots before complete blackness set in. Eyes straining, we inched around the cliff face, hurrying on as the last rays of daylight vanished. It was impossible now to see the onward path but our luck held. A group of locals hailed us and, on learning we planned to return the same way on the morrow, trustingly lent us a torch. We walked through several villages, knowing only that Metera was somewhere along the route. In absolute darkness, we called out "Selamat Malam" loudly, anxious not to startle locals.

As the rain turned off and on, convinced we had missed the ceremony, we sought relief in an empty street stall. We had barely closed our eyes when we were woken by the glare of fiery torches. A flame was flung to the ground in terror and a young girl sprinted off into the darkness. Jim had our torch shining on my beard – in the gloomy night, a terrible sight! Happily, the rest of the walkers laughed, the ice was broken, and we were guided all the way to Metera, just a kilometre ahead. And from the heart of a gathering crowd appeared Nyoman, smiling broadly.

The Wayang Kulit stage stood in the middle of the street, a white cloth screen stretching across the front of a bamboo hut, with a platform behind to seat the gamelan and the players, and a fine sloping roof to keep out the rain. Jim and I had no such privileges!

Still new to the *Ramayana* story, I understood little of the plot but enjoyed it immensely, as clearly did the audience of about 300 villagers. Screams of delight followed fight scenes, and cries of laughter accompanied much of the dialogue. But the tour de force was the Dalang (puppeteer). He sat in one position for the three-hour duration, related the entire dialogue, as well as conducting the orchestra of four xylophones (gender wayang). To do his job, he had to know the entire *Ramayana*; for other performances, he had also to know the other great Indian epic, the *Mahabharata*. On top of this, he was required to be an ordained priest, possessing the power to ward off evil influences.

The Dalang began the play by striking three times on the puppet box "to wake them up". Then, as the xylophones began to sound, the performance came to life, an oil lamp lit behind the centre of the screen eerily exaggerating the puppets' movements. Everything on stage was symbolic: the screen was the sky; the tree trunk, the earth; the lamp, the sun; the Dalang, the deity in control. The audience knew that all characters on their right were evil, that all characters on their left, were good. At centre screen, a finely textured tree was used to indicate episodes in the story, including the beginning and the end. How I longed for knowledge of Balinese!

Becoming bitterly cold and wet from the intermittent rain, I huddled against a brick wall for protection, but the performance was otherwise supreme, concluding a perfect day perfectly. Rarely had so much been accomplished in 24 hours. Afterwards, Jim and I shared a bed in a small house where Nyoman lived and shivered through what remained of the night.

In daylight, the walk out was not half so forbidding. After yet another temple, we began a descent through rice fields towards the road, which dropped rapidly away from us. The entire hillside was a maze, an intricate web designed to confuse. Eventually a farmer appeared who directed our path to the road – and rides. Back in Denpasar Jim and I calculated we had walked about 100km.

Hanuman to the rescue

Two weeks later I was in Jogjakarta on mainland Java. Jim had moved on and I was exploring alone this centre of Indonesian batik. Jogjakarta was known as the University City, an apt title, for students abounded, all wanting to stop and talk. Finding cheap accommodation was rarely so easy.

Jogja was a much smaller town than I expected. I almost immediately bumped into the familiar figure of Sue, the American who had led me through Thailand and Cambodia. Travelling at a startling pace, she had "done" Australia and New Zealand, and was now en route to the Philippines on her way home where yet another full passport might be displayed. Now travelling with an Englishman, Peter, she had met up with my mother in Christchurch and sharing this with me, as well as understandable travel reminiscences, claimed much of my day. Together, we plotted how to attend Indonesia's most famous *Ramayana* festival, a four-day open-air operatic dance performance that serendipitously coincided with our arrival.

The opera was performed annually over the period of a full moon – two days before, and two days after – only in a few months of the dry season. But under enduring downpour, the three of us began to doubt whether it would be held at all. Its setting was a ruined Hindu temple complex at nearby Prambanan. We bought tickets of the cheapest variety then returned to our losmen where a perfume cloud of marijuana wafted towards us.

At late afternoon, the three of us took a bus to Prambanan. The setting was magnificent. An outdoor theatre combined the old and the new, curving as a Coliseum with parabola seating before a large flat stage. Immediately behind, rose the tower of the 9th century Prambanan Temple, tall and tapered. Just as the performance was about to begin, it was floodlit and there was an almost audible tension as a packed audience awaited the cast.

As was to happen each night, the show began with a procession of high-stepping guards and delicately shuffling maidens, presenting offerings at centre stage. The audience was in this way reminded that the *Ramayana* was, first and foremost, a religious happening. Unlike in Bali, women played women and men played men, though heroes Rama and his brother Lakshmana retained all the feminine graces to be expected in classical Indonesian dance.

The story unfolded intricately, the principals accepting an unfair banishment without demur before an array of adventures that exceeded my sparse knowledge of the legend. But I watched enthralled at the unfolding of Hinduism's great epic: the banishment of god-king Rama and the repercussions of the abduction of Rama's bride Sita by Ravan (or Rawana), the lord of evil. It was a riveting start, including a dramatic scene in which monkey god Hanuman and his followers were blinded by Ravan before being rescued by godly intervention and their sight restored. From audience reaction, it was clear Hanuman was a favourite.

The second night belonging to Hanuman, fittingly, exploded with action. An overfilling theatre indicated that this was *the* night, with herds of children, and shrieks of anticipation from all compass points. To add to the excitement, before the appearance of any cast members, one could make out shadowy figures clambering eerily over the temple ruins behind the stage. Thanks to a bit of overnight reading, the tale was more easily followed: Hanuman sent by Rama to find the kidnapped Sita;

his discovery of Ravan's hideout on the isle of Langka; his subsequent capture and miraculous escape.

In a thrilling finale, huge fires were lit for Hanuman's immolation, but his escape was effected and Ravan's forces at the last routed. Every triumph over evil, every suspicion of action, was heralded by voluminous cries – whistles, cheers, hisses – and the actors responded, displaying leaping skills with breath-taking co-ordination. The previous night, the rain stopped shortly before the show began; tonight, the deluge began almost immediately at curtain call.

We had a long wait before a ride home. All private vehicles ignored us and those that were chauffeur driven, had upturned noses. Eventually a busload of schoolchildren from Semarang, inmates laughing uproariously, invited us on board, insisting in return that we sign a multitude of autographs.

Master puppeteer

The night was not yet over. Back in Jogja, we walked to the Sultan's Palace just in time for a midnight Wayang Kulit. There were hundreds in the audience, but only a handful, all Europeans, sitting in front. The seating that was jampacked was behind the screen, where all that could be seen was the manipulation of the puppets. It was the Dalang (puppeteer), not the shadow play that the locals had come to see.

Tonight's performance was matchless. The Dalang sat cross-legged for eight hours, reciting all dialogue, manipulating all puppets, repeating without hesitation his version of the *Mahabharata*, an epic tale of war between cousins overspilling with instruction of ethic and morality. At no stage did he falter, cough or yawn, the only possible quibble being the use of an electric light rather than traditional paraffin behind the screen. By show's end at 5am I was one of three remaining Europeans. I had fallen briefly asleep twice but woken to continue witnessing a rare performance.

Before the third opera evening I rejoined Sue and Peter at our favourite restaurant, along with an Australian, Rod, part of our losmen's scene, enjoying a meal until it was ruined by Rod's loudly arguing the cost of his share. We convinced him of his error but waiters were left with unflattering views of Europeans entrenched.

The *Ramayana* this night was fun, but the sheer ineptness of the child monkeys at centre stage detracted from the earlier enjoyment. On the first and second nights, their parts had been small and their slightly

82

off-key antics had provided amusement, coming from ones so young and with such little import in the overall plot. This night they performed repeatedly, and the show suffered. The full moon, however, was resplendent and, in religious terms, it was apparently the most important night of all.

Hoping for a good look at the temple in daylight, I caught an early bus for the final performance, arranging to meet up with the others shortly before the show began. Sadly, the Prambanan temple had been subjected to substantial pillage throughout the 19th and 20th centuries, its parts scattered around the world. While once it had comprised seven stunning towers, now, most had fallen. Outside the main entranceway a family of beggars lay in wait for the chauffeured Pontiacs that would soon berth nearby.

I approached the stage for the final time with trepidation. But third night failings were soon forgotten as the drama of the timeless epic unravelled. The final battles of the generals won the hearts of children and adults alike, especially when Rama accelerated from his usual classical poses to fight – and kill – the terrible Ravan. After more reading later I wondered whether the plot had deviated from legend, Ravan being invincible, but no defeat needed be absolute in this story of life balance between good and evil. Sue, Peter and I argued over fares home with competing bemo drivers, but we had our way, good triumphed over evil, and we reached home safely.

The 1960s in Sumatra saw the start of huge land grabs by pulp and paper companies, precursor to later devastating palm oil plantings, with widespread deforestation endangering once flourishing populations of elephant and tiger. Into the 1970s, Suharto's drive to "centralise" met fierce resistance from ethnic groups objecting to what was perceived as a neo-colonial government engineering influxes of Javanese migrants, with associated unfair distributions of income. 1973: throughout Indonesia, ethnic and religious tensions simmer.

VIII

The strange case of the missing Swede

Sumatra: a rocky start; where women rule the roost;
a hippie settlement where the tourists come to look at me;
and a drugs' reality check at the border.

Take one bowl, preferably large. Into it, put chunks of papaya, avocado, pineapple and banana. Sprinkle on top a liberal amount of diced coconut. Daub chocolate powder artistically across and, for flourish, conclude with a splash of sweetened condensed milk (Banana Susu *– famous recipe of Lake Toba*).

Rocky beginnings

Australian Paul looked the stereotypical hippie: flowing black hair cascaded about his shoulders and a lush moustache threaded the tangles. In strict Muslim territory, I knew immediately we would be the centre of unwanted attention.

At Merak, the ferry departure point from the tip of Java to Sumatra, there were two queues: one for the masses, one for the army. The former overflowed, the masses periodically prodded into shape by police with truncheons; at the latter, an occasional soldier sauntered for his purchase. After enduring the proletarian queue for some time, we broke ranks for the army side then calmly boarded our boat, worryingly named the Krakatau after the terrible 1883 eruption.

Joined by an American and a Canadian, Paul and I watched as small boys below begged us to throw down coins for them to dive for. What a sight we presented! The Canadian also had long hair, magnificently blonde, with a broken nose for added effect; the American had the build of a footballer; while my matted beard waved above faded jeans and a hole-ridden shirt. This was not an auspicious first entrance into strict Muslim territory.

On the Sumatran side, at Tanjung Karang, first one losmen then another had "full-up" signs, despite a dearth of visible guests suggesting otherwise. We were followed as we walked and watched in a manner that could in no way be described as friendly. Rocks were thrown and Paul was hit in the back. We turned, glowering, and that was the end of it. But it was enough of a scare for my three companions, who eased my discomfort by catching the night train to Palembang. Within minutes of their going, a student offered me bed at his home. Better still, I was woken in the morning with a breakfast of egg and rice, ample appetiser for the long train ride ahead to Palembang. There was slight awkwardness when my host requested "oleh oleh" but I satisfied his wont with a pair of socks and a photograph. He had initially requested "something small, like a jacket".

My carriage was full of soldiers. Military policemen escorted the ticket collectors, with pistols in leather holsters. They also had truncheons that they used to hurry passengers with. An officer in a nearby seat took a banana from my pile without so much as a beg-your-pardon. But otherwise, they were unthreatening.

Indonesia's constitution guaranteed the army a third of parliamentary seats and a quarter of Congress, thus ensuring their perpetual power. They were there to guide, protect, and watch over. They were God. Founding president Sukarno's policy of "*Guided* Democracy" extended down to even the individual soldier. A popular joke went: "a man in a crowded carriage asks a neighbour, 'Excuse me, are you in the army?' 'No,' the neighbour replies. 'Well then, is your father, brother, son or cousin?' 'No? Well then, are any of your friends in the army?' 'No? Then will you please get off my foot'!" The ludicrous was not far from the reality.

In Palembang, a teenager in a denim jacket shouted at me, "hello", but tight-lipped traditional Muslims walked by quickly. Once I was deliberately bumped. To the young I was a romantic adventurer; to a good proportion of the rest, I was a decadent hippie. I welcomed neither judgement: the English of many teenagers was limited to "prostitute", "Hell's Angels", "fuck", and "free love". "Hati ada penting [heart is what's important]," I would inadequately respond.

Bus ride from hell

I had been warned the 750km bus ride to Padang would be hell. And it was. After recent severe flooding, the first leg toward the eastern city of Jambi was impassable and we had first to head south, then west, on poorer and poorer roads in an ever-enlarging detour.

Our passage did not quicken. When the driver tired, we stopped to rest, when he became hungry, we stopped to eat. In between times, we crawled. It took most of the following day to reach Jambi, where the bus pointedly stopped outside an expensive hotel. Fortunately, I managed to convince the driver to let me sleep on the bus. I went with it to its night park beside an oil-logged pond that provided bathing for the company's workers, stripping with them, and sharing their rice meal.

The long last leg to Padang was agonising. We arrived at a bridgeless Batang Hari crossing point close to midnight under a massive downpour where our driver wisely delayed boarding the one-vehicle-at-a-time ferry till the deluge had subsided. When it finally did so, I crossed in the truck ahead of us with Peter, a Kenya-living Englishman, to give us time for a tea on the other side.

The next crossing point had a bridge, but of fragile slats, and most passengers chose to walk over. But Peter was asleep and I still glued to my seat – nervous as hell – as the bus inched and swayed its way over! Barely across, an oncoming truck squeezed against us, hitting the window where my head was resting. Our driver leapt from our vehicle screaming abuse, but the truck was gone. I was just bruised, but shaken. Lesson learned: when we came to further bridges of doubtful construction, I disembarked!

The next morning brought another early start but, on slightly sturdier roads, we plopped safely among Padang puddles shortly after midday. The 750kms had taken us three days.

The funicular-travelling Minangkabau

My breakfasting at a bicycle stall so perplexed a Chinese local she insisted on taking me to her house to eat comfortably. Later, an Indian less impressively accosted me with a surprising racist prattle. "The Indian is like the European," he said, "He has the same long nose, round face

86

and narrow cheek bones. We're dark, but that's because we come from a tropical climate. The Indonesian is different, with a squat, ungainly, stub nose and fat face."

A detour or so later, a painfully slow northbound train dropped me at a small town I failed to identify. Stepping on to the platform, I was welcomed effusively by the stationmaster who told me *no one* went this way by train. "You can continue as far as Padangpanjang," he said, "but the trip will take about eight hours as against 60 minutes by bus!" Excited at the appearance of a rare tourist, he insisted on buying me tea. I almost chose the bus – till I saw the train.

It was funicular *and* steam, ancient and picturesque, and I jumped aboard with alacrity. Inside were no passenger seats, no ticket collector and precious few passengers! Seating comprised wooden benches. The ride was uphill, slow and tortuous, with mechanical cogs assisting the train in its heavenly ascension, but rather than dwell on physics, I concentrated on breathing in the scenery amid the black coal dust that infiltrated the carriage.

Two elderly Minangkabau women insisted I share their meal of rice and chillied fish. From a rare matriarchal society, these women exuded confidence – no sporadic giggling from women earmarked for child rearing, but strong, assured conversation, even with a bule (foreigner). The women shared a saying with me: "water becomes round in bamboo" (peace comes from togetherness). Crime was almost unheard of to the Minangkabau, they said. When it did occur, however, everyone took responsibility and the offender continued to live within society. Of course, the lack of crime might equally be because Minangkabau men were notorious wanderers, reportedly the reason for a marked dispro-portion of the sexes.

We climbed, at times spectacularly, above cliffs and canyons, till thunder heralded a sudden deluge. The train halted, forcing passengers to huddle mid-aisle away from the pane-less windows. It was monsoon rain, brutal but short-lived and when the sun broke abruptly through, we warmed to the strains of birds reawakening, and the delicious scents of wafting durian. Into this setting walked an elderly Katib (Koran reader), bent spine, creaking limbs, and with deep lines etched across mountainous eyebrows. He shuffled, one hand authoritatively on a sharp hip, and began speaking, giving clearly important advice from below his black, Muslim cap. His teachings were recorded in a school exercise book, elaborately decorated with flourished penmanship.

Disembarking in miserable wet, I jumped aboard a bus to Bukit Tinggi where I found a high point with views of the town, looking way beyond to mountains and secret views of strange prow-shaped houses – these ones the traditional homes of the Minangkabau. My reverie was halted when I witnessed a group of men take pleasure at goading a caged civet with sticks. While my revulsion grew, I felt a small hand slip into mine and left the scene with a tearful child. My new friend and I drank ice drinks of Christmas hues and, when it was time to leave, I had someone to wave to.

Lake Toba

Gurning's losmen was perched right on the edge of Lake Toba. With a small veranda stretched out over the water, a willow birch providing shade and romance, it was not hard to fall for. I had passed into yet another tribal region, this time of the Batak, also possessors of prow-shaped houses, providing yet another apparent link with the Sulawesi inhabitants of Tanah Toraja. Swallows darted and bats emerged silently from crannies in the building's foundation. Miles above, falcons flew, always in pairs, while next to me the lilt of a flute reintroduced me to an Australian I knew from somewhere.

After booking in, I was set upon by two Englishwomen who bewailed Indonesia's poor sanitation. I told them I had found Indonesians to be exceptionally clean. Their pigs might mingle freely with their children but they swept their compounds every day, washed thoroughly – and their pigs cleaned up any remaining residue after them. In the morning, I escaped to the island Samosir, crossing with a middle-aged Australian and two Americans overladen with camera gear. Our ferryman was a Batak named Mongoloi whose reliance on sail provided us with time to enjoy millpond surrounds before landing at lake-edge Tomuk, a narrow kampong lost in island greenery.

At Mongoloi's – he also owned the losmen – I laid claim to space in an attic cranny then repaired to the lounge for a meal that was near identical to that served at Gurning's. But Mongoloi's was famous for one menu item, stories of which I had heard whispered about as far south as Jogjakarta, and I was eager to sample it. The Banana Susu – tropical fruits and avocado topped with diced coconut, chocolate powder and a liberal splurge of sweetened condensed milk – was unbearably addictive.

One day, uncomfortably bloated in Susu, I set out to cross the island. After an initial stiff climb to a plateau, I followed an easy path to Ronggurnihuta, a village that I hurried from when its children surrounded me. At Sijambur, however, a clatter of cymbals drew me in to a mini-festival where I was welcomed with friendly questions. "Berapa Umor?" "Twenty-four." "No, not yet married." "Why not?" "I'll think about it when my travels are over." "No children?" "Certainly not!" I glanced with mock horror at my questioner and my hosts fell into laughter. Without further ado, I was invited to share a meal of red rice and goat meat in a thick, blood gravy.

The path beyond widened, but far from easing the way, a hard rock base cut at my feet and my jandals provided little support. Wherever I walked, my presence evoked screams from the children. Sometimes, "Hello, Mister" was replaced by "Minta uang" or "Minta rokok", requests for money and cigarettes. When I stumbled into lakeside Pangaruran late afternoon, I gratefully gleaned relief from copious tea. But I was sore. Both my feet had split between big and middle toe and I was limping. I had walked nearly 40km. A stall keeper offered me a table as a bed and the floor became platform for impromptu English lessons. My "bed" was shared with one of the family.

My next stop was the much-anticipated hot springs of Pangaruran. I crossed a bridge, barely noticing the relatively large vessels below and had nearly completed a citrus peel climb around the side of a hill before realising I had crossed back onto mainland. The island and mainland had once been linked by a narrow isthmus that, at some point, had been severed to create a channel. Arriving at a river dotted with oxbow pools, I subsided in the hottest I could withstand. A rickety shed offering a bed at the edge of the water had one other guest. We slept in a private planetarium, an "upper floor" that was only partly rooved. The stars shone on us and the soft rustle of hot steam provided a subtle lullaby.

In the morning, I resumed walking around the lake edge. My feet were hurting badly, so I was grateful when an antique bus trumpeted its approach. A nanosecond squint at the overcrowded inside had me clambering onto the roof where two or three other unfortunates introduced me to the unique Samosir bridges, famed for their sporadic overhead ceilings – at a height just low enough to endanger the lives of anyone foolish enough to travel on top! The first ceiling came without warning. I barely had time to fling myself as low as I could as the roofing timber scraped centimetres above me. Four more such bridges followed. We top-riders posted a lookout to yell, "jambatan" ("bridge"), but the warnings were invariably late. Once I was reduced to an over-the-side fling, thrusting my feet inside into the faces of indignant passengers.

The bus route ended at Simanindo where I had no option but to resume my painful walk. But the ever-present lake soothed and a small boy gave me a present of an avocado mashed with sugar before, best of all, directing me to a shortcut to the next lakeside paradise I was seeking: Tuk Tuk. And just as rain began to fall, I strolled down to the lake edge into a losmen known as Bernard's. Dry!

A Banana Susu love affair

Propping myself within a dull marijuana ring, I sussed out my new roommates. Thanks to their head start they were aloof to me so I parked myself in a corner foregoing joints for a Banana Susu. The Tuk Tuk menu paralleled that at Tomuk, and it amused me when Bernard himself questioned me eagerly about Tomuk menu developments.

Clear head of the kitchen was Bernard's sister, Peppy, whose swashbuckling effervescence won everyone. She played favourites. When I arrived, her pet was a huge German called Thomas, with a long wispy beard and relentless banter. When he left, she chose me. When Banana Susus were served, it was always made clear, "this one is for Alan", and "this one" was invariably huge.

An American introduced himself to me as a disciple of "Eck", an abbreviation of Eckankar, a religion born out of the US in the mid-sixties. He proclaimed grandly that his soul could travel outside his body, becoming excited as he explained "life forces" – "Man, I feel so good!" It was ordained we had met. According to him, Plato was a member of Eck, so perhaps my current reading too, was ordained.

I loved Tuk Tuk, but an influx of tourists removed the appeal of remoteness and I was keen to return to Tomuk before departing Indonesia. When I made sombre farewells to Peppy, she cast an accusing eye at my treachery. I immediately missed her. Tall for a Batak, she was at times coyly feminine; at other times the tomboy emerged with playful punches. Busy days serving a full house of indolent Westerners did nothing to dissuade her jollity.

Returning to Mongoloi's at Tomuk, I reacquainted myself with familiar faces. Joe from Sulawesi, was here, and several-remembered Australians, all hooked on grass and Banana Susus. Larry, the Canadian on the boat to Sumatra was also here, also stoned. A tape recorder had manifested from somewhere, and the main house filled with chatter and music. I parked myself on the balcony, where Larry joined me.

Larry had left Canada as a 20-year-old after a modest inheritance; now 25, he was still wandering. With long blonde hair, he had many colourful tales of clashes with officialdom. He had been refused entry into England, had his hair forcibly cut in Panama, been jailed in Honduras (drugs), as well as other scrapes aplenty. Yet he bought meals for beggars and was a soft touch for anyone in need of a dollar. His sole dishonesty was a predilection for weed.

I began a daily routine. Awaking, I toileted, ignoring the pigs poised for my waste removal before bathing in the lake alongside children washing dishes, women scrubbing clothes, and water buffalo, just watching. Back at my balcony, I played chess with a yawning schoolchild (everyone played chess here!), then Banana Susu for breakfast, and more serious chess encounters with a lately risen Larry. As night fell and the chess set tired, I would watch the sun fade and the buffalo being herded slumberously to their pens under the houses.

A woman dies

Great excitement at Tomuk! A woman had died and a procession of European travellers keen to observe Batak custom invaded. The villagers showed little concern at the overwhelming presence until three shirtless Australians arrived. The religious leader waved them angrily away. Presumably because we were respectful, Larry and I were invited to remain, as were a Swedish couple. The body lay in a rough-hewn coffin, her face uncovered, lined but calm. But for a still-working carpenter hammering noisily at the cross, she might have been sleeping. An inked inscription read: "Tubu 1871", which, assuming this was the year of her birth, made her 103, Tomuk's grand old lady. "Tubu" is Indonesian for "body".

An odd setting this, a sacrificial goat tethered to a central tree while the preacher preached. A renowned orator, the latter soon had mourners sobbing – and laughing. At the height of the soliloquy a high-pitched scream signalled the arrival of a daughter of the deceased, and, as if on cue, villagers jumped to restrain her as she fell, prostrate, upon the body. A sombre procession left the kampong, stretching across strangely quiet padi fields to where a plain white tomb stood waiting. After the preacher had spoken once more, the corpse was pushed peremptorily to rest, the tomb slab slammed shut with finality.

Afterwards, we gorged ourselves on familiar red rice and buffalo meat while a trio of gendang (drum) and serune (flute) players entertained us. When night halted the performance, we retired with the players to a waterfront stall. The Swedish husband, a keen collector of music, requested one more performance. "We are tired," the flautist protested, but agreed to a tune or two for payment. The Swede placed his tape recorder and a fast-gathering audience whooped their appreciations.

Continuing long into the night, the music only ended when all tapes were full. Eager eyes swivelled towards the Swede's wallet. But when he produced just 200rp there was a ripple of resentment. The players had expected at least 3000 and the "donation" was not appreciated. I escaped to share a joint with Larry.

The hippies of Tomuk

The following days saw an influx of tourists, immaculate Americans and Europeans in batik shirts curiously photographing these long-haired creatures, dissolutely poised at chess or reading. A pamphlet advertising Tomuk was shown to me. It included: "Come see the hippies of Tomuk!"

Three well-dressed Indonesians also arrived, looking out of place, and a drug-addled suspicion spread of police "hippie infiltration". We kept our joints in our pockets. But on our balcony, Larry and I risked one, then another, then two more. We subsided in soft laughter, then louder giggling.

I could easily have stayed longer. Lake Toba and Samosir – its "island within an island" – was at the heart of the Indonesian section of the trail. Much of that had to do with the welcoming Bataks, in particular their entrepreneurial losmen owners at lakeside spots like Tomuk and Tuk Tuk providing beautiful and safe settings away from authoritarian eyes. "Hippies" were accepted, could live cheaply, and relax safely. But I was keenly aware of my fast-expiring visa. The Medan (Indonesia) to Penang (Malaysia) ferry service reportedly had been shut down and I needed time to suss out alternatives. Everyone I spoke to was resigned to having to fly this leg but I was determined to make a saving. So, after a couple more days, I moved to the next big town en route, Pematangsiantar, hoping to achieve a visa extension.

Inevitably, it was a holiday – Independence Day, anniversary of the start of the Indonesian National Revolution against the Dutch and the 1945 freedom proclamation – and Immigration was closed. But I was lucky to meet Syahdan, a tall Batak with long black hair and an intriguing limp, who offered me a bed at his home. That sorted, he took me to the city centre to enjoy the Independence Day celebrations, a series of rousing patriotic acts performed on an open-air stage, including a popular pair of comics who gave a disturbingly vicious send-up of the Chinese.

"I became crippled after falling from a tree," Syahdan told me. "It's left me with a limp and I can't grip rice with my fingers." He was not the only family member to have suffered. A brother who had gone to Czechoslovakia to study had been blocked from returning when Suharto took power. Another brother, an opposition politician, graced a Siantar prison. Though a devout Muslim, Syahdan was keen to explore Christianity. "There is only one God," he said.

The next morning, I interrupted Immigration officers from their game of table tennis, to be told briskly they could not extend visas. With no alternative, I caught the next bus to North Sumatran capital, Medan, where I found a cheap hostel with a cool roof sleep-out. And there was Larry and the Australians, and a Swede I had previously met somewhere down the line. There was grass. There was happiness.

Beating the ban

Every traveller I met despaired of reaching Penang by sea. Refusing to give up, I walked kilometres to the wharves where I unearthed two boats headed there, but both captains denied me passage, saying the Port Authority forbade passengers. When I produced my forged press card, the *Tapian Nauli* captain confessed to having room for *some* passengers, but I would need permission from the boat's agents. Of course, their offices were closed for the night.

On a long evening walk with Larry, we were shouted at rather too publicly, "Marijuana, mister? Hash"? Trying to look inconspicuous, we hurried on. When we sat at a stall, a pusher approached with some neatly packaged samples: "One kilo, two kilo? Sure!" Behind us, the fat restaurateur sat quietly listening and, when we rejected the pitch, joined us. "You must be very careful. These street salesmen are bad men," he said.

When the others flew out, I got busy. The shipping agent denied there was a boat going to Penang. I mentioned the *Taipan Nauli*. He said it was permitted to carry only cargo. I said I knew different. He said the boat was full. I showed my press card. He said only the manager could deal with me, but if I returned in an hour… Bit firmly between my teeth, I did so, arriving back just as a group of poorly dressed Europeans were shown the door. I asked if the manager was available and a smile passed me a ticket.

Elated, I presented myself to Immigration with my ticket in hand, only to be gestured to a seat and ignored. In a battle of wills, I sat unattended for more than three hours before officialdom finally caved and my visa was extended for two days – just long enough to cover my departure. With a leaving time of "about 7pm", I was left with nothing to do but loiter amid typically dreary wharf stalls and restaurants. Three prostitutes joined me and we wiled away the hours in conversation until work beckoned them. They left me with a card granting me one night's free admittance to a local club.

Looking down on the wharf as the last of the cargo was brought aboard, I watched a wharfie pilfer products while a policeman stood guard. At first it was a few bags of potatoes. Then other articles were taken: ornaments and chattels passed surreptitiously from hand to hand with cash clearly changing hands. In the middle of his work, one wharf worker glanced upwards, saw my wink (tact!), and continued his pilfering unconcerned.

I found sleeping space on a deck bench and, sometime after 11am, woke as our vessel steered through an island maze towards mainland Malaysia. A school of porpoises raced us effortlessly before turning south, whereupon flying fish took their place like vaudeville understudies. It was like returning home, this second visit to Malaysia, and I felt a sense of relief when, stepping ashore, no hawkers leapt at me, nor drug salesmen, pimps, students, the curious, nor conmen.

There was, however, a twist to my Sumatran adventure. Catching up with Larry a country or two later, I learned that the Swede of our Medan group had attempted to enter Malaysia with a kilo of hash rolled up in his sleeping bag. He had been at the back of the queue when they entered Customs. Larry and the Australians had waited for him, but he had failed to appear. Oh, did I forget to mention? Our Swedish friend had borrowed my solitary pair of presentable trousers in order to look smart at the airport customs. I never saw him – or my trousers – again.

In 1962, the US sent troops to aid Thai military dictator Kittikachorn against "communist" aggression, a presence that expanded with large bases built in support of the war in Vietnam. In 1968, a Pattani United Liberation Organisation was formed seeking secession for a Muslim state in south Thailand. 1973: the insurgency is officially declared "untrue" (a lie not to be dispelled till the escalating violence of the early 2000s). In Bangkok, thousands of students demonstrate against the central military dictatorship, 77 are killed, and a student uprising unseats the government.

IX

Why turtles cry

West Malaysia to Thailand: the infinite sadness of giant turtle motherhood; shutting my door on a city of prostitutes; and mapping an island paradise.

On he goes, the little one; bud of the universe; pediment of life; setting off somewhere, apparently; whither away brisk egg? His mother deposited him ... as if he was no more than droppings; and now he scuffles tinily past her as if she were an old rusty tin (D.H. Lawrence).

Turtle grande dames

Fifteen miles from Kuala Lumpur, the car in front accelerated just as a villager scurried across its path. There was an un-braked thump, metal against flesh. Neither car stopped. I strained to see if the man was okay, but my car too accelerated, the driver grim and making no comment. I recorded the offending number plate.

In Kuala Lumpur, I sought out a police station where a bored looking officer asked me where the accident had taken place and, as accurately as I could, I did so. "Oh, that's not in our jurisdiction," he replied. I expostulated acidly about a man's life being the consideration. Eying me strangely, he tore an edge off a sheet of scrap paper and recorded the number plate. As an afterthought, he took my name.

I did not stay long in KL. Hoping to witness giant turtles during their birthing season at Rantau Abang on Malaysia's east coast, I once more put out my thumb and, a couple of days later was arrived, my latest ride dropping me deliciously on a signposted "Beach of Whispering Love". Virgin white sands spread sensuously under leaning coconut trees – and a road sign announced the imminent construction of a new port. I had arrived just in time.

As I alighted under the inevitable coconut palm crochet, small boys led me to a line of tiny, sea-perched cabins. The floors were concrete, the beds – doubles – easily filling the entire room, and that was all. There was no electricity. But I had a roommate – an American named Fred. At one end of the cabins were stalls peddling coffee and bananas, at the other, a lone kedai that also sold meals. The stalls once a day sold a simple rice dish at a third of the kedai's price, so I ate there. The kedai however, became my resting place during daily inactivity, its 20c coconuts satiating the most avaricious of my mid-morning hungers.

Rantau Abang evidenced plenty of signs of neglect: discarded beer bottles, wrapping paper waste, empty food cans, and scattered banana skins. But in the turtles, it had a universal attraction. On the beachfront, alongside the inevitable activities of smoking and chess, was a wired-off compound reserved for anak penyu, the baby turtles, where the eggs were relocated after each daily collection to be scientifically recorded. Those due for hatching were caged separately.

A flurry of torches after 10pm led me to the hatchlings just emerged from their eggs. The tiny creatures buffeted their cages excitedly, flopping against each other, climbing over each other as they tried to nudge forward, primeval instincts working overtime. It was to be a long night. Not to be released till the morning, the tiny creatures kept struggling, no frolic, just an insane flapping, a desperate jerking of their heads.

At midnight another burst of human activity on the beach indicated the arrival of the night's first adult. This mother was enormous, how else to describe her? Her eggs had been laid but already cruelly collected from under her. The misguided creature had meticulously covered over an empty hole.

As she began her long haul back to sea, humans surrounded her, their torches shone curiously into her large, and I imagined, tear-filled eyes. Hands prodded her, with comments on the hardness of her shell.

They handled her flippers, and the under-flesh, commented on the softness ... not surprisingly, this grande dame pursued a zigzag course to lead everyone away from the hole, unknowing that her eggs had gone. It was a sorrowful delusion and every flipper stroke prolonged the agony.

At times, she stopped exhausted, her giant flippers thrashing the loose top sand, propelling her nowhere, but still, eager torches enforced the detour. An official stepped in to assist a hind flipper, and the beast spun seawards. There was a howl of protest from the audience but the intervention was a kindness. At times, her thrashing posed a danger to the throng. I estimated she was about 2 metres in length and her flippers were correspondingly large. I kept my distance. When she found open water, she sank rapturously, and disappeared.

Further along the beach, the government had leased areas to private enterprise. The eggs sold for M20c each on the market and, as a single turtle laid up to 140 eggs, the income to a fisherman was at least worthwhile. I found tank-sized tracks leading from the sea and it took just a short walk to find the next straining mother, yet to start her digging.

Using her flippers for shovels, she began hauling and emptying the sand in little piles. When she could reach sand no longer, a deep, almost human, sigh emanated. Her shell hunched and eggs began spilling at random. A local with a sack materialised and, while labour pains continued to wrack the turtle, skilfully flicked her produce onto dry land. As the laying neared completion, the eggs grew smaller, apparently yolkless, and these the collector discarded. This was heart-breaking stuff. I was left welling with indignation at the behaviour of a poor fisherman, etching his living as best he could.

Emerging from my cell mid-morning, I leapt into the sea and remained there. The water was tepid and it took quite an effort to eventually remove my body to land. Mid-afternoon saw me sitting lazily at a wooden bench facing the sea, poring over Thoreau's *Walden*. Defoe, Hemmingway, Coleridge, Thoreau… I pondered that each had had their retreats to the eternal, their escapes for reflection. Surely, I too, was entitled to my search for eternity.

A break for freedom

When I rose to leave, I found my sandals missing, which was devastating as the sand was near impossible to walk on. I crossed molten granules as far as the hatching compound without expecting to see anything in sunlit hours. Sadly, there were to be more dramas. I watched as a young turtle floundered against the netting and the unrequiting sun, before withering before me. In a neighbouring cage, another minute head peeped out of its shell, one tiny flipper followed, then the figure froze, instantly dead in an alien setting.

The scene was repeated again and again, plastic necks turned Lottishly to cadavers, whitened prehistoric creatures suspended in sudden stillness. I saw only one survivor, liberated from its cage in response to the urgings of onlookers. All my attention was now on one solitary break for freedom. Before the tiny creature lay a veritable desert with no oasis in between for respite.

In their natural state the young turtles erupted from their eggs in the evening, then, instinct-driven, followed the moon to the sea. But now, in mid-afternoon, this unguided 5cms of water-soft leather headed stubbornly inland. Somebody turned it around and its neurotic reaction was repeated. This might have gone on indefinitely if nature had not intervened, a wave cascading higher than those preceding, enough just to dampen, but what psychological moment this first energising life force provided!

If for Freud, birth was the greatest single, mind-shaking human experience, how much greater the shock for a turtle as it emerged from dankness to a world of overflowing sun before a second transformation at the crash of a wave and the pounding of surf. For now, it was safe. But the presence of predators virtually guaranteed this turtle would fail.

Toasting the miracle of birth over coffee, my attention was drawn to a large fin leaning threateningly 50 or so metres from shore. Someone shouted, "Ikan yu!" Thankfully, there was no one bathing. The shark lingered. Over a half hour period, this 2-metre-or-more monster swam up and down the beach area before leaving without notice. Others reported seeing two youngsters accompany her as she left: she too, was a mother. Why monster? I knew common perceptions were askew. We loved the porpoise, hated the shark. The former fed on small fish, the latter, large, hence perhaps, our horror.

A little guiltily I ordered a turtle's egg for my makan. It was boiled for more than 10 minutes, served with rice and a soya sauce. As I had been warned, the white had not fully congealed, though the yolk had hardened sufficiently to be palatable. The white was inherently tasteless but, spread with the rice, the whole was edible.

Next morning, another influx of baby turtles was released and a comic sequence re-enacted of a thousand Charlie Chaplins. They bumbled and bumped, flippers upturned as if penguins. They fell over, they collapsed then, as surf cascaded upon them, they turned somersaults, jumped, plunged out to sea, were washed back, and restarted. Already the young clowns had responsibilities. After a bare five minutes of gaiety, there was a need to face life.

Large numbers of tourists arrived for Hari Kebangsaan, the Malaysian anniversary, so Fred and I removed to a distant coffee stall. Telling me about growing up in America, he asserted black people were less intelligent than whites. "I'm not saying whites are superior," he said, "just different. It's a fact. If you can accept that races have evolved different physical features, why can't you accept that races may have evolved different brain structures?" His thesis was based on "studies and statistics". Wearying of a debate that went nowhere, I made my excuses and sought out a kedai where I bought new sandals then, back at the beach, discovered a local wearing my old ones. I now had two pairs of thongs: more guilt – I could have let him keep them.

The mass baby turtle release was repeated in the morning, comic relief and Shakespearean tragedy. How many would survive? No sharks were evident, nor the school of dolphins that had appeared briefly the day before, but swollen fishing boats and sea-bird entourages encircling the horizon indicated predators were present. They were not fishing speculatively.

It was time to move on. I had been travelling with only a small shoulder bag, washing my clothes nightly, so was looking forward to Penang where the rest of my gear awaited me in a storage locker. I was glad too to be rid of Fred's bigotry but, as it turned out, the presence of the Ugly Tourist was not easily cast aside.

My main ride was with a French couple, the husband a retired lawyer, the wife a retired journalist (neither tired of mentioning their professions). They carried a guidebook, which was their bible, and every kampong mentioned became reason to halt. Chendor had crocodiles and the grave of a mermaid; Cherating had cottage industry, driftwood sculptures ... on, on, on. Past Ular we stopped at a five-pointed red star where the book told us a baboon could be hired to fell coconuts. A Chinese family shared the hire cost. The poor creature scrambled on its long chain sending several large husks tumbling. The Chinese family accepted one coconut and left quietly; my Frenchwoman loudly insisted on claiming all that had fallen. "Damn it, I've paid for them!"

Hurry, short time!

A week later I was in border town Pedang Besar where I sneaked into a restaurant toilet to change clothes for the crossing into Thailand. My good work was nearly undone when I followed the shortcut directions of some boys to the Immigration Office – through a hole in the fence. Two immigration officers looked on disapprovingly. Nevertheless, I was allowed to enter Thailand and, almost immediately, caught a train to the southern city of Hat Yai.

It was a memorable ride, if only because eating excesses caught up with me. Already uncomfortable on the carriage's hard wooden seats, I now also had to contend with dashes to the end-of-carriage loo, an open outlet to the rails below. With no toilet paper, my only recourse was the pages of my latest book, Solzhenitsyn's *One Day in the Life of Ivan Denisovich*. If not for the discomfort, it might have been funny, as I pushed myself to the limits to keep ahead in my reading!

Hat Yai was a junction town but, more notably, famous for a certain type of profession. I was accosted immediately I stepped from the train. "Hurry, short time!" "Want a room? No charge! You just pay for the fuck!" "Want my daughter? Is good girl"! "20 baht, mister", "30 baht, mister", "100 baht, mister", "very cheap" … All Europeans "want fuck" it seemed. So too did the fat Malaysian businessmen who arrived with me and were already in the arms of 15-year-old children.

Still suffering, I struggled to find accommodation that was not a brothel and, eventually, gave up trying. As yet another proprietress indicated the extracurricular by pumping a finger enthusiastically between thumb and forefinger circle, I squeezed myself into the first room shown to me, and locked the door. And luckily, I remained ill enough to barely notice the knocks on my door throughout the night.

I saw no evidence of the Muslim insurgency taking shape in Hat Yai and further south, though heard talk of their fight for secession under the umbrella of the "Pattani United Liberation Organisation". When I asked a local about it, the response was an unequivocal "untrue", which I had no reason to doubt. It would not be till the early 2000s that mass killings and bombings would unequivocally demonstrate the lie.

I recovered at Phuket, where I had barely settled into a cheap hotel before finding familiar faces: Rob (a Kiwi from Kuantan), Karl (a German from Rantau Abang), and newcomer Jan (a Dutchman). Rob moved into my room – costs halved – with the others next door. Rob was nearly 2m tall with light hair well below shoulder level, thus encouraging a fair amount of attention wherever he ventured. Just 21 years old, little things unduly annoyed him. Karl was the opposite. Thirtyish, prematurely grey, always in trademark sunglasses, pink cap, faded jeans and T-shirt, he was the true "freak", wandering on grass, tripping on music, and forever smiling. Jan, a student on holiday, was determined to make the most of everything.

Mapping Koh Samui

Phuket? Much of the tourist hotspot we could not afford, but the beach we could. Eating and smoking prevailed, mainly in that order till, for no particular reason, Rob and I decided to move on, he for Bangkok, I for the island of Koh Samui. At the last minute, Karl and Jan decided to join me.

At Nathon on Koh Samui an affable Customs' official allowed us to leave our luggage in his office. The others planned to leave for Bangkok the next day but I decided to stay. Told I could leave my pack as long as I liked, I threw toothbrush and soap in my shoulder bag and set off on foot for nearby Lamlamai beach, recommended to me as solitary, my kind of destination.

Lamlamai was indeed near perfect: no houses, just a single store tucked out of sight of the beach. White sands presented a beautiful setting, with the best swimming from some polished rocks that could be sat on, slid off, or slept under. A youngster named Anothai peppered me with advice, starting each sentence with "You!" "You! Go swimming!" "You! Sit here!" When I told him I wanted to sleep on the beach, he insisted I stay at his friend's store. "No pay, mister!"

I swam, reddened appreciably, then joined a bevy of travellers who had arrived from somewhere and together we smoked a bong and relaxed even further. Not too stoned, but happy, I wandered across to the store where the owner, Anun and his wife, greeted me warmly and fed me on fried fish and oodles of coconut cake. I slept before a sea horizon on a sand floor.

In the morning, Anothai led me across yawning rice fields to his parents', stopping only to pluck a long green bean from a garden. "You try. Good!" He had a tendency to ignore the "s" sound, as in saying "ri" for "rice", and my impressing its importance conjured its appearance in all manner of phrases. "You! Goods!" His parents fed me, not unexpectedly, on fish and cake, then we returned to the beach where Anun was waiting with an aged Yamaha. "Come to market." We jolted along a coastal track to a coconut oil depot where we drank whisky and a wizened old man felt my arm muscles disparagingly. I had been presented.

Continuing to the home of Anun's parents, we sat on the porch chewing betel nut. Anun pasted the coarse red dye on the lime leaf and wrapped the nut within, all the time laughing wickedly. At first it tasted foul but, as I chewed, the nut fibres had a soothing effect, something like day-old chewing gum. I promised myself this would never become a habit. The rusted teeth of the old villagers were a terrible advertisement. Back at Lamlamai, Anothai appeared carrying a newly slaughtered hen. As Anun prepared the fowl, the sky erupted, the rain cascaded viciously, the house shook and our candles extinguished. Outside, a lone seagull beat futile passage against the wind before disappearing in reverse and a dozen waterfalls manifested on the bay's rock surrounds.

I sat throughout the next day under brilliant sun in my briefs, exposed on the hippopotamus rocks with my feet dripping in warm seawater, Uncle Toby (*The Life and Opinions of Tristram Shandy*) my only company. It occurred to me the mixture of salt and sun might have done wonders for Uncle Toby's groin! The next morning, refreshed, I set off clutching three hands of bananas through blotchy village streets, each with children chanting as far as their village boundaries: "bye bye".

Wanting to circumnavigate the island, I kept briskly on the move, through avenues of palms, though for a while was held back by a slow villager in front with an even slower baboon on a chain. It was only when the monkey and its owner stopped to perform their allotted task of felling coconuts that I managed to pass. "Hoo! Hoo!"

When I strolled past the coconut depot where employees were lined up for a morning briefing, I was mildly pleased when they broke decorum to wave. At Thong Takien, where seaward horizons were unlimited, I ignored the temptations of its coffee shop to begin a steady climb, from time to time refreshing myself with my bananas. An entire hand disappeared before memories of earlier problems encouraged me to ditch the remaining two.

To nowhere in particular

Villagers at Suing gave me copious coconut milk, leaving me feeling rather like a washing machine set on rinse. At Borpud, a horde of youngsters descended upon me but I found peace at a Walden-like pool on the beach where I soaked till a fishing boat spotted me, heading inshore to offer me a ride to nowhere in particular. I was dropped off at a rounded spit dividing the bays of Banmanum and Borpud, where the only life to be seen was a dog cavorting.

Caches of seashells straggled along the coast, for the most part broken by relentless surf but, by sifting carefully, I discovered some of rare beauty. I soon had an impressive collection. Then, on schedule, the heavens opened and I might have been savagely caught, if I had not stumbled on a line of bivouacs on the shoreline. I threw myself inside the nearest, huddling against the rear wall, for the roof was partially caved in.

From a rough plank bed, I looked out at a livid sunset, entranced by delicately lit-up fishing craft fluttering along the coast. I fell asleep then abruptly woke to see a canoe berthed outside my hut. As steps approached, I barked out frantically, "Sawatdee!" The fisherman jumped, startled, and crouched outside, where I hurriedly joined him. My inadequate Thai managed to elicit that he had further fishing to do, before he broke into a smile and waved me back to my slumbers.

When light came, I read a little (Thoreau, on winter!) then continued my island circumference to Banmanum. A growing thirst hurried me to the next stop, a tiny village where a gathering of townsfolk shared with me their Laow Khow whisky. From there, I set myself a westerly course along the beach. I found a long pole hidden in undergrowth that was used to reach and drop coconuts but my efforts at wielding it proved fruit-less. I also discovered a cave at the base of a cliff-face containing a rough bed and a supply of firewood. What man had claimed retreat here? Perhaps the coconut plucker needed a bolthole?

Now mid-afternoon and mindful of past weather patterns, I turned inland, trotting unnoticed through back gardens of several stilted houses till the rain came, along with a sudden burst of thunder. An abandoned house provided all the shelter I required. At Banlamhoi, children took me to their schoolhouse where I spent the rest of the afternoon playing table tennis until, victorious, I was offered a ride all the way back to Nathon on the back of a motorcycle. Circumnavigation over!

Booking into the modest Santegasem Hotel on the seaside, I straightway won over the proprietress by producing my collection of shells. Suang Kawotai, thin to gawkiness, her smile several sizes too big, was gorgeous. When I made her a gift of the collection, she promptly exhibited them in a foyer display cabinet. A card I had been using as a bookmark won me further brownie points: seeing it bore an outline of

Koh Samui, she made a request beyond refusal. "Draw for me, please, a map for the hotel." Drawing was not a strong point of mine but I was foreign and therefore talented, so I yielded! My skewed attempt was pinned prominently in the foyer and benefits immediately accrued: a large seafood dinner followed by continuous snack offerings for the remainder of my stay.

Writers are not welcome in Burma

It was not easy to move on from Koh Samui, one more island paradise to have wooed and won me. But a week later found me once again entrenched in the Bangkok youth hostel. I explored the Thieves' Market, then the weekend market and, with Nepal trekking in mind, bought some US army boots and a good knife, as well as managing a good book exchange: a Hermann Hesse (*Narcissus and Goldmund*) for an Alistair MacLean.

My immediate plan was to have another go at Laos but, looking ahead, first sought a visa for Burma, only to be curtly rejected. When I asked why, I was alerted to my listed occupation – "writer" – an unwelcome notation for the Burmese government. At a time when passports required an occupation, I had chosen my profession badly. I had had my reasons. Fearing entry into Israel might be problematic after any side forays into Arab countries, I had applied for a second passport on the grounds I was, indeed, a writer. And, though valid for one year only, it had been granted.

Israel had long ago stopped being my destination. Nevertheless, the second passport had proved immeasurably useful. Already, it was almost full, which mitigated any difficulties in having to renew on the hoof. But today, the downside – no visa! My pleas eventually saw me led into the ambassadorial chambers, all the while stressing I was no longer a writer, where a stern-faced man in starch agreed to cable Rangoon for permission. I was advised to return the following day. And this time, I was successful. It wasn't a significant score, of course. As for every other traveller at this time, the maximum time period permitted in Burma was seven days. But first, Laos.

In the 1960s the US extensively bombed Laos to shut down North Vietnamese supply line the Ho Chi Minh trail – dropping more bombs than during the whole of World War II. The "communist" Pathet Lao were backed by the North Vietnamese, who repeatedly invaded. 1973: In Laos, the ceasefire divides power between the communists and the royalists in a nominally coalition government. The North Vietnamese, however, remain and the Pathet Lao have much of the ruling power.

X

He reholstered his revolver, slowly

Laos: running a Mekong gauntlet of trigger-happy Pathet Lao; rejoining the "trail"; the folly of using personal documents as bookmarks; and the varied temptations of Vientiane.

Laos had emerged from the Indo-China war at least nominally independent. But sovereignty did not make this roadless stretch of land viable. The French had kept it going as an idyllic back water … the Americans set about transforming it into an anti-Communist bulwark (Crozier, B, *South-East Asia in Turmoil*).

A wine-drinking pilot and an indignant pig

I looked apprehensively across the Mekong at the rugged spine that was Laos. At its edge hunched a thin fringe of houses, veil to a nation where peace had not been known for a very long time. The war had officially ended. The government forces had shaken hands with the Pathet Lao and a failed recent coup attempt had been laid at the door of neither side. But neither had yet yielded and, according to officials, Laos was still "unsafe".

A dinghy carried me across the river to Ban Houei Sai where Immigration was a shed, its solitary official asleep at an outside desk. He jolted awake, stamped my passport, then laid down his head again, oblivious to some German travellers who sauntered passed without bothering about immigration niceties. Wanting to cut costs, I held back from booking into the town's single hotel, instead finding a seat overlooking the river to spot new arrivals. Soon all manner of familiar faces materialised: an Englishman, a Swiss and a Canadian, all met previously along the trail. I booked a room with Nick, the Canadian.

Military were everywhere, straggles of undisciplined soldiers with fearsome M16s slung casually over their shoulders. They laughed and argued good-humouredly, punching each other on the shoulders, with little evidence of work or duty. For a while it was fun to sit and watch. But with a visa allowing just two weeks' stay, I had to quickly spring into action. I approached Air Lao for a ticket to the old royal capital of Luang Prabang, but the plane was full. I had lots of questions for officials. Was the road open? Were there boats available? A truckload of negatives soon had me discouraged and I consoled myself with two Frenchmen in the same predicament.

It was time for some lateral thinking. The next morning, I walked with the Frenchmen out of town to the local Air America base, optimistically hoping to hitch a flight in the manner of a war correspondent. We spotted two unattended helicopters, and a groundsman who assured us a pilot was due "sooner or later", so we waited patiently. In due course he arrived – and apologised politely. "Sorry guys, but they'd have my arse if I carried you. If word got back to Vientiane…"

But serendipitously, Air Lao had last minute cancellations and all of us found places for later that afternoon on an ancient DC3. Though I was nearly turned away by a zealous Customs official who found a bag of maté tea in my pack that he squeezed and sniffed before letting me passed. I climbed aboard over a squealing pig and some live chickens, and sat uneasily in the first fitting-less aeroplane I had had the pleasure to travel in.

On take-off, a hostess pushed cuspidor bags onto each of our laps before, unnervingly, an effusively jolly captain appeared in the aisle with a glass of wine in his hand. "They call me Poppa," he said. Poppa was a pilot of 30 years' experience on a single run, Vientiane to Luang Prabang to Ban Houei Sai and back again, though the service had till recently been war-interrupted. I noticed his face was flushed and prayed there was a teetotal co-pilot up front.

Below, spread Laos, rugged and uninhabited. Fancifully, my eyes searched for the Ho Chi Minh trail, the route by which the Viet Cong had outflanked the American and South Vietnamese armies. Occasionally, I thought I could see a secretive mountain path but the subconsciously hoped-for glimpse of exiting – or arriving – Pathet Lao armies did not eventuate. Eventually a blanket of white cloud forbade further viewing and after a brief moment of excitement when the pig threatened to break loose, I fell asleep.

In Luang Prabang, I found floor space at *Jodie's*, the home of a young American that was favoured by freaks. Outdoors, the market was in full swing, with large numbers of hill-tribespeople dressed in black trousers and long-sleeved jerkins, red waist and headbands, their shoulder bags, prisms of colour. The ever-present military slouched, some with short hair, some long, but all carried guns. In contrast, the hordes of trishaw riders wore black or blue "Mao" style jackets, with caps and mildly threatening sunglasses.

A bicycle with a sidecar swung into view, the outrider beating a drum as the driver shouted his news: per the peace agreement, the Pathet Lao were free to move their forces into the city from a two-week period, and two weeks was now.

A teenager stumbled past, both his legs artificial, and I was embarrassed to be caught staring. I saw other war victims, a leg missing, or two, an arm missing, a hand… They begged, but without obsequity. The "free world" stand against "communism" had clearly taken a terrible toll. I turned away. In the evening I joined a Canadian named Dave at a French restaurant where Bob Dylan blared, and left late, inexplicably happy in outwardly tragic Luang Prabang.

The American never heard of again

Over dinner, I was reacquainted with Joe and Wayne, integral members of the Samosir scene. They invited me back to their hotel for a smoke where, beneath a slivered moon, we inhaled while Joe plucked expertly on a guitar. Three uniformed Laotians joined us and the evening passed in peaceful relaxation.

Inevitably, our conversation explored reaching Vientiane overland. Travel by truck or boat would be dangerous, but the former, doubly so. Joe had heard that the Pathet Lao had recently captured two Australians and an American on the river ride: they had released the Australians but the American had not been heard from since. I was to hear this story several times. Perhaps it was apocryphal.

A paper had been signed, officially peace existed, but Pathet Lao acquiescence could not be taken for granted and, if a traveller was shot, there was no recourse. Reports were saying as much as four fifths of the country still lay in the hands of the communists. "There's no real truce, just a government surrender," Joe said. And none of us argued. We had heard time and time again that the Pathet Lao now controlled the country.

Luang Prabang was an addiction. It was easy to linger in the coffee shops, enjoying the food and the smokes, with occasional gentle strolls riverside. But its allure was diminishing as more and more tourists arrived, taking advantage of the newly opened borders. One morning Dave and I trekked beyond city outskirts to the hill villages where the tribespeople shone in their dresses and headbands, reds splashed against black. Heavy silver earrings tore at lankish earlobes, and stiff necks strained against supporting structures that resembled oxen yokes. How they loved their silver: bangles and opium pipes, scales and betel nut dye containers.

When Dave left by plane, I stirred from my indolence to obtain police permission for an overland journey. Even though I had no clear plans, it was a formality. The police philosophy appeared to be, "if you want to get shot, that's your business". Traveller chat indicated a couple of potentially imminent boat departures, and the prospects seemed good. Officially, the river was open. It remained only for someone to inform the Pathet Lao.

Setting out at 4am in pitch black for the dock, it was difficult to check directions under meagre street lighting. But I found the vessels, one named *Green Spot*, the other, *VT222*, like a serum batch. Neither stirred. At 5am a lamp was triggered and the boats were illumined but it was another hour before greyish figures emerged for their toiletries. At last in a position to approach people, I learned that the *VT222*, though not due to sail for a couple more days, had fewer stops, so immediately booked passage.

I spent the rest of my day in the Lao American library reading its copy of John O'Hara's *Appointment in Samarra*, using my police permission slip as a bookmark. At closing time, I dutifully replaced the book on the shelves – with bookmark still inside! By the time I was aware of my lapse, the building was deserted. In growing panic, I realised the centre was closed not only the next day, a Sunday, but also for the entire following week: Monday was Columbus Day, Friday marked the death of Buddha, and the week between was a public holiday. But thanks to an incestuous expat community, I was able the next morning to find the home of the Lao American Association's director. Even more wonderfully, he was willing to break into his weekend to rescue me.

Very slowly, he reholstered his gun

The *VT222* was half cargo, half houseboat, high roofed at its bow, high roofed at its stern, and sunken in the middle like a sway-backed pig. Corroded oil drums were stacked on the central roof, while below were piled car chassis, bicycle wheels, more oil drums, and miscellaneous iron scraps.

Simple sleeping quarters with chained wooden beds that rattled were available at each end of the boat, but these were reserved at bow (for crew) and stern (for privileged Lao). Lesser Lao spread their effects on a large mat between the kitchen and the engines. The few European passengers had to make do with the only place left for them − the roof. My travelling companions comprised a South African couple, two Germans, two Swiss and two Canadians. Most kept to themselves, though one of the Canadians, Clark, I warmed to.

As we cast off, I found a position at the rails, enjoying a scenery that switched magically from mango and banana pastureland to forest. Despite the advice given me, we stopped frequently. Each village had military offices with desks on muddy Mekong bank and, each time, a crewmember was required to run ashore to register and pay what I assumed was a token fee. Our captain had no record of traveller names, yet the bureaucracy of inspection was maintained, the "coffee money" given, a routine enacted.

Sometime before lunch we encountered our first Pathet Lao village, where the same procedure was enacted. Their military comprised three or four solemn-faced soldiers dressed in jungle green. Their shirts were squared at their base, and someone suggested that the only way to distinguish officer from rank and file was by noting whether the tail end was tucked in or left out. Perhaps this was so − certainly there was no evidence of epaulettes or badges.

But always in the centre of the group stood a soldier of immaculate bearing and dress, on his head a rounded cap with a thin lip, just as might be seen on the cover of *Time* or *Newsweek*. At his hip, always, was a holster. Perhaps irrationally, I became convinced he was from China. Similar scenes were repeated several times throughout the day − a straggle of villagers, a gaggle of mixed-dressed military, and a well-uniformed man with Chinese features.

At one such encampment I wandered ashore to fill my water bottle at a mountain stream and was paid little heed. At another, I identified the Pathet Lao flag: red horizontal stripe on dark blue, with a circular white disc at centre. This sight was not to be repeated but we often saw the stern, silent stares of Chinese-style clip jackets and round-lipped caps.

It was a strange situation existing in Laos. When the Pathet Lao moved into the cities, the country would effectively be theirs. The peace agreement accorded each side a deputy premier and five cabinet ministers: the loyalists had finance, defence, interior, health, and education; the Pathet Lao, foreign affairs, public works and transportation, information, economic planning, tourism and religion. The premier was to be "non-affiliated", which seemed to exclude all claimants bar neutralist Prince Souvanna Phouma. How could they possibly gel?

The agreement also required the removal of 200 American "experts", 8000 American-funded Thai mercenaries, and an estimated 60,000 North Vietnamese troops. In the light of the graphic Pathet Lao gains, one could only wonder at a reported Prince Souvanna comment: "The Laotian people are too easy-going to be communists!" I could see only a communist victory, a government capitulation if not surrender. But perhaps this would not be a bad solution to a meaningless war.

Shortly before 6pm, our captain slowed at the government-controlled village of Hoy Suey where we stopped for the night, further passage deemed "undesirable" in darkness. Here we picked up two French motorcyclists who had ridden from Vientiane to Luang Prabang, but broken down on the return journey. They boarded with signs of clear relief. Traveller complement was now 11 and the boat began to resemble a tourist cruiser. Two armchairs had appeared above the forward cabin and bodies and books were cluttered untidily everywhere.

A store near the riverbank sold Ovaltine, which we drank at an open-air table. Ovaltine! Back on the boat, the Germans had attached a large mosquito net over the two armchairs, subsiding underneath in luxurious sleeping bags, oblivious to local amazement. I fell asleep on a sheet of cardboard on the tin cabin roof.

We set sail at sunrise, with a straggle of sleeping bags still unravelled. From ashore, the sight must have been bizarre: an enormous mosquito net framed against the skyline, with befuddled European heads popping out from sleeping bags, like chickens from their shells. Within an hour we had reported at four military outposts, with most Europeans still in their beds. As if word had been telegraphed, crowds of villagers turned out to view the spectacle: strange people with heads buried in Cohen and Lawrence, Hesse, Forster and Huxley. Youngsters stared and pointed and even the usually dour officials were caught off guard, with sudden smiles that made a mockery of war.

Pathet Lao outposts alternated with royal government, and interface was at first limited to stares of surprise. Our journey so far had been a jaunt, eleven boys and girls having fun. Shortly before midday, we parked at a Pathet Lao village where the gathering of the troops took place as usual, at centre Clipped Jacket, silent and taciturn. Nothing out of the ordinary. Then one of the Frenchmen raised his camera.

When a German followed suit, the calm was shattered. Clipped Jacket lowered his right hand to his holster and began to withdraw his gun while, beside him, a colleague waved imperiously for the cameras to be lowered. The Frenchman put his down, the German covered his with a sarong, and that should have been the end of it. But the German attempted to sneak a shot, his glinting telescopic lens peeping from beneath its batik cover, and the movement was detected.

A soldier began shouting and the officer, more purposefully this time, again went for his gun. Seated next to the German, I flung myself hard right while the quick-thinking South African grasped the camera and threw it along the cabin roof. Slowly, very slowly, the officer reholstered his revolver and the *VT222*, already shunting to midstream, breathed a sigh of relief.

As our trip continued, the countryside became more rugged and stops became less frequent. But the trip became more interesting thanks to one of the French motorcyclists, a fluent Lao speaker, who translated conversations for us. When Pathet Lao boarded, we learned that they asked if there were any Americans on board, and that the captain had reassuringly replied in the negative.

This day was a long one. Our captain eager to spend the night under the auspices of royal government forces, we bypassed the sizeable town of Pak Law, then continued through doubtful territories with the moon, almost full, providing brilliant highway for late travel. Thailand appeared on our starboard bow, a succession of well-lit towns highlighting Thais' relative affluence – electric lightbulbs and cars. The outskirts of Chiang Khan were marked by a fairground where loudspeakers out-shouted our thudding engine.

We parked for the night on the Laotian side, Sanakham, an obvious contrast to the opposite bank. And told there would be no more Pathet Lao, we slept peacefully. Sanakham had a lively market that sold crickets, kingfishers and sea snakes, all of which I declined to sample. Before continuing the next day, we were joined by a group of fleeing Yao hilltribe refugees who, according to our French translators, had been cajoled into fighting the Pathet Lao with promises of money and now were afraid. Perhaps with good reason.

Vientiane appeared at 4.30pm, a village by sight, city by proportion. We docked twice, once for the refugees, again for ourselves, clambering ashore stiffly, weakened from our prolonged inactivity.

City of sin

Clark and I sought out the Lido Hotel, by repute the cheapest accommodation in town. It doubled as an opium house and a brothel. Comfort indeed! I was conscious my visa had expired, but it was getting late, and I did not feel like a frantic rush to Immigration before a 5 o'clock closing. So after settling, we caught up with the Germans and some familiar Luang Prabang faces for an extravagant French cuisine.

Vientiane had a romantic air: "Paris in Asia", the Folies Bergère with sarongs and brocade. Alas, only the name conjured romance. The poorly sealed roads, edged with pathways of dust, provided polluted passage. Citroens, Volkswagens and Toyotas busily mounted footpaths while hapless pedestrians leapt frantically aside. Armies of German Shepherds patrolled the streets, Cassio-lean and, though neither molested nor eaten, I recognised their desire.

This city of sin had prostitutes in copious quantities and, on pleasant days, they could be viewed, arm-in-arm with self-conscious Europeans strolling the Mekong promenade. Their work was a performance, though whispered obscenities aimed at titillation often fell flat, for the words were borrowed from movies and servicemen. The drug scene too was a heavy one. The deathly thin heroin addict could be seen stumbling, stark contrast to the many fortunates merely playing with grass or opium. All the travellers smoked weed. Vientiane in 1973 had little else to offer.

As soon as I could, I called on Immigration, whose officials were unconcerned at my overstay and granted me a further two weeks. I wandered down to the Mekong with Clark, an Australian girl, and a Canadian called George, where a carnival was in full swing. Ferris wheels spun and a wall of death roared, while stalls peddled whisky and coconuts. We tried our skill with rifles with clearly bent sights, then jostled with a growing crowd for the best position to watch the weekend's highlight, dragon boat races.

All the while George talked of his sexual conquests. He was full of bravado. A day earlier, his room had been burgled and Clark had generously lent him enough money to reach Bangkok. I knew Clark had lost his money, but could not tell him so. A prostitute joined us, and George found enough coin to collect a wife for the weekend. Clark and I returned to our hotel, sidestepping the numerous Nepalese stalls selling jade, sapphires and bronzeware, everything "precious" and "antique". These itinerant salesmen spread their mats throughout South Asia. They were friendly if outrageous salesmen, but that was their business.

Back at the hotel George and "girlfriend" Lilly appeared with another hooker in tow, whereupon Lilly teased us by dropping her sarong. But neither Clark nor myself were willing to participate. When George and Lilly left, the newcomer remained, till Clark smacked her behind and she took the hint.

George had his benefits. He bought large numbers of newspapers that he passed on and, for the first time, the scope of current world horror was revealed to me: a coup attempt in Thailand, Israel at war, US Vice-President Spiro Agnew's resignation, and the Watergate scandal heightening. It seemed possible that in Laos, I was on safer ground than in all those places! The Pathet Lao had still not entered the cities, though the papers reported China had offered to airlift them into Vientiane and Luang Prabang.

Returning to my hotel room, I found Clark stoned. He insisted on lighting a pipe for me. One pipe, two, a third, and I too, was star-borne. I awoke late the next morning still feeling high. Later, I met up with Joe, an Australian who had cropped up at various points on my travels. We had never travelled together but if I were seated alone in a restaurant, he had often appeared, always with polite restraint: "Do you mind if I sit here?" This evening, he was high, and I not, so our conversation comprised many silences.

George was not yet gone. He, Clark and Lilly played gin rummy while I set off on a round of duties that included the collection of my Thai visa and my application for a Laotian exit visa. Those achieved, I dodged a downpour in coffee stalls reading Forster's *Passage to India*. Clark went nightclubbing, taking our key with him, and I might have been left homeless for the night but for a smart piece of breaking and entering. Clark had been "whoring", as he later put it.

Lilly came to pay court. In her early thirties, she was by no means beautiful, but had a goddess-like smile. She kissed me, punched me sisterly, then passed to reverie with her fingers knitting patterns in my hair. She seemed more like a mother than a prostitute and it was easy to believe she liked me. When evening fell, I went for a walk. The Nepalese salesmen had long since packed up, but the coffee shop behind was just beginning to flourish. "Ovaltine, hon! Fried eggs, ning!" The calls went out and the customers filed in, the hungry and the satiated, the lonely and the gregarious. The woman who roasted bananas had gone, but the corner Vietnamese restaurant had begun a steady trade and, perched above its window, two screaming mynah birds competed raucously with the singing cash register.

I tired of Clark. We had discussed travelling together to Paksane, a crossing point back into Thailand, but he would give no indication of when he wanted to go and I decided to make my own way. In the morning I paid my share of the bill and set off for Paksane, blissfully unaware of how to get there. A receptionist had suggested trucks might be leaving from the 6km mark, so I took him at his word and presented myself at a wayward coffee stand, early-morning-shivering behind a sign helpfully proclaiming, "6KM".

A boat capsizes

When no trucks appeared, I was in a quandary. I knew nothing of the route ahead, whether Pathet Lao lingered, or hobbits. No travellers I had met had travelled this way. Now also knowing trucks were an irregular appearance, I decided to hitchhike.

My first lift brought stern moralising: "Who told you this is the road to Paksane? It goes only to jungle and North Vietnam. Have you got police permission? You'd better take the next taxi back to town!" I almost obeyed this well-dressed businessman but, after checking this was indeed the right road, continued heedlessly. As it turned out, the route revealed no dangers, but I was reminded of the amount of emotion – and fatalism – aroused by the term "overland" in 1970s' Laos. The excitement was contagious. I felt keyed up, almost elated, as I bravely strolled to war.

A landrover gave me another start. We stopped several times for the driver to practise his marksmanship with a long-barrelled rifle and once had to backtrack to reclaim live bullets scattered after he carelessly left them on the bonnet. Importantly, he took me past a northern junction, from where there was little chance of losing my way.

A ride on the back of a Ford pick-up, a raft river crossing, a ride in the back of a truck with three young Laotian girls dressed in their finery, elegant blue sarongs, shining plastic handbags and cartons of fish and vegetables, and I found myself at another river crossing, this one a spindly branch spanned by an army pontoon with a hole blasted in the middle. A canoe paddled by a youngster carried passengers across one at a time. When it came to my turn, the boy impatiently risked three passengers and the overladen craft capsized. Scrambling ashore in knee-deep mud, I lost a sandal.

As I curled up in an empty street stall, some workmen interrupted me to share their meal of sticky rice and chicken. They shared also their laow khow (whisky) and I was watched carefully for my reaction as I drained my glass in the customary single gulp. I fell asleep on a riverbank veranda, unconcerned at a squadron of mosquitos.

In the morning, I joined the men at their bathing from a raft buoyed by thick iron buckets, leaning over the side to scoop river water with a borrowed pail. The water was black. Almost clean, I was fed a breakfast of congealed, sticky rice and fish. As I ate, I was bombarded with questions, all in un-understandable Lao. But when "America" was mentioned, I gathered they were guessing my origin, and my little-acquired Lao assisted my fervent denials.

My final ride came from a van crammed with a cargo of rice. But it drove fast through numerous police posts, and it was barely midday before I was at Paksane. I found a cheap hotel where I bathed making use of a large barrel of water in its courtyard while a group of giggling schoolchildren turned out to watch. The next morning, I jumped on a ferry and changed nations. At Bung Kan, Thai Immigration greeted me unkindly with a weekend service fee that left me without any Thai money. But I was able to board a bus for the larger Udon Thani, thanks to a genial conductor who took my word that I would change money and pay him as soon as we arrived.

In the early 1970s, escalating protests by struggling Thai farmers demanded fair rice prices and debt reduction. This so-called "Farmers' Revolt" was the precursor of the "10-day War", a student-led challenge that, with royal support, overthrew the government. 1973: the dramatic 10-day uprising sees students challenging tanks and leads to the sudden flight of key military leaders, including PM Thanom Kittikachorn. And in just three years, the last US Air Force bases servicing Vietnam operations will finally be shut down.

XI

Gunshots, screams and
a national anthem

Thailand: overtaken by an unexpected "10-day" war;
the Bangkok aftermath of a student revolution;
and renewing my forged documentation.

Dozens of people have been killed in the Thai capital of Bangkok in street
battles between government troops and demonstrators … violence broke out
when several thousand students took to the streets demanding the military government
step down … Bangkok is now under a state of emergency
(BBC News, *14 October 1973, Thai army shoots protestors*).

Facing guns and tanks

Bangkok was eerily calm. The once bustling youth hostel I frequented was barely occupied, its Triem Udom School grounds strangely removed from the furore of the last few days. But furore there had been. During my brief absence in Laos, an uprising led by students I remembered as docile had overthrown their government. Newspapers were calling it "the 10-day war". The city was in shock.

I soon learned that hundreds of people had died and strongman Prime Minister Thanom Kittikachorn had resigned. As a result, a long-promised constitution and free elections had leapt forward from three years away to a foreseeable six months.

I was stunned by the actions of the Thai students. The hostel I was staying at was perched innocuously between a distant corner of the Triem Udom School and the Chulalongkorn university adjunct. The main school building was a pale two-storey block servicing Bangkok's elite families and known as a "preparatory" institution for the university. Its main entrance was at one end of the grounds, the youth hostel at the other. A small gate nearby allowed hostellers entrance and exit during school hours; outside school hours, arrowed pikes stood sentry duty above the gate and the fence was topped with barbed wire.

Every morning of my earlier stay, I had watched the school pupils marching in a rigid cadet drill, half goose step, while an audience clapped. How proud everyone seemed! And how rigid! It was common for us worldly hostellers to mock the apparent homage to authoritarianism. We commented on the suppression of individuality and, though without empirical evidence, presumed the same of their tertiary colleagues next door.

How wrong we were. In 10 short days students had mounted protest after protest, facing guns and tanks, and overthrown a despotic military government.

It was hard to get a handle of what had unfolded, let alone the political detail, in an atmosphere that was now of closed, empty streets. But I made the effort to talk to people, listened to English-language radio broadcasts, and collected newspaper articles. And, years later, I was able to piece together a mixture of history and recollections for a commemorative piece in Christchurch's *The Press* (8.4.81).

An earlier upheaval in Thailand

"Sawatdee." The Thai student holds his hands as if in supplication, stiffly bows to his teacher, then enters the classroom. Once the room is full the pupils, unprompted, stand grimly at attention then fervently proclaim the national anthem.

Everything is ordered and correct. Obedience is a virtue and the Western observer is left with the indelible impression that the young Thai will, if so instructed, run to the end of the earth and back – without question.

It is the first week of October, 1973. In a few days' time a small group of students and activists will be arrested for distributing pamphlets calling for a free constitution. The universities will erupt...

On April 1, 1981, a group of Thai generals launched a "peaceful" coup, ousting the Prime Minister, General Prem Tinsulanonda, banning political gatherings, and dissolving the constitution and Parliament. This action from the military provided no new experience for the long-suffering Thai people.

That coup failed. But the present government, itself a militaristic one, might recall the story-book "10 days" of upheaval in 1973, when a group of students from a Bangkok university sparked a public fury that toppled that year's military rulers. It could happen again.

Thanom Kittikachorn seized power on November 17, 1971. It was a bloodless coup, carried out against his own constitution, cabinet and Parliament. He was already premier of an elected government that had been running the country for just two years, nine months.

The reason for the coup, according to Premier Thanom, was the threat of communist insurgency at a time when the Vietnam war was overspilling. The new military government promised to return the country to democratic rule as soon as "internal security had been restored." By 1973, the level of insurgency had not markedly increased, yet the government had shown no sign of restoring democracy. Because of this, a new political movement was formed. Its aim? To put pressure on the government to introduce a constitution.

The group vowed to use peaceful means. It hoped via public seminars and the like, to provoke public discussion and thereby encourage the government to change. It distributed pamphlets.

DAY 1 (Saturday)

Special branch agents today arrested former student leader, Thirayudh Boonmee and 10 other activists as they distributed leaflets urging support for a movement aimed at the early promulgation of a permanent constitution. They are being held on initial charges of violation of a National Executive Council decree which forbids more than five people gathering for political purposes ... (Bangkok Post)

The 11 were subsequently charged with "inciting the public to act against the Government." The arrests were ordered by the deputy premier, Praphat Charusathien. The 11 were taken into custody at 2pm, later escorted to their homes where extensive searches were carried out. Leaflets were confiscated.

DAY 2 (Sunday)

The National Student Centre of Thailand threatened some sort of reaction against the police. A twelfth activist was arrested.

DAY 3 (Monday)

Deputy premier Field Marshall Praphat dropped a bombshell this morning when he announced that police have uncovered plans which showed that the 12 arrested were involved in a plot to oust the Government ... (Bangkok Post)

DAY 4 (Tuesday)

Tension flared up at the Thammasat University this morning as some 2000 students congregated for Hyde Park style rallies to attack the government, and threatened to march on Bang Ken (where the activists were detained) (Bangkok Post). In response, the whole Metropolitan Police force was put on full alert.

The university called off examinations as thousands of students missed classes and joined the mass rallies. Anti-government posters began to appear and student leaders began planning strategy. Talks included "how to set up moveable toilets" – essential amenities if the protest was to last.

DAY 5 (Wednesday)

More than 300 students continued the rally at Thammasat. Many had kept an all-night vigil on campus, despite light rain. The students now demanded the release of "13 persons" and a permanent constitution by Constitution Day, December 10. The thirteenth arrested student was named publicly.

DAY 6 (Thursday)

A student delegation delivered an ultimatum to the government: release of the 13, or "action". Military units all over Thailand were placed on full alert. Field Marshall Praphat promised a constitution within 20 months and advised that police would arrest "only those who used the constitutional movement as a cover to overthrow the

Government". The 13 began a hunger strike.

DAY 7 (Friday)

By midday, "tens of thousands" of students had entered the grounds of Thammasat University and an announcement was made that all schools in Bangkok had been closed indefinitely. The students proclaimed a 24-hour deadline for the activists' release.

The Government, in its turn, called an emergency cabinet meeting as the tension built up at Thammasat. The students began a countdown towards the release deadline... On radio that night: "*Bail will be granted to the 13 activists*." A constitution was promised by "next October". All 13 refused bail, demanding unconditional release.

DAY 8 (Saturday)

The students now demanded unconditional release by noon. Twelve students were subsequently forced to leave their cell (the thirteenth was kept separate). They sat on the kerbing outside.

Shortly after midday, about 200,000 people marched from the university. This was the start of the biggest ever demonstration in Thailand's history. It was no longer just a matter for students – it involved everyone.

All metropolitan police forces were immediately mobilised along the route of the march. The King, involving himself for the first time, met student leaders. As the demonstration spread to the northern city, Chiang Mai, he called for "a return to normalcy".

DAY 9 (Sunday)

Just after midnight, the protestors reached the palace. They were told that the 13 had been unconditionally released and that a draft constitution would be introduced by next October. Half the gathering dispersed, the rest remained, unsatisfied with the delayed constitution.

Then suddenly a series of tear gas explosions scattered the marchers (now about 25,000). The police had closed one exit road to direct all marchers out along a single route. Some had refused to move.

Sub-machine gunshots were heard, and screams, and word filtered back that three girls were dead. The marchers, panicking, sprinted back towards Thammasat, grabbing branches and sticks as weapons. A group set fire to a police booth. Protestors seized government departments and surrounded a local police station. A policeman was wounded. The police hit back, firing indiscriminately at the protestors, who scattered before the onslaught. Several were killed as the police regained control of all buildings and the university.

The Government announced that the campus would be kept as a "safe place" and thousands gathered there. Soldiers fired through the fence, killing at least three more people. The students fought back with pieces of wood. They set fire to official vehicles and lobbed 'bottle bombs' at the military. They were killed.

The end was as unbelievable as the beginning. At 6pm, the government abruptly resigned. Professor Sanya Thammasakdi was appointed Prime Minister. Thousands of students shouting "victory" gathered at the central Democracy monument. Others turned furiously on police headquarters.

They were fired upon and, suddenly, the fighting escalated. The new premier tried to stop the violence with promises of a constitution and elections within six months; the King broadcast a plea for "peace and unity". Supreme Commander Kittikachorn, though no longer premier, ordered all forces to "fight to their full capacity..."

DAY 10 (Monday)

Hard-core students, ignoring their leaders, tried to attack police headquarters, using sticks and bottle bombs. The rioting spread, with widespread burning of police booths, buses and cars. On radio, the Supreme Military Command declared that the riot had been organised by communist terrorists.

Peace came with incredible abruptness. The army under General Krit Sivara simply refused to support further repression. At 8.45pm, Radio Thailand made the stunning announcement that former premier Thanom and deputy Praphat had fled the country. It was suddenly quiet.

DAY 11 (the day after)

There was an eerie feel to Bangkok that morning. Few people ventured from their houses, except a few student groups attempting to clean up. Some wreaths had been tacked on the gates of Thammasat University. Broken buses littered the streets. There was not a policeman in sight.

It wasn't a happy ending. To the revolution's timeline, I added subsequent events that signalled more unrest, more threats to Thai democracy. Sure, in March 1974 a new draft constitution was introduced. But five months later again, a student leader was murdered, the first sign of another rightward swing.

In December 1974, Thanom slipped back into the country. His arrival, however, sparked massive demonstrations and he was expelled. In August 1976, Praphat returned. After more demonstrations, he left voluntarily. One month later, Thanom once again returned, this time as a monk, and it was unlikely to have been coincidence that two students putting up anti-Thanom posters were strangled.

In October, Thailand reeled under yet another armed forces' coup that saw Parliament dissolved, the fledgling constitution revoked, and heavy censorship imposed. More than 300 students, labour leaders and intellectuals were arrested. A few decades later, the country would experience a very different type of upheaval, as Muslim separatists took their war in the south to new levels. But in October 1973 there was abundant, if cautious, hope. The 10-day war had dissipated as abruptly as it had started. Premier Thanom and deputy Praphat were gone, and an eerie stillness lingered over central Bangkok.

Still deathly quiet

Wary of venturing too deeply into the CBD, I exhausted my first morning back washing clothes but curiosity soon had me outside school grounds. The iron gates and fences of the neighbouring Chulalongkorn University were smothered in floral wreaths: peony, lavender, daisy and rose, suffusing colours spread over and beyond university limits. Chulalongkorn was not the heart of the uprising. That honour fell to Thammasat University, but its sacrifices were similarly heavy – 30 of its students were killed in the toppling of the military regime.

Early in the afternoon, I set out across town for Thammasat. It too was closed, its gates also bedecked with evocative flower garland wreaths. A bus carrying no passengers went past with its windows shattered, a live memorial, and I abruptly felt an immense respect for all the students of Bangkok. Down the road, still deathly quiet, I noticed an overturned bus, a couple of crashed cars, but no sign of police or military. It was hard to find an eating stall open for business.

Within a week, however, Bangkok was back to its crazy, bustling normal. Busy work went on as it had before, as did the schoolwork.

Impassive Thai faces showed no excitement, nor was the issue of democracy raised in discussion. I watched on perplexed as the Triem Udom students began their days once more fervently singing their national anthem. Perhaps the need for talk had become redundant. It seemed to me too, that a "wait and see" attitude prevailed, a pervading reluctance to believe in victory until the new constitution was passed – and adhered to thereafter.

Yet, at the very least, no government in Thailand could henceforth smugly rule, assume its power as a right – all that followed would be aware that the people were in control. They would remember 10 days, an aeon of achievement, culminating in the resignation of Kitticachorn on October 14, 1973. Surely!

An army for sale

For sheer size, Bangkok's Weekend Market had to be one of the most imposing of its kind in the world. Spread over nine acres of parkland, it circled large sections of the city like a giant equator belt, including a dusty central courtyard where children delighted in skidding their bicycles on self-fashioned racetracks.

I was here for a reason. Among numerous offerings, the most astonishing was that of army surplus equipment. Every conceivable military item could be bought. I saw gas masks, war helmets, collapsible military shovels, privates' jackets, generals' jackets, army mosquito nets, penknives, bayonets, strong serge socks, boots, woollen underwear, ambush trousers, and even army-issue pens! Much of that available was brand new. I was sure if I had asked for a Sherman tank, it would have been produced.

With Nepal trekking in mind, I settled for a pair of army boots, an army-green T-shirt, a warm woollen under-shirt, and a water bottle. Over the next few days, teamed up with an Australian, Steve, I exhausted a series of long-neglected tasks: renewal of vaccinations for cholera, typhoid and smallpox, and the registering of my imminent Burmese flight with U.B.A (Union of Burma Airways).

Those out of the way, Steve and I alternated between ice cream delicacies from street stalls, and ganja, the latter shared with two Japanese hostellers. This "Buddha grass" was powerful medicine and it took little inhaling to reduce the four of us to a state of infinite relaxation. Still under the influence, Steve and I sought out the traveller-fashionable high-rise "Malaysian" hotel, where a great proportion of like-minded seemed to congregate, all looking for a little luxury after the hardships of India or Indonesia.

Without much difficulty, I found the entrepreneurial tradesman who fashioned student cards and prevailed on him for a forged renewal sticker for my nearly expired forged card before searching out a nearby stall that specialised in blended fruit drinks. A banana milkshake – ganja – bed! Despite just-ended disruptions, the next day was a holiday. Frustrated inquiries revealed it marked the anniversary of the death of King Rama V, aka King Chulalongkorn, a man famed for his liberal reforms – including the abolition of slavery – who had died as recently as 1910. No children came to school and all businesses were closed.

On my final night in Bangkok, I and a small group of hostellers went to the movies. It was a very silly, very American action movie titled *Walking Tall* with action fast and plentiful. The story was of one man's fight against the "system's" corruption, his setbacks and eventual triumph as the people learned to stand together. Bangkok's story had been almost as unbelievable! As the film ended with the American townsfolk burning casino equipment a message was flashed across the screen: "Please Pay Homage to H.M. the King", a clear response to the recent overthrow of the government, and its meaning was taken to heart by the audience. As the King's features appeared on screen for the customary concluding national anthem, the whole audience snapped to their feet and bowed their heads. I stood too. Only a small European boy in the front row allowed his head to wander.

After a 1962 coup, General Ne Win declared Burma socialist, nationalised key industry and banned foreign media. In 1972, the economy stagnant, he quit the army but continued to run the country. 1973: facing rebellion, he sets up a "People's Assembly", himself as first president, but shortages continue. "For a quarter century Burma … has remained aloof … a blend of ardent Buddhism and fuzzy Socialism. Now after a decade of military dictatorship, Burma is not sure it can survive in isolation" (*New Yorker*, 20.8.1973).

XII

Seven Burmese days

Burma to Nepal: a week's dash nervously paid for by a bottle of whisky; paranoia upon encountering a perceived police spy; a scam prophetically rebutted; and rejoining old friends and freaks in Calcutta.

By the old Moulmein Pagoda, lookin' eastward to the sea; There's a Burma girl a-settin', and I know she thinks o' me; For the wind is in the palm-trees, and the temple-bells they say: Come you back, you British soldier; come you back to Mandalay! (Rudyard Kipling, *Mandalay*).

Black market rules

Rangoon airport outperformed others bureaucratically by a country mile. After filling out forms in triplicate at numerous departmental desks, I thought of a number, entered my finances, swore with conviction that what I had entered was true, and put my life in the hands of a military regime. Along with every other traveller, my passport was stamped for a maximum stay of just seven days.

Rangoon displayed olden, golden charms – elegant-leaved, thin-branched trees, wavy reflecting ponds – and all human-built structures were museums. The cars were pre-war models that required cranking to start, the street stalls cooked over charcoal, the houses were yellowed and ancient, and the locals went about their business in crisp white shirts above chequered longyis (sarongs),

It was as if nothing had changed since World War II, except that Burma was independent and the prevailing dictatorship strangely called itself a "people's" republic. If the Burmese "socialism" warranted exploration, the market provided an early insight. In Singapore, a US dollar could be exchanged for 20 Burmese Kyats, Burmese banks gave 4.67, the black market, nine! Numerous forms had to be filled in at exchanges, always with warnings that all money spent must be accounted for. Arriving passengers changed money at the official airport counter, but I walked by. Forewarned, I carried a trump card – a bottle of whisky.

A lovely YMCA building of tall, blue-white squares agreed to store my luggage but, conscious of the seven-day restriction, I did not book in. Instead, I began my onward travel immediately with two likeminded others: Glenn, a thin, head-shaven South African dressed in bright colours, and Lida, Dutch, clean-cut, straight-looking but with laughing eyes. After the barest of introductions, we ran to the town centre carrying nothing but shoulder bags, dodging coffee vendors, book wallahs, street urchins, saffron-robed monks, businessmen (always white shirts outside their longyis), numerous soldiers, and hungry canines, in a frantic start to our cross-country dash across Burma.

We stopped for breath at the sight of the gold-towered Sule pagoda, bestriding the main thoroughfare like a beacon. With little time for reflection, we hurried onwards past an out-of-place Raquel Welch poster (starring locally in *Flare Up*) to the railway station where we purchased tickets north to Mandalay and, at 2.20pm (precisely), were aboard carriages from another era. The station was cluttered with human bodies, many attempting to climb through carriage windows, but our seats were secure, and we settled on hard wood seating and awaited the future. At frequent station stops, vendors bombarded us with savoury delicacies, the stallholder heads half-hidden beneath red-glazed pots with dippers. But the stops were always brief.

We reached Mandalay – Kipling's Mandalay – in the early hours and staggered on to the platform stiffly, unable to form early impressions for aches and yawns. We did not attempt to compete with departing hordes, just waited for calm before submitting to the inevitable registering of our passports and questions about our Mandalay movements.

Glenn had an address, a Baptist church offering free accommodation, and finding it was our first goal. Wide, dusty streets parted at our approach while humped Brahman bulls stared past us without interest. We took directions from children who shook our hands vigorously, screaming with glee at our every word. The church was very English: square frontage and a tall grey spire. The sole Burmese characteristic was a sea of mud surround but we were happy to accept roof and a bed and, when mosquito nets were produced, our comfort was assured.

On Johnnie Walker

Still with no local money, I persuaded the others to follow me to a coffee stall where I exposed my bottle of whisky – and made immediate sale. The buyer was a middle-aged man who questioned the wisdom of having a bottle of hard liquor in open view. "It is not wise to risk being seen," he told me frankly. I replied honestly enough that I had not much money and he made me an offer. It wasn't a huge sum, but it paid for nearly all of my Burmese Days.

Spotting a weed-filled moat around a long, low brick wall we began a long walk to circumnavigate what turned out to belong to the royal palace. This had been home in British times to Burma's last sovereign, Thibaw Min, and I couldn't help but think of Kipling:

> *Er petticoat was yaller an' 'er little cap was green*
> *An' 'er name was Supi-yaw-lat – jes' the same as Theebaw's Queen.*

At the main entrance, a large collection box discouraged us, but three friendly off-duty policemen emerged to squirrel us inside via a small side entrance passed a suddenly very respectful sentry.

The palace complex was enormous: kilometre upon kilometre of unkempt grassland with, everywhere, monuments, not to Buddha, but to the People's Republic of Burma. The shining courtesans' pathways had been cleared, the sparkling ponds filled in and replaced by hut billets for the military. Allied bombs in World War II had destroyed much and the government had done little by way of restoration.

We climbed to the top of Mandalay Hill – *thousands* of steps (1729, to be precise) – winding upwards till our breath came in spurts. At top, the view was breathtaking. We gazed silently from marble floor over barely discernible townships far in the distance, a winding river retreat, valleys and mountains, all as a backdrop to one mighty alluvial plain.

Here we came across a squatting Indian sadhu, small, wizened, and clad in frail white linen, the loose trousered dhoti and shirt of Hindu manhood. He had in front of him a mat, his life possessions around him, including a large astrological chart. His eyes were piercing and probing but he was friendly and we were soon comfortable in his company. We shared rough Indian tobacco from a chillum then Glenn brought out his grass while a light sunset from the west gently invaded our – and his – senses.

Between smokes, we supped salty tea and the sadhu, Sandi, made predictions from our palms. Of course, he was bogus but the occasion felt genuine, though Lida, who did not smoke, sat uncomfortably apart. Another man sharply addressed us: "What is it that you are smoking?" Despite our befuddlements, we were aware of danger – he had an air of the military – and stood up to leave. Our peace was further jarred when Sandi demanded payment and Glenn, perhaps foolishly, obliged. Stumbling down the steps, minds blown, Glenn assumed symptoms of paranoia. The questioner was police and out to get us! The priest where we had stayed had earlier asked too many questions! Informers and undercover cops were everywhere! "Move man, move!"

Back at our church, the elderly resident minister prayed for our souls and castigated heathen Buddhists. We were woken with further prayers. The minister was determined to reform us, possibly having already detected signs of decay in our souls, or perhaps just kindly worrying about the exposures we were likely to suffer at the hands of Buddhist idols. He was paradoxically likeable, but it was sad to hear such outmoded "Christian" doctrine: "Oh God, please protect these young travellers from heathen idols…"

The floating isles of Inle

We drank coffee, were reminded again that the Burmese brew was the best in Asia, then caught a train to Thazi, a small southern town at the centre of a map line between at one end, Shwenyaung, at the other, the ruined city of Pagan. We arbitrarily chose Shwenyaung as our first goal. It was the nearest stop to Lake Inle, in more affluent times a thriving resort renowned for its "floating islands".

After waiting several hours at Thazi for a connection, we twice raised our thumbs, and twice, antique behemoths crashed passed, spattering us in pools of mud and dust. We eventually caught the eventually arriving train connection, but arrived at Shwenyaung far too late to continue so hired camp beds from the stationmaster and set up house inside the ticket office. Under a flickering light I read Hermann Hesse's *Narcissus and Goldmund*, its plot sagely emphasising the importance of experiencing all facets of existence. Only by experiencing, Hesse shouted at me, could one appreciate life.

The next morning, a wicked-eyed Indian cab driver offered us passage to the lake. When we laughed at his exorbitant fee, he gave us a free ride to the Shwenyaung outskirts, from where we caught a bus to Nyaungshwe, the closest village. Half way, the bus died. Our luck held, however, a rescue bus plucking us from our meanderings. Even better, a sympathetic conductor refrained from charging us.

A boatman agreed to take us to a bungalow-bathing site in the middle of the lake and we were soon speeding through an everglade world of flower fields in reds, whites and violets. We continued along weed-congested canals, passing villagers propelling their cargos in shallow canoes with large, single oars propelled by their feet. Disgracefully, we continued to hasten. Seven days!

We burst suddenly from weeds into a clear lake expanse, with bordering settlements uncannily attached to what ground there was. In the middle of the lake, was our promised bungalow. We could see no land serving as a foundation, just this single watery apparition grown from the depths. We hurriedly stripped. I lathered in soap, sharing the waters with a million guppies, then sunbathed alongside Lida who had changed into a bikini of disconcerting brevity.

All too soon, our excursion was done. The lake still glinted, the sun still shone, but our schedule remained. Seven days! While our pilot pointed his prow towards shore, we cursed the Burmese government. And as we again passed the foot-propelled longboats, we at last encountered the phenomenon Lake Inle was famous for – its floating islands. There were several, unconnected, cultivated land clumps that villagers pushed from on top using long bamboo poles. Why they needed moving, was unclear. I spoke to several townsmen but none enlightened me, leaving me only with visions of torsos heaving, and land mass shifting. At least I had encountered – albeit briefly – the famed floating islands of Lake Inle.

We made another attempt at hitching, this time aiming for Meiktila, a step on the way to Pagan. But when not even buses would stop, it slowly dawned we needed prior tickets which, of course, were only available from a depot, the nearest of which was in Taunggyi, an hour's drive away. One of us had to hitch there and I was elected. I reached Taunggyi much earlier than expected though had to wait a couple of hours for a return ride. But it drove fast and we caught our bus.

As evening settled in, a fellow passenger produced a guitar and Glenn was prevailed upon to entertain. Once a professional musician, he was well equipped for the task and the evening rocked away with an odd mixture of *Neil Diamond* and *The Who*. We were showered with attention. Cake followed fruit, but the pièce de resistance was a large bottle of banana wine passed around the passengers. A Chinese woman added to the largesse, sharing her bananas and guavas.

When we reached Thazi just before midnight, Lida left us, anxious to head home to the Netherlands. Glenn and I continued to Meiktila, a sprawling city where we were fortunate the driver was willing to take us beyond the final stop to his depot at the town outskirts. We were assured there would be at least one more vehicle passing through that night. And so it proved. In post-midnight pitch, we boarded a truck and plunged on nightmarishly. Seven days!

City of a million pagodas

Dropped unkindly at 3am at a meaningless intersection, we collapsed on a grass verge on the roadside. A dog discovered our hiding place, a succession of growls exploding to barks as we hurried further afield for another attempt at a roadside sleep. This time we were undisturbed.

Woken two hours later by a squall of rain, I ran to find cover while Glenn, unshakable, continued to sleep. A bicycle passed, an astounded head swivelled, then ploughed swiftly away. Across from us, a morning stall yawned beneath the slowly brightening sunlight, a finger waved at us alarmingly, and I rushed across to alleviate fears. I explained our plight and the proprietress exploded in laughter. Her elderly father accompanied me to stare at the mute corpse that was Glenn, then he too began laughing and I was beckoned to their home to wash and recover. When Glenn finally joined us, we sat nibbling fried flour cakes, all complimentary, till a truck thoughtfully stopped for us.

Dropped off amid ties and cufflinks, terylene trousers and sunglasses, it was clear we were close to Pagan. Horse-driven carriages plied for hire, with cries of "Pagan, mister? Five kyats, mister! No bus." A quick query, however, revealed a truck service for a tenth of their fares and a few minutes later Pagan emerged splendidly from behind vistas of white, red and gold, but with high weeds and grasses choking the 40 square kms of ruins the ancient city was famous for.

Pagan was known as the city of a million pagodas, and it seemed to us entirely possible that the claim was a true one. Its origins dated back to 874AD but the writings and frescoes that dominated its landscape, emerged later, in the 11th century AD, when Mon monks introduced to Burma their alphabet and their scriptures.

Glenn and I tramped many paths this day, strolling through countless temples till Buddhas blurred and white temple stone merged opaquely with red clay brick, till the beauty was beyond comprehension. Atop the giant Gawdaw Palin temple, a massive white structure of the 12th century, we looked down with awe on the powerful Irrawaddy River, beside it, the majestic remains of the deceased empire that was Pagan. Incredible structures emerged mystically in every direction, a graveyard green against the rust-red of fallen walls and broken pagodas.

We bathed for an hour or two in the Irrawaddy, a necessary reprieve from truck and temple lurches, before again seeking solace in the past, trekking through the Ananda temple complex, another massive structure whose cloisters, unlike most of its neighbours, remained largely unpillaged. Dodging tourist shops, our trek became a run. Each time we slowed, locals attempted to buy from us our clothes – and Glenn's watch – and we counted ourselves lucky to get a ride out of town almost as soon as our thumbs were raised. Seven days!

At a satellite town, we dined on curried bean then boarded a crowded bus with room only on the roof. The bus broke down. It was revived, but failed repeatedly, and I was mildly alarmed when the driver asked me if I could do the repairs. I could not! Our route was interminably long and interminably slow, our bus stopping at every village along the way to take on board farm produce bound for market. On the roof, Glenn and I shivered in the gathering gloom, enduring the road's eccentricities and despairing of ever reaching Meiktila, let alone Thazi, from whence we knew a train could be caught to Rangoon.

Arriving in Meiktila in darkness, heedless of improbabilities, we ran through town with our thumbs out in hope of an onward ride. Once, we clung to the back of a town bus, and several times took wrong directions. At 11pm we halted despondently at the city outskirts outside a large factory, grandly signposted, "The Peoples Textiles Mill". A manager appeared with the glorious news that a passenger truck would be leaving for Thazi that night and further, optimistically, that the Rangoon train from there was liable to long delays, often not leaving till well after midnight. Seven days!

As we waited for our truck, he treated us to coffee and we, in turn, were treated to the sight of his multitudinous employees hanging behind broad iron gates like zoo animals. A whistle blew, an all-pervading shriek, the portals swung wide, and the uniformed factory girls sprinted to waiting buses. They worked seven days a week in eight-hour shifts, the manager told us. According to the sign, the mill belonged to them. Their behaviour suggested otherwise.

We shared the truck with those of the girls that were from Thazi and chivalrously gave them space to stretch out by suspending ourselves uncomfortably from the back duckboard. Miraculously, Thazi did arrive and, even more miraculously, the Rangoon-bound train had yet to arrive at the station. The sole problem now was a singular lack of funds that brooked no miracles. At 1.30am, without tickets, we leapt aboard and marched down the aisles, futilely seeking seats. Inspired, I climbed into a rare section of hat rack not occupied by bodies or baggage and Glenn copied me. Neither of us had slept properly since Mandalay, and it took little time to nod off. It was tight and uncomfortable but at least we were stretched at full length and a semblance of sleep was possible.

When morning rays penetrated, we climbed down to seats that had been vacated. We sat nervously, unsure whether ticket collections had gone or were coming and practised looking confident. When the collector came, I was a study of pathos. I explained our circumstances sadly: bus broken down; train almost missed; frantic rush; nowhere to buy tickets! His eyes rolled perceptibly as he advised us to get tickets at the next stop, which was an hour away, plenty of time to recline in our wooden seats without a glimmer of guilt. Sitting next to us was a soldier who had observed the whole performance. He seemed amused but said nothing.

We purchased our tickets as if the stop was our starting point – one third of the original price – and relaxed regally and legally to enjoy familiar out-of-window scenes of velvet rice fields and carpeted pasture that adorned so much of this road from Mandalay.

At Pegu (Bago), we had time to wander a station platform overflowing with a noisy band of flutes, drums and clackers. At its heart were two heavily cosmeticised dancers, one a girl of about 10, the other an exaggeratedly camp character of middle age. The contrast was ludicrous: the girl elegantly caressing the air with her wrists; the man waggling his bolstered posterior, grinning inanely from beneath thick rouged lips. Just in time, we jumped back on board. Seven days!

Time stood still

Rangoon was awash with character colonial homes, its streets smothered in greenery, ivy and trees, and the 100 per cent-saronged populace had not forgotten how to smile. The Burmese path to socialism had brought a total time stall: its cars, its people, its attitudes, all were pre-war and, for this, the tourist might be grateful. But even from my short sojourn it was clear its citizens were resentful towards their government, many hate-filled.

We had one last task: Shwedagon pagoda was heralded here as one of the Seven Wonders of the World. At 100m, it was the world's highest pagoda, taller even than the mighty Chedi at Nakhorn Pathom in Thailand. Supposedly built as early as 585BC, its entire surface was covered in gold leaf, reflecting at each quarter face, brilliant gold Buddhas. We climbed to the top of its outer walls from where Rangoon unfolded as a vast plain. And there we sat and stared for an aeon before leaving, reluctantly, at dusk. I carried the musings of a Burmese poet:

In this patent poetry of gold, Behold!; The image of a flower bud; On a stalk atop a pair of hands; Cupped and lifted high in fervent prayer.

Due to my irritating logic, the prayer was denied me, the experience, not. Our haste had given us the bonus of a final day to enjoy Rangoon. Midday found us on the river port frontage, where black marketers pestered us. Amazingly, I was offered 240 Indian rupees for US$20, so greedily accompanied my benefactor to the grounds of an official-looking building for the exchange. "Give me the money. You wait here. I'll get the rupees!" I declined this see-through arrangement and the disgruntled changer severed our agreement. His intentions were so blatant a child could have seen through him. I instead changed US$10 – legally.

The rest of the day was a meander. In a gem shop, a salesman talked to us about exiled former Prime Minister U Nu and an impending referendum designed to introduce a long-promised constitution. "No opposition will ever be allowed here," he said sadly. He spoke in whispers, for informers were a very real threat in the Democratic People's Republic of Burma.

This meeting rather summed up Burma. There was the government and there were the people: two coexisting extremes, one autocratic and fanatical, the other outgoing and warm. Our week had been a tremendous experience, if exhaustingly quick, but now it was over we wanted only departure. And that part was easy. I had worried for a week over how I would explain my lack of spending to airport Customs, but no one asked.

What a contrast was Calcutta! Glenn and I booked into freak favourite the *Paragon Hotel*, in the Newmarket area, which gave us a spacious room with its own bathroom. Glenn had a bong, an American guest had grass, so we merged effortlessly with the pale of evening, without any sense of danger, till hunger pangs attacked us. It was an amazing feeling, walking stoned metropolis, neon lights like shattered glass, the people mere bewildering shadows. Happy to be back on the trail, we plotted Nepal.

From the mid-1950s till 1972, King Mahendra ruled Nepal under a partyless system in which communists, backed by India, participated. But after the 1962 Sino-Indian war, India's support was withdrawn. As Mahendra cracked down on them, Maoist rebels took control of outlying areas, which became off-limits to travellers. 1973: Hoping to fund a revolution, activists hijack a plane carrying US$400,000 of Bank of Nepal money. Under new monarch Birendra, they are arrested, but insurgency continues and "Maoist" areas remain off limits.

XIII

An idiot's guide to Everest

Nepal: Everest in shorts, jandals and tennis shoes, and no jacket;
a trek almost abandoned when unbroken boots lead to torn,
suppurating heels; a telling off from a high-altitude nurse;
and surrounded by the world's highest peaks.

*Hillary stepped on top first. And I stepped up after him ... many of my own people
... have given a great and false importance to the idea that it is I who was "first".
These people have been good and wonderful to me, and I owe them much. But
I owe more to Everest – and to the truth* (Tenzing Norgay, *Man of Everest*).

Lameroo and lemon meringue pie
Once a resident of Darwin's infamous Lameroo Beach freak settlement, Glenn had discovered old friends. And not only had Alice and Guy just had a baby, but this very day, here just outside Kathmandu, they were getting married. My first sight of the bride was of her bathing naked at a well, an hour before the ceremony in a secluded garden we had reached by a two-hour bicycle ride. Seeing Glenn, she screamed, and promptly invited us both to the wedding.

An hour later we watched on as an alarmingly young lama behind graduate spectacles blessed the happy pair. He pressed the base of a small copper kettle against their temples, scattered a light-coloured powder at their feet, and they were man and wife. There followed a party about which I remember little, except a conversation largely confined to passing the chillum. An American began playing the sitar, another increased the volume on the record player, and that was that.

Over the following days, I spent long hours in cafés reading. And smoking. Some prodigious smoking was done at a street where the cafés dangerously specialised in lemon meringue pies. Glenn introduced me to another Lameroo expat, "Peter the Greek", who would grin wickedly from a shocking thatch of wire-brush hair then beckon you to his lair where he dispatched hash chillums. Never had I seen a man smoke as much. "Who'll boomsucker?" he would ask, handing the pipe over and preparing the matches.

At our favourite restaurant, *Jimi Hendrix* blared while a 12-year-old maître-d' managed the customers. Giving the impression he didn't give a damn, he would smile, "I give order quickly", and then shout stupendously: "Porridge banana – oyota – eggs poached – toast jam – milk tea – cream curd, oyota!" Then he would remind the cook: "Hey! Eggs poached – oyota!"

When Glenn departed, I was sorry to see him go. He could be alarmingly intense and cynical. He often expressed his distaste of freaks yet was forever dressed in flour bag trousers, red floral shirt and a breasted Nepalese jacket. But he was good company. In his absence, Peter joined me for breakfast, inviting an elderly Nepalese to join us, and paid for him, an act of generosity that surprised me. "Good fellow," he explained. "Smokes!"

A cribbed bookshop map

One random morning, I left excess gear at my hotel and set off for Everest. I caught a bus to Dolalghat (610m) a common trek starting point, and began a long walk to Dumre (1310m), the first village in a list I had cribbed from an uncomplicated bookshop map. The map also helpfully provided estimated times for the trekking between.

DAY 1: Dumre (altitude, c1200m)

My first day in my stiff, unbroken army boots was difficult, so I was relieved to reach what I thought was Dumre, first village on my list, at a reasonable hour. Unaware, I had already passed it by. But a teenager and an older man playing chess outside a house offered me sleeping space on their floor and later fed me on rice, dhal and sac (spinach). Asked what caste I belonged to, I endeavoured to give a neutral answer! It had grown suddenly cold so I huddled early in my sleeping bag.

DAY 2: Risingo (c1370m)

Unsure of protocol, I offered payment. "No money, please, it is not our custom," said Kedar as he passed me the "famous Nepalese breakfast" – a dry serving of maize popcorn and purple-husked soya bean.

The climb to Chaubas (Chyaubas) was hard, but I reached it early so kept walking, galloping along a high ridge till the Himalayas came splendidly into view, most dominant, probably, Dorje Lhakpa and Phurbi Chyachu, 6666m and 6657m respectively. Along the way I met numerous villagers heading oppositely, burdened under heavy basketed loads strapped from their foreheads.

After encountering my first mountain horn, a man-sized tuba with a funnel-like mouth that was blown resoundingly, I ground to a halt at a hilltop bench. My heels had rubbed badly and I bandaged them, a painful process watched curiously by a barefooted local. When I continued walking, he slowed to keep near me. Unaccustomed to track formalities, when I arrived at Risingo, I sat on the path, whereupon a clod was thrown at me and I was invited to stay the night at a local house. I drank gallons of ciya (tea), arak (rice spirit), then gorged on rice and sac at this, my first traditional "truck stop" on the Nepalese trail.

DAY 3: Manga Deurali (c1525m)

Nursing my sore heels, the start of the day's trek was a limp. A long downhill stretch was followed by a hard climb. I reached Phedi (2040m), a town of curious stares, carrying on straightway in search of Chitre (1540m). This stage was a long one, exacerbated by starting on a wrong path and necessitating a hard catch-up climb. Back on track, I slowed badly.

Instead of Chitre, I found myself at a mountain hideout called Manga Deurali where I was offered space on an outdoor veranda. This village had a precarious facade that was strikingly beautiful, curving stone walls teetering across a precipitous mountain pass.

DAY 4: Kirantichap (1280m)

Though off the bookshop trail I wasn't too worried as I knew the names of the villages en route. At Kata Koti a boy begged me for medicines, reflecting an enormous faith in European drugs that never ceased to amaze me. I stumbled into a mountain horn-led procession which, at bidding, I joined. Progress was slow, more so when it merged with another group, this one bearing a body draped eerily in white with a thin string of flowers adorning.

Two boys directed me to a rickety suspension bridge where my way was blocked by an ape, which thankfully took flight. I lost my way again in open pasture but was rescued by a shout. Incredibly, I recognised the caller from a Kathmandu coffee shop and gratefully followed him to Kirantichap, a small hilltop settlement where I joined the villagers at cards and ganja till the evening paled. Stoned, Mahorn and I watched a glorious mountain sunset before returning for our evening meal – and two more chillums.

DAY 5: Sikri Khola (1830m)

I was overcharged – mildly – but it left a slightly bitter taste. Mahorn tied two beads about my wrist, possibly as placation, but I suspected his was the influence that had caused the price inflation.

I passed Busti, rugged mountain quarters above a crashing Tamba Khosi river, where an Australian and an American were struggling with breakfast yawns, then continued up a sculpted staircase to Yarsa before a climb of more than 600 bitter metres to a pass with glorious views of Gauri Shankar (6850m) and Melungtse (7200m). As I walked, I recited my latest reading (Coleridge): "… *deep heartfelt inward joy that closely clings …*"

At Sikri Khola, I received a royal welcome. Children excitedly showed me their English exam papers and I went through the answers with them. After dinner, I curled up in my sleeping bag next to an elderly woman who coughed raucously all night.

DAY 6: Thodung cheese factory (3126m)

Crossing a frothing river via a slippery log – one inch at a time – I stumbled upon a freak asleep on the side of the track. Fearing for his safety, I called out, "are you okay?" "Protein, man, protein," he responded. He called himself "Walking Horse", today at least a misnomer, and we shared provisions. He ate my biscuits and quoted Homer at me; I sampled his grass. Walking Horse was a mine of information: where marijuana grew, where to stay, where Everest would first appear… He had a *Time* magazine, which took up more of my time, then it was onwards alone to Those Megchan, a mediaeval collection of stone houses with strange wooden balconies. A long but easy walk along the Khimti Khola's pebble banks ensued, before another hard ascent. My feet were hurting badly.

Reaching a hilltop marked: "Cheese Factory 1 Hour's Climb", I felt dizzy. This was easily the highest I had been and I took frequent rests, my climb taking nearly two hours. Then I was there, a sign at the gate proclaiming, "3126 metres" – above the danger level for altitude sickness.

A roaring fire and a meal of ham and hot mashed potatoes, cream curd and much tea welcomed me. Utopia! Others were here: Americans, English, and even a Kiwi. Sunset was a torrid flush that illuminated Gauri Shankar, red pearl necklaces dripping intensely over snowy apron. I retired to my room where a fire blazed and, for the first time on my trek, was truly warm.

DAY 7: Thodung cheese factory

The other guests departed; I decided to linger. I breakfasted on fried eggs and fresh baked bread, then retired to my room in front of the fire with a volume of *Biggles*. It was either that or *Grass and the Dairy Cow*.

At sunset, Gauri Shankar was eclipsed by cloud and the sky appeared as a Van Gough playground. Truly, this place was amazing. In the absence of the father of the family who was in Kathmandu on business, the mother was in charge of both factory and their three young children. No new guests arrived.

DAY 8: Thodung cheese factory

Two Americans arrived, bought cheese, and resumed their trek with barely a wave. I too visited the factory, buying a kilo of rich cheddar for my onward travel. The high factory site, set up by the Swiss, had been chosen to negate the need for refrigeration, and the thick slab delicacies hanging in the storeroom indicated the success of the venture.

Finally, some guests arrived. A loud Australian voice echoed, "Thank God! We're here!" It was a couple I knew well, our paths having crossed in Indonesia, Laos and Burma, and we had a great reunion. Their trek was near an end and we talked long about conditions ahead.

DAY 9: Sete (2560m)

Though frosty and crust-hard underfoot, I quickly reached the main Chyangma track. Along the way, I met two Canadians who asked me, "Are you the New Zealander who was in Cambodia?" I had been discussed. At Phedi, a last meandering village before a long stretch ahead, I was easily persuaded to have tea, then began a forewarned ascent that would last into a second day.

Stoically enduring the pain of my heels, I was relieved to arrive early at Sete, an outpost containing little more than a guesthouse and a monastery, each offering accommodation. In need of spoiling, I opted for the guesthouse comfort. My heels were now giving me a lot of trouble. On top of innumerous Band-Aids, I had resorted to stuffing cardboard between sock and boot, which at least alleviated pressure enough to make walking possible. My feet were unable to bear my body's weight till blood had recirculated.

DAY 10: Junbesi (2820m)

I began a hard climb to the towering Lamjura Pass, reputedly the hardest stage of the trek, enjoyment of scenery quickly dissipating in grunts. Worse, my heels started to pierce jaggedly at each reluctant step. I inserted new cardboard pieces behind the offending areas but still slowed to a crawl.

Trudging through jarring frozen snow, evidence of 3350m-plus, almost at a standstill, it was a relief to finally reach the bottleneck Lamjura Pass. As the wind whistled viciously, I sought refuge on a seat just below the peak occupied by two Swiss travellers who I knew from Laos. After we parted, my walk became a jarring fall. But I caught up with three trekkers met earlier in Sete, and thence it was an easy walk to Junbesi, a valley town of rugged stone houses. At the "hotel", we dined magnificently on shyakpa (Sherpa stew).

Midway through the meal a ragged Englishman arrived, frozen-damp like an Antarctic explorer, an apparition with long hair and a moustache that crackled. John regaled us with a frightening tale of how, after taking a wrong turn, he had slept rough for four days. We slept in a huge room resembling a Rembrandt painting, on plank beds that creaked. Ancient Tibetan thangkas adorned the walls, and occasional wood print blocks leaned from the floor. Given an unfortunate bed near the door, I shivered all night.

DAY 11: Junbesi

Finally finding the courage to bare my wounds, I soaked them in warm water. I was in a much worse state than I had thought. The flesh had been torn loose and the wound was suppurating. I knew I could not wear my boots again and was pessimistic about further travel – whichever direction – without shoes.

The others opted to stay the day with me and little was accomplished. We sharpened our knives; we admired the rolling plain that spread out before us like a flat pancake; someone washed in the river but the rest of us were much too conscious of wintry chill! When night came, we ate hungrily of shyakpa and smoked ganja and hash. When we ordered tea, John slyly slipped quantities of Kukri rum into our glasses. And at the last, our host brought me good news: in two days he was going to a market at neighbouring Salleri where he would try to buy tennis shoes for me. Meantime, I must wait, but this was no bad thing. I could no longer walk in my boots.

DAY 12: Junbesi

After my good companions left, my host took me to the village medic where my wounds were treated professionally. "If you were American or Japanese, I would charge you," I was told. "But because you are a New Zealander …" Everest conqueror Hillary was well known in the region for his work building schools, hospitals, and bridges and I was grateful for my antipodean birth.

My host's wife found a chair for me to enjoy the midday sun and kept me supplied with tea, which she prepared in a large, cylindrical churn, a work of art in fine black wood with copper ring supports. The husband too, was busy. He had placed in my room a crude copper still, which was bubbling merrily. When steam escaped, his wife sprinted for cow dung to plug the leak. Dinner was a glorious finale to the day: shyakpa, with potato, pumpkin, cabbage, and corn. Before turn-in, my host traced my feet for a template to assist his purchase. If he could not find shoes big enough at the Salleri market, I would be at a loss.

DAY 13: Junbesi

Almost everyone had gone to Salleri. Only the ever-working wife remained. She was first up to lay fire and cook, all the time watching over her baby. She fed the hens, picked the day's vegetables, and drove the oxen and goats to pasture. The house needed sweeping of course, and the family's clothes had to be washed early to make use of a short-timing sun.

The children, all wearing black trousers torn at the groin, wallowed happily in ample Junbesi mud. They played catch with cloth balls and I was encouraged to join in, sitting in my chair returning passes. An American researching a rare breed of monkeys called and offered to buy my boots. I anticipated an invitation to his home, but none came. I kept my boots! At night, my host returned clutching a pair of jandals. "Number 10," he announced. The market had had no tennis shoes big enough! It remained only to be seen if the Everest hinterland could be tackled in jandals.

DAY 14: Manidingma (Nuntale) (2195m)

I set out in my socks and jandals along a gentle slope high above a river gorge to be rewarded with enthralling views of the Himalayas. At extreme left, the unmistakeable Sagarmatha (Everest) bestrode majestically, Lhotse to its right, and a little further, the towering Nuptse.

After arriving early at Salung, I was faced with another big climb. A teashop at Ringmu tempted but did not halt me and I continued up to the high Taksindu Pass, a summit marked by a bright stupa, its white flag fluttering atop a tall wooden pole. From here, I had a long downhill stretch to Manidingma. My map confusingly proclaimed "Nuntale", but I learned the former was a Sherpa name, the latter Nepali. Though not yet 3pm, I slung my pack inside a house marked, "restaurant", and ordered tea. Sherpas here drank chyang (corn beer), which the host prepared onsite, crushing the fermented kernels by hand and straining the juices through a conical filter. I declined to join them, just ate my fill of "famous Sherpa dish shyakpa", then slept.

DAY 15: Kharte (2700m)

Walking on inch-thick autumn leaves that served amply for carpet, I made good time. After Phuleli, a thunder akin to ocean surf informed me I had reached the mighty Dudh Kosi, a thrashing river torrent that would lead all the way to Namche Bazaar. After crossing a shaky suspension bridge, I sat long in admiration of the force that had formed such an incredible crevice.

After a brief climb to Choubing, a confusingly spread-out agricultural settlement, I found the path, climbing over a hill spur to a similar-looking Kharikhola where I was greeted by a mini-procession led by an enthusiastic drummer. Three more hours of hard ascent had me in Kharte, a collection of about three huts that in the gathering gloom reminded me of cattle quarters. I toyed with the idea of continuing, but at the "welcome" sign of a guesthouse, had to have tea. Then, of course, it was impossible to move.

DAY 16: Phakding (2610m)

I began at dawn and somehow never quite stopped. Initially, there was a hard rise to the Bhanjyang Pass at over 3050m, then a rocky drop to Puiyan, a flimsy looking teashop perched above a Dudh Kosi tributary. Frost still dominated, yet I was happy in my walking, far freer in jandals than ever in my army boots.

Surkye, perched like a Wild West camp, provided me with tsampa, a powdered Tibetan gruel soaked in tea. From there, I revelled in a level trek following the Dudh Kosi. Never had I walked for so long in a day! I stopped in dark at Phakding at a shack proclaiming "Sherpa Hotel", which was good enough for me. I had walked for more than 10 hours. There were four Americans here, clear evidence I had passed the turnoff for the Lukla airstrip – the beginning of the abbreviated Everest trek.

DAY 17: Namche Bazaar (3440m)

Loping along an increasingly touristy gorge, each Sherpa I greeted looked at me feigning amazement and the questions became clichés: "Sherpa, no? Porter, no?" Lukla tourists passed by oppositely and I envied them their numerous porters. The first of the "Hillary bridges" led me across another Dudh Kosi torrent, then I stopped for tea at Monjo, a home whose walls sported an array of old copper plates and with a series of plank beds around the interior circumference.

After a second Hillary bridge, at Jorsale, I began the day's single climb, to Namche Bazaar, in earlier days, base camp for Everest. There, not yet midday, I found accommodation in the least patronised of the town's three hotels. By now I knew I could not continue for long in my jandals. Namche had shops but no tennis shoes big enough for me and I had to make do with a pair of rough-sewn leather Sherpa boots for the glacial path to come. I resigned myself to not completing the trek and lounged long in brilliant sun before shadows from the frozen ice flows on an adjacent cliff face put an end to my reveries.

DAY 18: Namche Bazaar

I set off on a day hike with the Americans from Lukla to the Japanese-built *Everest View Hotel* with its renowned views of the three great Himalayan peaks: Nuptse, Everest and Lhotse. But it was Ama Dablam that took my breath, perched on a slant like a be-throned Queen Victoria, her royal train outflowing.

Everest View was a startling hotel, not just for its extravagant (for 1973!) US$60 a day fee, but for the way its stone facade effortlessly merged with the towering surrounds. We drank tea bravely, one pot costing 8rp, giving us just over half a cup each, but regally, in sunken armchairs before a huge central fire that we shared with some Bollywood movie stars here filming an epic to be called *Love! Love! Love!*

We walked home late, with the sun dropping spectacularly. I again treated my heels, then a final shop visit uncovered some large-sized tennis shoes: a consignment had just arrived. Good fortune, I reasoned, must now lie ahead. The trek was go!

DAY 19: Pheriche (4300m)

Tengboche was the conclusion of a long ascent alongside Ama Dablam, a settlement around the famous monastery of the same name. It should have been an oasis of calm, but today was akin to a fairground – the Bollywood actors had arrived by helicopter ahead of us and were cavorting in their sophisticated gear.

At Pheriche, a Canadian nurse gave me cortisone for my heels, but berated me for my "stupidity" in walking from Namche in one day. "It's quite a walk, but not one you should be proud of. You have heard of altitude sickness?" she asked acidly. "It's a real risk travelling so fast over 10,000ft (3050m) without acclimatising." She was right but I was glad I was here, for the sooner I was up, the sooner I was down. I knew I was inadequately dressed or prepared for the conditions.

The owner of the hotel here was drunk, which was not uncommon, for Sherpas liked their liquor, and who could blame them in such temperatures! Hillary was eulogised everywhere, but this night I heard a different view. Three years a cook at the Hillary-built hospital at Kunde, my host had asked for a raise. "Please, Mr Hillary…!" But Mr Hillary had refused, saying free food, mountain clothing, and accommodation were a fair recompense. "I hate him," my host said. I sympathetically ordered tea. My host reached for the pot – and fell in a stupor. I moved his head a safe distance from the fire.

DAY 20: Lobuche (4940m)

The long day before had taken its toll but I was determined to carry on quickly, for the cold was infiltrating my bones and I was not certain my onward resolve would last much longer. The nurse too had taken toll, and I was walking a little scared of altitude sickness. But that passed when sparse tussock parted to reveal the beautiful blue of the Kumbu Glacier. In my oversized Sherpa boots, it was a hard hike, especially when I was forced to walk on glacial ice. The track was barely discernible and, more than once, I slipped badly. This was the Kumbu moraine, the glacier leading to Sagarmatha (Everest).

This section passed agonisingly slowly, including a tricky frozen river crossing that necessitated throwing my pack to the far bank. The ice looked dangerously thin, with a fast-flowing current below. Though not yet midday, I stopped at Lobuche, two huts tucked in a cleft, surrounded by mountains, mere toddlers of 5000 to 6000m. I was sitting outside under a strong sun when two Swiss girls arrived and shared with me their meal of boiled potatoes.

The second hut was a storehouse, its shelves laden with "Processed Cheese", "Instant Plum Pudding" and, to cap all, a large supply of ravioli. There was also abundant mountain gear. All bore Italian brand names, cast-offs from a recent Italian expedition – one Hillary had sarcastically termed, "a triumph of technology". Three Americans here had just climbed Kala Patthar, the "trekkers' peak" of 5500m, and they fed me advice about conditions ahead. Three more Americans appeared with porters, speaking grandly of snow to waist level and "Class 4" climbs. Class 4 required ropes! I slept with my shoes and water bottle inside my barely-functioning sleeping bag.

DAY 21: Gorak Shep (5200m)

The water in my canteen was one solid ice block. But the sky was clear. I had borrowed snow glasses off the Swiss girls they had hired at Pheriche, so was at least a little bit prepared for the bleached desert ahead. For the first time, I wore long pants, so was tolerably warm and it was wonderful to be walking without my pack, which I had left in the hut. When possible, I walked on boulders, for my tennis shoes were hopeless in the ice and the snow. My oversized Sherpa boots and jandals were barely more adequate!

Gorak Shep comprised two stone huts that could be spotted from a distance thanks to a bright yellow tent beside. The final valley of my walk was circled by the Kumbu glacial range. I was completely enclosed by the world's largest peaks: Nuptse (7850m), towering and dominant; Lhotse (8510m), a little behind; and between, a splinter of Everest (8850m). A thin wisp of steam glistened above Everest like a halo. Further east hovered Ama Dablam, not so splendid from here and, oppositely, Pumori (7150m). The valley itself was a magnificent whitewash, its centre a platypus-shaped lake encrusted in thick ice.

Rising from the Gorak Shep huts, under the shadow of Pumori, rose a minor peak, a rocky tower above a snow-lined ridge. Kala Patthar. I introduced myself to the four occupants of the tent, well-equipped Americans, and they pointed out the route to the summit. It was not a hard climb. A first ridge was devoid of snow and, slightly higher, the full-frontal Everest facade revealed itself. Everest, tilting between Nuptse and Lhotse, was now clearly dominant though, thanks to fierce winds, it oddly lacked snow at its highest.

I reached the top after perhaps an hour's climb, to a summit marked by three rocky cairns, a yellow bootlace and an empty orangeade can. The wind whistled shrilly, so my stay at the peak was necessarily brief. A little below I treated the world to a rendition of Coleridge's *Self-Knowledge*: "...*what hast thou, man, that thou dar'st call thine own?*" I answered, "nothing at all", before clambering awkwardly down.

Further up the valley, lay the modern-day Everest Base Camp, but I had been forewarned that no greater views would materialise, and the area was legendary for the garbage from a hundred expeditions. My vanity was already well fed from my summit climb of 5550m. Base Camp was at least 60m lower! It was also getting late. I walked back quickly, bypassing Gorak Shep and reached Lobuche well after sunset. Terribly cold, I huddled with the tent crew around a meagre fire.

I looked at the Americans and their equipment of ropes and picks. I could barely lift one of their packs, which its owner proudly noted weighed "well over 60lbs"! They too had scaled Kala Patthar, no more, but in boots, down jackets, and down trousers. I wore tennis shoes and had no jacket. I was terribly cold – but terribly happy!

Seven Sherpas died in 1922 attempting the "impossible peak". Until 1965, only nine more deaths occurred. By the end of 1973, however, another 12 died, from avalanche, frostbite, pneumonia, exhaustion, falling rocks and "disappeared". 1973: a huge Italian expedition uses helicopters to haul gear up the icefall and, with 100 Sherpas, gets eight of its climbers to the summit. A little later, a big Japanese party puts two on top, though loses a Sherpa in an avalanche. Both expeditions attract fierce criticism for their extravagance.

XIV

The legend of a mad Kiwi

Nepal: Homeward bound: another sharp but justified telling off from the high-altitude nurse; Christmas at 3000m-plus; my first shower in more than a month; and I discover I am an uncle.

I felt ... weariness beyond muscular fatigue and beyond the vague lassitude of mountain sickness. By the time we reached the moraine I had a bad headache. In the tent at last I was tired and shivering and there spent a fevered night (George Mallory, cited in Unsworth, *Everest: The Ultimate Book of the Ultimate Mountain*).

A bitter pill to swallow

The incentive now to reach a warmer clime, I ran insanely, reaching Pheriche by 10am. I made a point of seeking out the nurse to thank her for her medicines and, in return, was again berated strongly. It was a bitter pill to swallow, but she was correct. If something had gone wrong, I would have been high on the *Greatest Trekking Idiots of All Time* list.

DAY 22: Namche Bazaar (3440m)

I continued my flight along still sleeping pastures, ignoring even Ama Dablam, so impatient was I to reach the warmth of a Namche

147

Bazaar hearth. Tengboche appeared in early afternoon and I was sorely tempted to stop. But Namche beckoned. I flew passed an elderly Sherpa calling his yak herd to roost, his ear-splitting cry rising out of mountain silence. And when Namche arrived coldly around a corner, I booked into the *Sherpa Hotel* to be greeted by the Americans and the lost Englishman from Thodung. After a single passed pipe, I excused myself and collapsed, instantly asleep.

DAY 23: Namche Bazaar

Stopping for the day was not a hard decision. Sadly, my Thodung friends had flown out, despite our pact to reunite at the cheese factory. Now it appeared as if I alone would see out the Christmas promise and, frankly, I was wavering!

With some newly arrived trekkers, a discussion began of trek characters, of whom "Walking Horse" featured prominently. He had been tramping this terrain "for months, never more than 20rps in his pocket", begging meals off fellow trekkers. Next was "Space Blanket", who had travelled without a sleeping bag and, when questioned, would admit to having been "slightly cold"! "Lost John" also featured, he who had missed the Lamjura Pass yet somehow managed to progress from Thodung to Junbesi, albeit over four days!

A fourth character was mentioned, a Kiwi laid up in Junbesi with torn heels and no shoes, hopelessly entrapped in his Himalayan surrounds. Thus were legends forged! Much later, I encountered tales of a Kiwi who climbed Kala Patthar in tennis shoes, and no jacket! Meanwhile, my left heel was still infected, I still limped and, more than ever, was feeling the cold. I had to decide whether to walk out or fly. Once again, I was terribly cold and coughed all night. It should have been an easy decision.

DAY 24: Surke (1545m)

There was no way I would fly! I gave Namche just one farewell glance as I ran out of sight through the narrow entrance pass. My much-treated heels gave me little pain but now the soles of my feet began to ache from the constant rock pounding. I made good time, however, reaching Chaurikharka shortly after noon before continuing as far as river station, Surke, where I stopped at the "hotel" for the night. Here the elderly Sherpa woman in charge bustled me importantly to the fireside, a privilege I shared with her 6-year-old granddaughter whose task was to blow mightily to keep the fire ablaze. She sat primly next to me and moved only once – to eject a calf that had wandered indoors.

The girl's father was in charge of the cooking. I was fed a Sherpa porridge called "gue", then rice and chicken – *chicken!* – before being directed to the bed nearest the fire with a blanket under-sheet. This night was the warmest I had spent since Kathmandu.

DAY 25: Kharikhola (2220m)

My morning started with a difficult ascent but, feeling strong, found myself passing Sherpa porters with relative ease. They, of course, were rather more laden than I but it was still a thrill to nod greetings as I nudged ahead and they seemed surprised at the pace I set. I met many hikers heading oppositely: some Englishmen anxious about conditions ahead; an American group who peppered me with questions; two Canadians who donated me their excess Thodung factory cheese; and a huge line of Sherpa porters transporting goods for a weekend market. Some of the porters were harshly overladen, trudging in bare feet over grim frost pathways.

I bought from the porters as many suntala as I could eat. It had been weeks since I had enjoyed citrus fruit and I revelled in vitamin C. After Bhanjyang Pass I was content to coast for my next stop, Kharikhola, was in sight. From there, it was a mere two days' walk to Junbesi, two more to Thodung – and, hopefully, Christmas. At Kharikhola, I stopped at a school that doubled as hotel and received a royal welcome – spiced boiled potatoes with spinach, washed down with Sherpa salt tea.

DAY 26: Ringmu (2855m)

The day started easily enough, with Dudh Kosi, previously a wrathful torrent, now seeming quite tame. The sun however burned cruelly and I began to wonder if any sort of target could be reached. At Manidingma, a teahouse proprietor confounded my plan to stop with the news it was not yet midday. So I continued, lunging towards the high Taksindu Pass like a man possessed. I was exhausted but knew I was making good time. This latest rise was one of the hardest yet: an unladen Sherpa family passed me and I was perversely encouraged to see them similarly perspiring.

At Taksindu, like Tengboche built around an important monastery, a soft-spoken lama offered me tea without expectations of payment and I made him a gift of the army boots I knew I would never wear again. He directed me to a shortcut pass from which I ambled happily down, noting superciliously some struggling Europeans in the ascent. Their porter being unsure of the route, I advised them, then skipped a mere half hour to the familiar Ringmu teahouse. I examined my map. In a single day I had climbed from the Dudh Kosi at 1500m to the Taksindu Pass at a colossal near-4300m. Lamjura Pass was touted as the hardest obstacle of the inward trek, rising from 2135m to 3530m, an ascent of nearly 1400m. Today's climb had been about 2800m.

"New Zealand? Ah, Hillary," the teahouse proprietress quizzed me, and I was made welcome, none more so than by a small black puppy, blind in one eye, that sat in my lap and tried to eat me. A little boy in monk's robes watched on eagerly then joined in the game, and the three of us teased each other throughout the remaining hour of sunlight.

DAY 27: Junbesi (2820m)

The path to Junbesi was frost-caked and I walked slowly. It was bitterly cold, especially as I persisted in wearing short pants. At Salung, a youngster took me to his house, saying it was being converted into a hotel. He asked me for a suitable name. Looking out at the framed peaks of Nuptse, Sagarmatha and Lhotse and the eternal Himalayas beyond, it was an easy call. Why not the *Sagarmatha*? He squealed with glee, producing a piece of paper already inscribed, *Sagarmatha Hotel*. I felt guilty for not stopping but I had friends at Junbesi who had helped me greatly in my days of immobility.

In its windswept valley plain, Junbesi too was cold, but my first glimpse of the town's prominent centre stupa had me quickening my step. "Namaste!", I greeted a Sherpa and the response was of laughter. "Nam-she-day," came the rejoinder, a comical mimicry of European mispronunciation, but the jibe was well meant. I settled happily in the rest house, drank gallons of Sherpa tea then tackled two giant chapattis. The husband was in Salleri for market but his wife welcomed me, with much concern about the state of my feet.

DAY 28: Kenja (1630m)

A Tibetan monk interrupted my slog. Shamefully underclad, he was of a type I had sometimes seen wandering the countryside in small refugee-like bands. His right hand lacked a thumb and the gap was wrapped inadequately in stained swathing bandage. He eyed my gloves enviously, made a motion of request and I, staunch opposer of begging, passed them over.

My feet were hurting again but I had no choice but continue. Thankfully, the high Lamjura Pass was not so imposing from this side and once over the summit I changed back into jandals for an easy passage, despite icy footpaths. After a tea break at Sete, I ran downhill to Kenja (Phedi) and stopped there. It was market day and wares were spread out invitingly. I was offered soap, biscuits, crystal-like candies and, inevitably, raksi but, tired, rejected everything except for tea and a fireside seat at the resthouse. I changed into long pants and struggled into my oversized Sherpa footwear. By the time night took control all present had filed passed, just for a glance at size 10 feet in Sherpa wrappings. Everyone with a modicum of English inquired as to the price of my purchase, nodding the information to his neighbour.

DAY 29: Thodung (3125m)
Christmas Eve. I climbed, exertion upon exertion, but the effort was worth it and I was happy enough when I passed a summit spur with glorious views of the fertile valley of Bandar hanging below. I strolled down to the river but from there the walk grew harder. The valley was long and uncompromising and I found this latest uphill haul deceiving and taxing.

Thodung came. It had to. But I was not prepared for the early hour and, in consequence, plunged into teas and cream curds rather carelessly, sitting outdoors under a benign sun with husband Parsay. He had studied in Taranaki and had much to show me: photographs, a Kiwi badge, and an embossed postcard of Christmas greetings from the Hillary family. He asked me what a New Zealand Christmas was like and, a little homesick, I did my best to convey the occasion. "Most important, is family," I told him. "Christmas is all about family." And perhaps that was why, alone at a remote cheese factory at nigh-on 3350m, I felt suddenly lonely and went to bed early.

DAY 30: Thodung
"Happy Christmas," they said, expecting some sort of festive reaction. I showed none. I sat quietly with my thoughts in front

of a huge log fire when a broad Australian voice broke the calm: "Anyone else 'ere?" There was indeed, and I rose from my chair to pass yuletide greetings. Soon there were three more, an Austrian an American and, finally, an Englishwoman. All intended to continue but, possessed of extraordinary powers of persuasion, I convinced all that the 25th was not a day to be spent trekking. A New Zealander arrived and we joined forces to convince him too to stay. All had guides and porters, but these were happy to be dismissed for the evening, opting for a party of their own at a neighbouring village. One Sherpa had engaged a porter for himself out of his wages, but I was not into mockery, this most festive of days.

We began the day by demolishing the factory's cream curd supplies. We drank coffee out of china teacups then devoured cheese with freshly baked crusted breads. Afterwards, we sat in the sun and explored each other's adventures. A middle-aged Englishman in Nepal to recruit Ghurkhas for the English army arrived. It was interesting the English still had pulling power in independent Nepal. But much foreign exchange was apparently generated. He was a trifle condescending, however, and no one was disappointed when he decided to continue to the next village.

I shared my favourite view of primrose Gauri Shankar at sunset, drug free, then we adjourned to the lounge fire till the call for dinner had us filing expectantly to the kitchen. Before us were consommé soups, enormous plates of ham steaks, chips and grated white radish. All this at a remote cheese factory at more than 3000m, aeons from cars, flush toilets and electricity, aeons from home! We scraped our plates then spontaneously began crooning Christmas "carols", slaughtering such extremes as *Silent Night* and *Click go the Shears*. After raksi was produced, I attempted a Māori haka. Our hosts chipped in with an enthusiastic rendition of a children's song featuring animal noises and we responded competitively with *Sweet Molly Malone*. A little tipsy, we concluded with *Auld Lang Syne*.

Back in our outhouse, we huddled around a fire and continued the hilarity. There was even a gift unwrapping, for the Kiwi had been carrying a present from home, with a message asserting the contents would be "sorely needed" by this stage of the trek. Predictably, it was cologne, and we Dean Martin-ishly passed the bottle around. We did sleep. I am sure we did, for the final reward to the evening's frolic was a kiss from the English girl, Lynne, and there could have been no more fitting finale to an extraordinary day. In lieu of mistletoe, we had hung the Australian's polka dot underbriefs from a roof beam.

DAY 31: Those (1930m)

Ready for the onward trek, I caused a bit of a furore when I appeared in short pants and jandals. The others all sported woollen jumpers, jackets, thick woollen socks, and imposing tramping boots designed for the Everest summit. Tagged "the mad New Zealander", I became the target of a frightening array of cinematic machinery. After fond farewells to the Thodung staff we all climbed down to the Bandar Pass summit where my friends turned left and I turned right. Their Everest adventures lay before them; mine were almost done. I had no great desire now to cover great distances so descended with frequent rest stops. I shared my cheese with a passing Sherpa then refound valley floor where I wandered dreamfully till Those persuaded my halt.

Those was a strange antiquity. Its houses, all two or three storeys, faced each other, and the way between was of such trifling breadth that a museum arcade rather than a township was indicated. I found a teahouse, unconcerned that midday had barely arrived.

DAY 32: Busti (1275m)

After a hard, quick climb before Chisopani the trail became easier though I still struggled, pausing frequently to rid my footwear of thick limpets of red clay. Two Swiss youngsters greeted me hopefully: "Hello, are you Swiss?" Once, I raced along a wrong trail, to be rescued by a woman in a red velvet jacket and light blue sarong, with a gold ring through her nostrils and looping earrings through her lobes. Before steering me on the right path, she gave me some suntala oranges. Travelling in reverse, only the villages now were familiar: Yarsa, Kabhre, Namdu, all in pastoral settings, and I was forced to dodge processions of goats, cows and water buffalo. But with few hard climbs I walked for longer than my norm, tiring markedly before arriving at Busti at the end of a long, downhill stretch.

Beautiful Busti comprised a few houses perched above the Tamba Kosi, a pastel river that flowed abundantly below. Looking down, I could see a suspension bridge crossing; Busti itself was almost hidden amid fern and scrub. It had a solitary teahouse that I shared with a

Sherpa family whose path I had crossed frequently, swapping lead on five or six occasions. They laughed to see me ahead of them and talked about me at length with all who cared to listen.

DAY 33: Shere (1220m)

Though in no mood for heavy walking, I began early, grunting beneath morning cloud till over a ridge from where Kirantichap made belated appearance. After refreshments, I began an immediate climb to a spur high above the Choksila plain. All land now bore the mark of cultivation. I stopped once to find that the price of tea was down, the price of oranges up, and knew that Kathmandu could not be far distant. I was now in unfamiliar territory for Kirantichap was a crossroads: down to my trek starting point, Dolalghat, or new-territory-up to Lamosangu. I chose Lamosangu.

I walked a little further to an enclave called Shere and, though still early, stopped for the night. The capital city was no incentive for haste. Besides, I was physically and psychologically spent.

DAY 34: Lamosangu (1370m)

The morning track bent cruelly upwards and I took refuge in far too many teashops. Because it was the last day of my trek, these skyward paths felt harder than they perhaps were and I found it helpful to pace myself behind a soldier. After Nigalam, a sharp descent ensued down a staircase pathway, a detour track built after the recent completion of the Kodari highway to Tibet. When I realised I was nearing my objective, I slowed to enjoy what little of the countryside was not yet under shadow. Then it was over. It ended as simply as that. Concrete steps guided my last paces, and with superior gait I strolled into a surprisingly shanty Lamosangu, a *roadside* village that shivered at the centre of a large Chinese-built hydroelectric scheme.

Tales of exhaustion and woe

The first stall I encountered sported a sewing machine so my jeans, split unashamedly from here to there, were immediately repaired, then I retreated from a plea for baksheesh, knowing for sure my trek was over. The time was exactly 3.50 pm and, with near-perfect timing, I boarded the 4 o'clock bus for Kathmandu.

Of course, the bus broke down. Somewhere after Dolalghat, I spent one hour shivering before another vehicle arrived, two busloads packed into one. Further on, our headlights packed in, but this proved repairable with the aid of some silver foil from a passenger's cigarette packet.

When we reached Kathmandu, it was after 11pm. I persuaded a restaurant in its dying throes to serve me rice, miraculously finding my companions of early Thodung and Namche still dining. I filled them with exaggerated tales of exhaustion and woe! On many occasions after, I tried lamely to tell friends how much Everest had meant to me, taking heart from similar struggles expressed by Tenzing in the concluding paragraphs of his *Man of Everest* autobiography. He wrote:

> *One of my friends asks, "Well, what is it like? How do you feel about it now?" But I cannot answer them. I can only answer in my heart, and to Everest itself, as I did on that morning when I bent and laid a red-and-blue pencil in the summit snow: Thuji chey, Chomolungma. I am grateful.*

My old hotel, *The Ganga Lodge*, was welcoming, despite my waking them with mighty door hammering. I had just walked to Kala Patthar – and back again! I tactfully thanked Christ and Buddha and Krishna it was over, smugly triumphant in my achievement. The trek, begun on November 26, 1973, had taken me 34 days.

Pokhara but no trekking!

Interminably weary, feet still aching, and with small sores broken out on my face, I made a point of passing my dirty clothing on to laundries – I had earned that luxury – then paid for a hot shower, my first in nearly 12 months. I had little motivation to move but managed a long post office queue to find three glorious letters waiting for me. Belatedly realising I had no identification on me to claim them I surreptitiously inserted them down the cuff of my Sherpa boots and made my escape outdoors where I soaked in home news. What news! I had become an uncle, to Michaela Anne. I celebrated at a lemon meringue pie shop.

I lingered another week before shipping my pack home: I would in future rely on my tiny Nepali shoulder bag for all occasions. I moved on to Pokhara, but not for the trekking the region was famous for. Over several glorious weeks I hardly ventured from a guesthouse on the edge of Lake Phewa under the shadow of beautiful Mt Machapuchare in the Annapurna range. My body slowly recovered.

PART B: OTHER SORTS OF HIGH

S.N. Goenka, the leader of Vipassana meditation
courses, magnet to thousands of hippie-trailers
in northern India. (Photo: Jim Duane.)

Kumbh Mela occur three-yearly at four river sites, returning every 12 years: Haridwar (Ganges); Prayag/Allahabad (confluence of Yamuna, Ganges, Saraswati); Ujjain (Kshipra); and Nasik (Godavari). *Maha* Kumbh mela are held at Allahabad once every 144 years! At Prayag in 1954, the first mela after independence, in a crowd of five million, 800 died in the crush. Crowds have since grown to tens of millions. Other mela exist, most claiming to be Triveni Sangam (sacred confluences of three rivers). 1974: a mela in Chitwan National Park just inside Nepal attracts an estimated 300,000-plus pilgrims.

XV

Mela

Nepal and India: a mela transforms a village of a few hundred
into a city of 300,000 overnight; tracing the source of
the inspiration underlying the Ramayana epic; before
treading a vast Indian river plain of reflection.

Cleansed from every vestige of sin and corruption by these holy waters
which make utterly pure whatsoever thing they touch, even the dead and
the rotten. It is wonderful, the power of faith like that, that can make
multitudes upon multitudes of the old and weak and the young and frail
enter without hesitation (Mark Twain, *Following the Equator*).

Please be careful

A mela, a religious gathering of great moment, was due "sometime soon" in Chitwan National Park on the Nepalese side of the border, at a village called Triveni (also, Tribeni, Treveni). I had heard much about mela. The most famous, talked about reverentially, was the Allahabad Mela Kumbh, held in Allahabad in north India's Uttar Pradesh state once every 12 years, reputedly attended by tens of millions.

With nothing but a name and some clumsy directions, I left Pokhara on a prayer with American couple, Alan and Terry. Two long bus rides landed us unkindly short at Barghat Bazaar, an evening glow-worm conglomerate of lighting-up teahouses. There were no more buses: to reach Triveni from here we would have to walk. We set off in the morning, our small band now including another American couple (John and wife), plus an Englishman (Nick), and a German (Gangalf), met overnight. Following loose advice from our hotel, we found a checkpost where an officer was unsure whether Triveni was in Nepal or India, but assigned us a soldier to lead us part-way across confusing pastures.

With lungi-clad residents, Brahman bulls, and villages of straw bivouacs and yellow clay walls, we might have been back in India. Green parakeets swooped over our heads and, once, we were forced to jump from our path when an elephant approached rather too directly. Just as our soldier guide left us, a bell introduced us to a long-skirted, furiously pedalling Englishwoman from a nearby Christian mission. Though wary of a crusader, we accepted her invitation to tea at the mission where she served us with china cups and a tea cosy.

Triveni was situated where the River Narayani flowed down from the Siwalik ranges into the wider plains of the Ganges. Meaning "three streams", the name referred to the joining of the larger Narayani with the Sona and Pancha rivers. The mela was held on Magh Krishna Amabasya, or the dark night (no moon), in the month of Magh (January) – beginning in three days' time and just 15km from where we were. Our timing was perfect!

Following oxcarts across a broad canal that carried Ganges head-waters to the lower reaches of Nepal and India, we halted at the small village of Panarewa, finding free accommodation at its "Malaria Eradication Depot". Nick, Alan and I set out to explore. The village streets were lined with huge clay pots for parboiling grain, numerous straw stacks, and long lines of tidily arranged clumps of cow dung. Teashops offered bhuja, pacowdi, and the dried lentil, chunna. We carefully noted where ganja could be bought. Dotted pilgrim camps grew before us, fires burning, and rice and dhal steaming. Campfires littered the skyline and smoke permeated as if in the aftermath of a bombing raid. Small herd-boys covered their mouths as they drove their oxen home. Two elephants that rumbled passed were fortunately responsive to their minute drivers.

The following morning, we drifted in an increasingly seething current of humanity, for the pilgrim course was now well plotted. Brahman bulls with their carts haughtily nudged us aside while their drivers dozed, and quick-fingered villagers pillaged firewood and sugarcane from the rumbling loads. Nick and I forded some mud flats, stumbling as we did so upon a moribund cow watched over by a flock of sharp-eyed vultures.

The path was a hotchpotch of characters: the sadhu in ochre lungi, dull red markings on his forehead, and hair in thick matted strands, or shaven with a twist of a pigtail at the back; the smiling Bhutanese, inquisitive eyes straining to take in a thousand strange sights, beneath a proudly worn monkey-fur cap; the Indian villager, accompanied by a fussing wife, their belongings slung in her sarong folds; the deformed pilgrim, legless, inching determinedly along the trail on his hands, wooden handles sufficing as "foot" wear.

At invitation, we stopped for raksi (spirit) and the others caught up with us for a lengthy stop, knowing that Triveni could not be more than a kilometre or two away. It was barely midday. We entered Triveni as Good Companions, seven Westerners bursting upon an exploding fairground. Leafy bivouac stalls had been hurriedly erected everywhere along the way, offering teas, pacowdi and "beedis". And ganja.

A worried-looking policeman examined our passports and asked where we planned to sleep. "There is nowhere," he said. But incredibly, John had attended the mela two years' previously and found us space at a teashop that remembered him. We were fortunate indeed. We asked the policeman how many people were expected, and were told, "conservatively, three lakhs" (300,000), an almost unimaginable amount for the tiny village setting. His last words to us were, "please be careful".

A python around his neck
The river headwaters passed by just 200 metres from our sleeping quarters. A concreted canal at this stretch, carved steps down, provided access for laundry and bathing. Religious "offerings" were already on sale with ragged tents offering plait-stranding services as well as brilliant red-orange dyes to be implanted on foreheads.

The path was lined with tea stalls, tables of rich candies, pastries, and hot, simmering curries. The pathway between was taken over by plastics, trinkets, curries, and the whining of toys swirled on large poles by the youngest of the ever-increasing throng. Everything was noise. Loudspeakers roared and the wealthy contributed with off-key transistors, always turned up to the loudest volume. A sadhu with a python about his neck tried to elicit baksheesh, then left, disgruntled when I showed no interest. The day was full beyond compare, and it was almost a relief when night fell. I settled on a straw mattress.

At the village outskirts, camp divisions had been roughly plotted and prepared for the influx of pilgrims and, though the village was already shuddering, these areas were still sparsely occupied. Further on, a forested area was home to some huge encampments in the making. The mela officially began in two days' time. Many thousands had yet to arrive.

I awoke the next morning in darkness but darkness did not prevent an ever-rising human tide from crushing available space, nor preclude loudspeakers from blaring. Morning toiletries were the first problem to be faced. I walked briskly passed the rough-thatched teashops and food stands, stumbling passed makeshift mud compounds where whole families now resided – cane packs, oxen and ox carts, horses, cows, and long lines of washing asymmetrically drying on damp flooring.

Whole villages had pooled resources to come here, and the resulting encampments evoked America's wild west. Two, sometimes three, covered wagons would be parked in a group, backs to the wind, the "settlers" squatting or carrying out duties such as washing clothes or collecting water. At this hour, there was a potent smell of cooking pots – simmering rice and steam curries.

A few rusted hand pumps were available where dishes were scrubbed, and teeth, and feet. Resuming one's path, one sank in mud pools and all good work was undone. The forest glade mercifully appeared, but enjoyment was tempered by the impossibility of avoiding people. The pilgrim tide was far from abated. I somewhere found my necessary privacy, then sought out a water pump to wash, fighting to keep my place in the queue.

Overnight, the village had become a city. Stalls continued to sprout startlingly, and unsophisticated pilgrims were easily induced to part with their money. Throngs of wide-eyed women bought cheap cottons in garish colours and junk jewellery, while their husbands were attracted to pocketknives and clay chillums that broke easily, before retiring for raksi. One of the most popular stalls sold betel. The customer could choose from a selection of dyes, nut additives, and juice extractions that came in red, orange and green bottles.

In the afternoon, I spotted a bevy of ancient-looking wooden barques pushing slowly upriver towards us. The about 6m-long vessels fought a difficult counter-current with long poles levered from aft. When a light wind arose, the leading vessel erected a curved canvas that was more patch than original. Other boats followed suit and it was not long before the fleet disappeared from our view.

I struck up a conversation with a Kathmandu man here to fulfil his late grandfather's wish of "going to heaven". He told me he had been instructed to attend the mela every year to distribute clothing and foodstuffs to the poor. "My father came here every year until his death, and since, I too have been coming," he said. "This is my fourth time." He had a system for dispensing his philanthropy. "I approach the first beggar I see on the day of the new moon, give to him a large proportion of what I have, then pass out what remains to all-comers."

Of significance to Hindus and Buddhists, Triveni was indelibly linked to the *Ramayana* scripture. Near here, the sage Valmiki had reputedly recorded the epic, sometime between 500BC and 500AD. According to legend, the point where the three rivers joined – where we now sat – was where god-prince Rama had bathed. And from where, doubting his wife Sita's purity, he had banished her. It also marked where (according to Sanskrit text Varaha Purana) an elephant wading to find lotus flowers for worship, was seized by an alligator. Hearing the elephant's cry for help, Lord Vishnu had descended from heaven and killed the alligator. On countless posters around India, the elephant could be seen with tears cascading from its eyes.

Nottingham Forest

I shared a joint with Alan before unsurprisingly heading towards the Indian sweet stores. The vendors created amazing confectionaries – light fudges, sugar crystals, syrup doughs kneaded into balls and squares, and all manner of other shapes and sizes.

We detoured to the sadhu encampment, the section of ground where the "holy" population had gathered. It was dark by now, with glistening campfires spewing smoke eerily. Green wood fog hung over our faces and, occasionally, a spurting flame illuminated the mystical surround. We approached one hearth where two longhaired proponents stood swaying. Apart from narrow G-strings, they were completely naked. Somewhere nearby, cymbals clashed discordantly and, as if in response to a challenge, one of the sadhus imperiously exposed his genitals. Much stoned, Alan and I returned to bed.

Hoping to escape the madness, in the morning I again sought out the forest. It was rather like Nottingham in the days of Robin Hood and I half expected to be surprised by outlaws in green. Cattle carts lay splattered in their encampments, their wooden wheels and frames giving no indication of this century. Wood fires and a smoky mist added to a sense of unreality and half-naked pilgrims made a convincing case that the centuries had indeed been rolled back.

Astonishingly, even more people had arrived. It was difficult to breathe, let alone make progress. I stopped for a while by a barber's mat whose custom was a group of shaven-headed sadhu, his long, cutthroat razor dismissing remaining hair shadow, a final preparation for the morning's ceremony. This day was the "new moon" and the bathing ritual was underway. For bathers from all over Nepal and India, this was the crowning point of their pilgrimage.

Further along the path, a dance troupe twisted sinuously at the centre of a gypsy-like campground. These people were darker skinned than most and I was surprised by the undisguised sexuality of the female principal. She was dressed in a vivid red sari, voluptuously thrown about her body so that no curve remained hidden, her stomach and back bared. Unlike the men, her movements were graceful and slow. She eyed them with contempt.

Faced with an ever-swelling human tide, I headed for the riverbank where I clambered along the embankment wall to watch the frantic activity below. Every available inch of riverfront was occupied. Every-where, men and women squatted to urinate. There was no privacy, nor could there be, and almost everyone present was in various stages of undress. Over all, hung a shrouding mist, the far side bank hardly visible, bar shadows about the water edges. But the morning sun rose, a brilliant saffron sphere, and the subtle effect of cloud on light caused a strange shimmering that may have had great spiritual significance for the pilgrims.

Throughout the morning, the tide remained impenetrable. The menfolk struggled to water wearing but loose "pyjamas" or modern underbriefs, and the women followed bravely in their footsteps in simple saris or petticoat shifts. The women sought their purification hurriedly, dropping sari tops and rinsing before putting them back in place; the men were more rigorous, dunking themselves entirely before surfacing to scrub.

Bundles and baskets littered the riverside and, at one point, I saw a poster warning in English, "Beware of pick-pockets". Occasionally, the bustle and constant discourse of thousands would be interrupted by a drumbeat or cymbal clash. A young sadhu carried a casket of coins he had earned by fingering red dye on foreheads. The general picture was one of incredible colour: a sea of pastels, crimsons, aqua blues, ochres, violets, and greens. There were now thousands bathing below and the swarm showed little sign of abating. Some women entered the water immaculately dressed, evening saris and society sequins floating below the current, but most were simply attired.

The sadhus provided contrast, bathing in simple white-ochre pyjamas, though a few wore yellow. Two entered the stream naked but for their G-strings. They waded out further than most, threw grains in the water, and only then began washing. As the bathing continued, I inadvertently found myself the voyeur as maidens adjusted their toiletries, then stared, fascinated, as a deformed and partially paralysed pilgrim struggled to shore on his stumps and his hands.

Long queues filed down the high, concrete steps and equally long queues returned, presumably, physically and spiritually refreshed. This was indeed a gathering of the people. I reflected that a thousand years ago, the scene might have been identical: except, that is, for the businessman in a chequered suit who had somehow intruded upon my field of vision. A sadhu replaced him, clutching a steel trident. His hair was in thick matted strands that collapsed untidily about his back, and with a long beard of the same constituency. From his waist, on a smudged red tassel, hung a brass bell that he kneed continuously. As well as poppy-seed bangles and necklaces, he carried an enormous gold figurine with a grotesque red tongue. A policeman stood close throughout his performance. There were evidently sadhus and sadhus!

I left my watchtower cautiously, climbing over sheets of drying saris and lungis then, reaching ground level, every movement was a battle. The procession of new arrivals had achieved a new intensity. I had never seen so many people. Yet families managed to lay mats, and delectable odours soon wafted about me: curries or simple fried vegetable dishes eaten with rice or chapatti. Gangalf joined me for breakfast and I learned with dismay he had had stolen from him his spectacles, watch, and cash. Oppressed sleeping indoors, he had moved outside. He had been wearing his watch. His money and spectacles had been inside his sleeping bag! He decided to leave.

The village now unbearable, Alan, Terry and I retreated to the forest with our books. Pilgrims approached and stared but eventually moved on, leaving us with at least a modicum of peace. It was late in the day before we returned to Triveni where the crowds had thinned. At last it was possible to move, to breathe. The new moon bathing was done.

With Gangalf gone, and Nick in the process of moving into a tent, the remaining of us squeezed into our still-narrow sleeping quarters and, to the man and woman, slept fitfully. We were all decided to leave. John was not feeling well and, without his and his wife's energy, Alan and Terry were easily convinced to accompany them.

I was sad to see Alan and Terry go. Alan was 31, rebelling somewhat after two years serving in Vietnam. He wore his hair long and paraded himself in embroidered Levi jackets and bangles. Nothing was sacred to him but his jibes were never serious. Terry, just 19, had a dry wit that was a perfect foil. But they moved at a different pace than I and our parting was inevitable. They often bemoaned the hardships. Neither had bothered to view the bathing ceremony – it required too early a rising. But we had become friends and Alan, uncharacteristically, told me: "At the risk of being emotional, I'll miss you." Terry kissed me.

Suddenly lonely, I breakfasted on curried potato while a sadhu tried to embarrass me for baksheesh by remaining close at my side while crowds gathered. Another passed by with a calf in tow that had fifth and sixth legs hanging at each side of its neck, and I saw that his begging bowl was full. A medicine man unravelled gruesome mats laden with dried snakes, rotted bird beaks, putrefied lizards, and other strange fauna.

Triveni had provided a rare excitement. For here was life. The one street paved the way for bureaucrat, holy man, snake charmer, shop-keeper, tinker, pickpocket, beggar, soldier, Hindu, Buddhist, sightseer, cow, goat, duck, hen, buffalo, horse, elephant, monkey – even the python was not out of place! Everyone was going somewhere, a forceful, persistent, tide that brooked no opposition.

I made a slow start. For a long time, I chatted with a man who, seeing me writing, invited me to record his life history. I declined, but earned a free breakfast. Then I packed my meagre possessions and began walking along the embankment towards the large Gandak dam just visible in the distance. Behind me, a few shanty mela camps persisted, though acres of temporary leaf bivouacs had been deserted.

Valmiki's Ashram

Reaching the dam, I looked around carefully for an immigration post for a Nepal exit stamp. Seeing none, I walked across the dam and into India. The other side was equally barren of officialdom, but locals guided me to a hatbox where an immigration man was woken, and I was invited into a bedroom that also served as office. He appeared nervous at having an overseas' customer but stamped my passport after I patiently lied that British citizens did not require visas. He did not notice my deficient Nepalese entries!

I was apparently at Baisha Lotan, or nearly so, for to reach there required a further 2km walk. The town also went under the name, Valmiki Nagar. There were roads here, and learning there was a bus service to reach civilisation, I breathed a sigh of relief. I had been travelling blind.

Then, armed with directions from a shack with a sign proclaiming "tourist office", I set off on foot in search of the Valmiki Ashram, which, confusingly, was back in Nepal. This time I met no immigration, just followed directions, crossing rivers and unseen borders. It was a walk of about five kilometres, through open pastureland where bright white, but black-faced monkeys crashed insanely in foliage above me and the occasional ox peered passed me incuriously.

Apart from its name, the ashram was not an impressive complex. I briefly surveyed the half-acre compound, its cattle-gnawed tussock patchily encircled by a cord from which hung triangles of coloured paper. Brick piles indicated started-but-forgotten building and it took but a moment to wander a few unsophisticated shrines. Some crumbling statuettes lay against a brick fence and, at centre, the thatch sleeping quarters of a resident sadhu.

Withall, the ashram was supremely significant as the home of sage Valmiki, the attributed author-poet of the *Ramayana*. To Hindu and Buddhist, the epic was scripture, the story heroic, much as Homer's *Odyssey*, drawing its significance not just from the tale, but the ethic, the guiding paths of good versus evil, with little doubt left about which was advisable. In the *Ramayana* the forces of light are led by Rama, those of darkness, by Ravan (Rawana). Good, of course, overcomes evil, though the latter is never eliminated, only balance maintained.

Wandering back to Valmiki Nagar across the ridiculous border back into India, I was interrupted again by an eruption of white monkeys and it seemed plausible that Valmiki had drawn from this unique population for his fabulous character Hanuman, the epic's white monkey god. It was possible I was viewing descendants of the very beast!

My tourist office shack offered me a bed. Before turning in, I distinguished myself by falling ungracefully in a mud puddle. A stall owner rescued me, provided me with water to wash, then fed me on dhal and vegetable and a sour savoury called "pinkel" made from mango. As I ate, he asked me, rapid-fire, my opinions on Hinduism, Christianity, communism and hippies. His final question was: "Do you hate black men?"

A river plain "long-cut"

Reaching Varanasi, the tourist officer said, would require a complicated bus hop through at least four towns before a train could be caught. The stall owner, however, recommended a "simpler" route, one involving a trek across a river plain to the town of Chhitauni, from where a train would be available for the rest of the way. "However, it will not be easy and will take much walking," he said. He had me won!

From Bagahar (one bus ride), I began walking across a huge alluvial plain, feeling slightly like Lawrence of Arabia amid burning white sands. After about 5km, it was necessary to cross the Narayani river on a bloated bowl of a ferry that seemed out of place in this Indian Gobi. I paid a small sum to the ferryman, leaping precariously aboard as two boys poled the craft the 20m or so to the opposite shore. There, two men clasped my baggage, propelling me to a horse and carriage royally waiting to carry passengers across the remaining river basin preceding Chhitauni.

I declined the ride to incredulous stares. "Don't you know Chhitauni is more than dos (10) km distant?" A slight, balding man, family in tow, walked with me, peppering me with the usual questions. And, as usual, I made the error of trying to answer honestly. "All religions are good," I said piously. "My belief comes from within." The man immediately assumed I was a holy man – he used the word "saint" – and asked me for pamphlets! We continued through endless desert, tripping through rivulets, and our talking at least reduced the strain of what had amounted to somewhat more than 10km. We ground to a halt at one final, unbroachable stream, where we huddled tiredly amid an already gathered group awaiting another far side ferry.

While we waited, my current reading – Alphonso-Karkala's *Anthology of Indian Literature* – was eyed with awe when the words *Veda* and *Bhagavad Gita* were recognised. I was sitting cross-legged, Indian style, and this and my wearing of mala (prayer beads) was clear proof I was indeed holy! When the ferry arrived, I was helped gingerly aboard and my baggage passed gently to a dry section of the boat.

The plain was now exhausted. Never had I seen a river plain of such size and it took little imagination to picture an impenetrable torrent sweeping all before during the monsoon season. Nor did it take much imagination to envisage a contrary season in which livestock and man failed to find sustenance.

It was but a short walk now to Chhitauni, a bundle of market stalls huddled under the auspices of a large sugar mill. After staking bed space at the railway station, I wandered, coming across a school performance of a rousing Hindustani song shouted with clenched fists and grim faces. January 26 was the anniversary of India's constitution drawn up by the Congress of 1950, three years after independence was gained from the British. The leader most revered for that achievement, I was several times reminded, was India's first president, Rajendra Prasad. Then Prime Minister, Jawaharlal Nehru, received no mention.

With morning came an inescapable Indian sun in a vast, fathomless sky. Reading the epics, it was easy to imagine sun god Surya and his goddess-of-the-sky mother Aditi overseeing all existence. The expanse above was endless; the expanse below was endless. It was as if this country had been built for reflection and no one could doubt the illusoriness of human endeavour. Christianity, Judaism, and Islam were all desert religions. Perhaps the grasping of the unknown depended on such a geography, where one's own minuteness was so starkly evident.

From here, the railway line shunted on to inland India and I would soon be aboard. But with time to burn before my train, I scrambled once more down to the vast river paddocks of silver sand. Magically, a long line of wooden barques, just as at Triveni, chose that moment to pass in battle file along the Narayani, their broad sails flashing before disappearing from view.

Cremations, defecating bathers and industry polluters of the Ganges threaten not just humans but some 200 fish and endangered dolphin species. In 1962, a committee was set up to "end pollution" but, apart from mounting levels of faecal coliform, nothing changed. 1974: India's first environmental legislation, Water (Prevention and Control of Pollution) Act promises to "prevent and control pollution and maintain or restore the wholesomeness of water". Due to "bureaucracy, lack of support from religious and local authorities, and corruption", it fails.

XVI

The home of God

Varanasi, India: where God actually lives and mortals go to die; I imbibe the essence of Buddhism at a deer park, and of Hinduism at a university; and take a long walk along the Ganges riverbank with a holy man.

Flowers and rivers, the blowing of conch shells, the heavy rain of the Indian July, or the parching heat, are images of the moods of that heart in union or in separation; and a man sitting in a boat upon a river playing upon a lute, like one of those figures full of mysterious meaning in a Chinese picture is God Himself (W.B Yeats, introduction to Rabindranath Tagore, *Gitanjali*).

Life is suffering

Outside my Varanasi (aka Benares, aka Kashi) hotel, busy bazaar streets provided intolerable temptations. "Chapatti, mister?" "Cha?" "Dahi" (yoghurt)? On each occasion, I nodded enthusiastically, reacclimatising myself to the delights of big Indian city – alongside frantic motor traffic competing noisily and dustily with fleets of rickshaws and large populations of cows, donkeys and water buffalo.

A New Zealander seeking to exchange books sought me out and we dined together. His travels had taken him through the Americas, Europe and Africa and he was now heading home overland. I was impressed – till he said he had been away from home for just a couple of months. Still, it was great to hear his news that New Zealand's Dick Tayler had won the first gold medal (10,000m) at the Christchurch Commonwealth Games.

The next morning, I began a modest pilgrimage to satellite town Sarnath, birthplace and home of the Buddhist movement. It was a longer walk than anticipated, through confusing bazaar mazes, oil-lined streets of light industry, and innumerable bus depots. When I stopped for tea, a young Englishwoman joined me. A resident at a nearby commune, her conversation hovered prosaically on drugs and, despite my best efforts, an articulate conversation did not eventuate.

A Mecca for pilgrims and tourists, Sarnath had more than its share of curio stalls, of the kind that cling to religious centres. Prominent among the pilgrims were Tibetans and Sherpas who had found haven from their mountain homes, gravitating to here, the very source of their beliefs. Enthusiastically scurrying from holy place to holy place, they were easily identifiable for their traditional woollen jackets and long, rust-red skirts over dark trousers, uncaring of the fierce lowland heat.

The most important features of Sarnath related to Buddha's first sermon. The heralded spot, in a nearby deer park, was marked by a 30m stupa dating from the 5th or 6th century AD. The Dhamekha Stupa was built above the remains of an earlier structure reportedly dating back to the reign of King Ashoka (Maurya Dynasty), possibly a couple of hundred years before the birth of Christ. The sermon, marking the beginning of "the path", was of immense importance to Buddhists – and Hindus. Repeated again and again to me, it introduced the Buddha's "Kingdom of Righteousness", outlining the Buddhist "middle way". This was his famous prescription for living, the "eightfold path" to Nirvana comprising right views, right aspirations, right speech, right conduct, right livelihood, right effort, right mindfulness and right contemplation. Simple!

Navigating that path depended on the acceptance of "four noble truths": that existence was one of suffering; that suffering derived from cravings; that suffering could only be alleviated by setting aside cravings; and that the method to achieve this, was by the above eightfold path. Buddha offered a "threefold realisation" to accomplishing each step: the recognition of the truth, the need to comprehend it, and its practical realisation. Simple!

I had bumped constantly into Buddhist doctrine from Thailand to Cambodia to Burma, but had not till now taken the time to explore it. In part this was because I had observed it being fashionably followed by hordes of travellers with chillums, or criticised by groupings of Christian zealots, neither of which had spurred me. But I was becoming fascinated.

I struck up a conversation with an articulate holy man, and was taken by his explanation of how "suffering" should be understood. While Westerners might see this view of existence as rather depressing, this man asserted most failed to grasp the breadth of the word's meaning. "Everything in life affects you, touches on you to some degree – that you *suffer*," he said. "Buddha's message is simply a guide to living with equanimity." Viewed this way, "suffering" might be better expressed as "experiencing".

I lay half asleep in arbour shade practising Hindi numbers with a youngster when an English monk came over to talk. A student at Dharamsala, home of the Dalai Lama-in-exile, he gave me an enthusiastic account of Buddha's life and teachings. He also invited me to enlist in a course under his guru, which I gave serious consideration to, but declined.

Where God lives

Over the next few weeks, it wasn't hard to fall under the spell of Varanasi, from the markets spilling wares across the streets, to the mendicants with disfigured limbs pushing aluminium bowls forward imploringly, and the sadhus, who were everywhere. The last, typically accompanied by the discordant whine of flutes and the clashing of cymbals heralding yet another pilgrimage to the holy waters of the Ganges, were a constant reminder of the city's heavenly status.

Large numbers of beggars collected at the bottom of a crescent, where wide, yellow brick steps led down to the river. As I began walking the long riverbank, an elderly sadhu joined me "to share his joy", and I followed him along the embankment to together enjoy this great, crumbling frontage of stone from another era. I absorbed much from this man: under gentle eyes, each word uttered was considered and spoken with sincerity. "Benares", he told me, meant "forest of happiness", which was logical for, in this city, "everyone" was happy. "The beggars are happy, the cows are happy, the vendors are happy, the policemen are happy, and so are you and I."

There was a reason for this. "Benares is the home of God," he said. "The Lord reigns over the whole universe but he lives in Benares." It was hard to gainsay: that was why so many pilgrims came. They came to bathe in the holy waters, to spend their declining years within holy precincts, and to die! We stopped by the famous riverside crematorium, today sporting a flaming bundle of sticks with a corpse on top. The body, clearly that of an old man, was covered by plain cloth, though its head and feet lay exposed and consuming flames promised a quick immolation.

A misty smoke, drifted in rings over the motionless river, completing an aura of unreality that bordered on the mystical. "Have you noticed there are no unpleasant smells?" asked my holy man. Just as the waters of the Ganges would never lose their purity, so bodies cremated here, would never putrefy, he said. "For the Hindu, to be burned here is the highest reward possible and ensures with certainty their ascension to heaven."

We moved on passed gaily-painted houseboats and, from one of these, I was hailed merrily: "Hey! Ganja?" It was not the river referred to. Another bend and we interrupted a small party of dignified-looking businessmen in plain white robes for their bathing, the culmination to their pilgrimage. They splashed the river waters on their bodies with great seriousness then proceeded to pass grains to a flock of swans that had eagerly gathered about them.

"This is heaven," repeated the sadhu. "Varanasi", he said, was a recent name for the city, coined from its river boundaries, the "Varuna" and the "Asi". A herd of buffalo, almost unrecognisable for their white sand coatings, were tethered along our route, their dung collected in neat lines for drying. Closely adjacent, squatted long rows of washerwomen. Their washing done, it remained only for them to guard the acreages of colourful saris and lungis as they dried spread out above the dusty steps down to the river.

"All religions are good," my sadhu told me. "Do you know that Mahatma Gandhi borrowed from Christianity? If you give me blows on this side of the face, I must turn to offer you the other side. India expelled the Europeans without firing a single gun. We won the war without fighting!"

Above us rose a stark, yellow brick citadel, the area about thick with various-hued sadhu. This, he said, was the city's refuge for holy men. "Any man can live here free of charge in any of the rooms available, but

171

for four nights only. Then he must move on – if only to a neighbouring room!" Music drifted hypnotically down from the turrets, a wavering choral distinctive for the oft-repeated proclamation, "Ram".

He told me the *Ramayana* was written here, which I questioned, to be quickly assured the epic had been first written *in Hindi* here – by a *reincarnation* of sage Valmiki. Previously, the epic had been known only in Sanskrit, he said. The title's first two syllables were significant: "Ra" and "Ma", together formed "Ram", and "Ram" was God.

Leaving built-up Varanasi behind, we were confronted with a tributary trickle that etched random patterns in sand at a miniature delta-merge with the mother river. This was the Asi, so here did Varanasi end. "On this side is paradise, on this side heaven," my sadhu told me. He gestured towards a great walled fortress on the other Ganges shore. "That," he said, "is Ram Nagar, the City of Kings". But God was Benares' sole ruler. No monarch could compete and all of India's historic dynasties in consequence therefore had had to be established outside the city.

As the shadows lengthened, the holy man spread out his possessions – a single change of clothing, a solitary brass bowl – on his platform by the river. For protection he erected an umbrella of flax, and squatted underneath, yoga fashion. He had already left me.

City of Kings

Each day, town and river beckoned me. The long approach, though by now thoroughly familiar, still appealed and I was happy amid familiar faces: the booksellers, the fruit vendors, the sadhus, and the donkeys. The last walked a constant passage along the main thoroughfare, tied in teams, heavily laden with grain sacks – or cement. They brayed horribly, great gasping bellows begging for sympathy. Brightly decked horse carriages scurried more quietly through the traffic, they too hauling heavy loads of dry goods or people, and from them came not a word of complaint.

The river frontage too, did not change. The houseboats clung determinedly to their highly sought-after moorings, and a continuing eddy of pilgrims and sadhus, hawkers and ordinary townsfolk swirled confusingly along and about the riverbank. I passed the cremation spot ("no smells, Father Gossamer!"), crawled through oxen herds, and tripped clumsily across near-unbroachable webs of drying laundry.

One day a fleet of wooden barges came ashore to unload their silvery sand cargo. Lines of barefooted workmen became a human conveyor belt, jogging to the boats, filling their flaxen baskets to capacity then, loads on heads, struggling tortuously uphill and out of sight. At the next turn, a grounded barque was being pushed back to water by 50 or more willing shoulders. There was a chant leader to inspire, a willing chorus to echo a rejoinder, "Ah yai, ah yai!", and the great tarred hulk moved an inch closer to the Ganges.

I set out to visit Ram Nagar, crossing a narrow bridge to the far side bank, puzzled at a construction that had been built so low that little river traffic could pass beneath. The result was one life above stream, another below.

Ram Nagar was indeed a fortress. Its tall, red turrets rose above a high citadel wall, unwelcoming, but promising a rare security within. Soldiers stood impressive guard, but the overall effect was lost for me when I realised this was now little more than a museum. For a while, I sat outside taking in the sights. A train of camels haughtily picked their passage passed me, long, supercilious necks craning. They wore heavy wooden saddles, though only the lead animal bore a rider, a small, wizened man who sat motionless, staring ahead expressionlessly, leaving direction entirely to the creature below.

I wandered as far as some rice fields to be interrupted by an untended elephant that strode ahead of me before veering frighteningly between two frail teashops, in front of which was an old-fashioned water pump. The shopkeepers seemed uninterested as the elephant held its trunk to the pump spout, pouring the refreshment inward with a loud, impolite gargle. One step to the left, one step to the right, the result would have been equally disastrous, for neither teashop was of a permanent nature! Satiated, the beast shuffled backwards, turned, and walked unconcernedly out of town. India!

The next few days I filled gluttonously with food and reading. For the latter, I alternated between Tolstoy's short stories and my *Anthology of Indian Literature*, which warranted rather more concentration than my overladen belly could bear. The words of the Buddha did not help:

He who lives looking for pleasures only, his senses uncontrolled, immoderate in his food ... Mara (the tempter) will certainly overthrow him, as the wind throws down a weak tree!

Tolstoy enthralled me, his *The Death of Ivan Ilyich* and *The Kreutzer Sonata* among the finest short stories I had read. The former explored "ignoble death", together with questions of life and hereafter in the minds of the dying; the latter was a potent account of marriage, society, and attitudes to women. No wonder Gandhi, in discussing "satyagraha" (the power to be gleaned from adherence to truth) had commented: "Tolstoy was the best and brightest exponent of the doctrine. He not only expounded it, but lived according to it."

My Anthology too gave me a lot to think about, exposing me to the teachings of the *Vedas*, the *Upanishads*, the *Bhagavad Gita* and the *Dhammapada*. With new insights into some of the great and earliest Eastern philosophies, I was surprised to find that much that I had read of Plato appeared to have had earlier origin in these Oriental works. I was also introduced to the writings of 20th century Bengali poet Rabindranath Tagore:

> *Where the mind is without fear and the head is held high; Where knowledge is free; Where the world has not been broken up into fragments by narrow domestic walls; Where words come out from the depth of truth; Where tireless striving stretches its arms towards perfection; Where the clear stream of reason has not lost its way into the dreary desert sand of dead habit; Where the mind is led forward by thee into ever-widening thought and action – into that heaven of freedom, my Father, let my country awake.*

Regardless of whether or not his *Gitanjali* was to be accepted as a "glimpse of heaven", it was a beautiful poem. It was not a surprise to learn from its introduction how much of an inspiration Tagore had been to W.B. Yeats.

A loaf of bread

Weak-willed, I took a trishaw to the Hindu University and was immeasurably grateful for the ride, for the road was a much, much longer one than appeared on my map. The university was famous throughout India. Situated on more than 1000 acres, it would probably count among the biggest in the world – Indians insisted it was also the most beautiful. It was certainly huge, each department set apart from its neighbour and comfortably shaded under avenues of trees.

Founded comparatively recently by a barrister who spent a lifetime squeezing capital from reluctant donors, it listed first among its founding donations a loaf of bread from a beggar. The bread was later auctioned for about $1500. Here to visit the university's Shiva Temple, I was unimpressed with passing groups of young men in dark blue suits who peered disdainfully at this badly dressed European in his beads and flip-flops. I caught the word "hippie" but long used to summary judgements, continued to the temple unbothered.

Shiva, "Destroyer of Evil", was originally worshipped as a symbolic manifestation of Hinduism's supreme, cosmic energy – hence the phallic symbol, the "lingam", associated with him. But this temple was an expression of a wide range of belief – including Buddhist – and it seemed the only justification in the name lay in the proximity of the buildings to Varanasi, the city of Shiva, the city of God.

Along the temple's upstairs' walls, were scriptural quotations of moral significance. Often, these were repeated in English, starting with a broad enunciation of the Hindu concept of God (K. Upanishad 1/8):

He is one and only one God; That almighty, all pervading God is Brahma, the creative form; Vishnu the protective form, and Shiva, the destructive form; He is Indra; he is immortal; he is self-existent and self-effulgent; He is form, he is time, he is fire and he is moon.

Other quotations emanated from the *Bhagavad Gita*, the *Upanishads*, and even the Buddhist *Dhammapada*:

Abstinence from all evil, fulfilment of good, purification of one's mind, this is the teaching of the Buddhas.

I wondered if there was anywhere else in the world where a place of worship existed so tolerant of all beliefs, and was becoming convinced that the Hindu philosophy underlay much Western thought. The Vedas were claimed to have been written as early as 1000 BC; the Upanishads, sophisticated philosophies and metaphysical statements, sometime between 200 and 800 BC; though the Bhagavad Gita was conceived as recently as between 200 and 400 BC! I read:

Therefore, without attachment, constantly perform action which is duty, for, by performing action without attachment, man verily reacheth the supreme.

What price my life so far?

I took a trishaw back to the central Varanasi market where I bought a paper and pored eagerly over the final results of the Christchurch games. Local hero, John Walker's performance in taking the 1500m silver medal behind Tanzanian Filbert Bayi was stunning news, his staggering time the second fastest ever recorded.

Walking home, I became caught in a lengthy procession of paper models of mosques and domes borne grandly above long bamboo poles. Grandly, that is, till they became entangled in power lines and chaos ensued. Guided by horses clad in splendid white robes and with procession leaders loudly chanting mantras, the march regathered its composure. The celebration was the Muslim holiday, "Muharram", the first month of the Islamic calendar, one of the faith's four sacred months of the year, the next holiest after Ramadan. This faith, too, was accepted.

Back in my hotel room, I paradoxically began reading *Mein Kampf*, if nothing else, a fascinating exploration of a darker side, when I was disturbed by a sudden outburst of Hindu incantations propelled unbearably over a loudspeaker from the building next door. Played at full volume, these continued all night: "Hare Rama; Hare Krishna; Hare Ram; Hare Ram"! Cymbals and bells clanged discordantly and I had little sleep. Further detracting from my "inner peace", my hotel manager began to walk into my room unannounced as if privileged, asking for gifts from my untidy array of unlikely possessions. When he began eating my bananas and using my washing powder, I chose to spend my days in town, unfazed at the long hour's walk to city centre.

I ran into old friends from Indonesia, Laos and Nepal, and hours passed in inconsequential reminiscences undisturbed by the backdrop of shouting trishaw drivers and hunting beggars. I experimented with new ways home along untried bazaar pathways, enjoying the thrill of the unexpected as processions interrupted me, invariably including elephants straddled by holy men waving posters.

My hotel room, however, still drowned in loudspeaker cacophony, "Hare Ram" and "Hare Krishna" impossible to avoid. It was time to move on. But I loved this city. For me the ancient town, with all its spiritual allure, had more appeal than a Rome or a Paris. This sacred heart of India was alive, its religious practices and beliefs just as vital for its people as they must have been thousands of years before the birth of Christ. There were no majestic ruins here, just ancient temples, ancient pathways frequented by sadhus with old-world austerity. The modern Hindu still made pilgrimages, discarded his grey flannel suit for simple white lungi, bathed, and sought spiritual refreshment. Only the European was new, he and his homegrown entourage of hotel touts, "guides", and sometimes, financiers!

On whim one morning, I parked my gear early at the railway station, and awaited service at a nearby chai shop, within earshot of the whistle that would signal the arrival of a train. And when a train arrived, I slipped unobtrusively into a sleeping carriage, claimed a berth, and waited. It was easier than I had imagined. Fifty paise slipped to the ticket collector enabled me to retain my seat.

As we crossed the metal span over the Ganga, I was treated to a perfect sunset, a gentle intermingling of red-gold with wintry mist. The river below drifted towards sea, reflecting beautifully the numerous yellow stone temples along her banks. The sun sank slowly, but decisively, while the train gathered momentum as it headed to the nighttime blackness of deeper India.

A little later and a pallid full moon rose just as surely as its opposite had fallen. Heaven was revealed, the Milky Way spread luxuriously across all horizons. Clearly, God was at home. And that was how I would remember Varanasi.

In 1959, the Dalai Lama fled occupied Tibet to set up an exile government in India. Titled the Kashag Government (later, the "Government of the Great Snow Land"), it was to be dissolved "as soon as freedom is restored". In 1965 the Chinese renamed Tibet, Xizang, as "a provincial autonomous Chinese region". 1974: on the anniversary of his flight, the Dalai Lama issues a statement that includes: "The cause of Tibet ... is the struggle of a people to determine their own identity. Until they are satisfied, the struggle for Tibet will continue."

XVII

The middle way

Bodh Gaya and Darjeeling, India: in the footsteps of the Dalai Lama and his Indian diaspora ... and a few others.

Would the Chinese destroy our holy city and massacre our people
if I went? ... everything was uncertain, except the compelling
anxiety of all my people to get me away before the orgy of
Chinese destruction and massacre began ... I decided to go
(Howarth, ed, *My Land and My People: The*
Autobiography of His Holiness the Dali Lama).

The next enlightened man

Just off the train at midnight, the only accommodation to be found in Gaya was an expensive tourist hotel. Joined by Irishman, Jim and Englishman, Harold, I managed to persuade the porter to allow us to sleep on the floor in the foyer. "No charge, but baksheesh would be appreciated," he said.

All the Buddhist nations had staked temple ground in Gaya, the believed site of the Buddha's enlightenment: China, Sri Lanka, Japan, Thailand and Burma. But it was Burma's edifice, hidden behind old iron railings and persistent ivy that was biggest magnet for travellers.

Meditation courses were regularly held there and its grounds were in consequence littered with European devotees.

First pilgrim port of call had to be the host country's Mahabodhi Temple for its famous, still effulgent, Bodhi tree, under whose shade the enlightenment had supposedly occurred. We approached the sacred compound down steep steps and there it was, the very tree under which Buddha had discovered his way, or sort of. In reality, it was a bit like Murphy's axe: it had been cut down many times during the 2500 or more years since Buddha chose its shade for his meditation. No matter. Rice paper fluttered as circling pilgrims solemnly intoned their timeless prayers or prostrated themselves before it.

For the pilgrims, it was important to pray at the precise spot where Buddha had knelt, where he had walked in contemplation, and at the lotus pond where he had bathed. Inside the temple, priests prayed at the feet of a gold Buddha; another was preoccupied pouring fine grains and a single pea on the back of a brass plate. The latter threw the mixture in patterns, contemplated his work, smudged it, and began again.

To be closer to the action, Jim and I moved to Bodh Gaya, 15km to the south, into an imposing "Tibetan Tent", a marquis complex that housed large numbers of refugees and pilgrims. Here we were fed all the familiar foods of Nepal: momo (dumpling), thukpa (noodle soup), and chow chow (noodles), and I was quickly at home with the smiling Sherpas I had come to know so well. Lodging was 50p a night – less than NZ10c.

Buddhists have four "most holy" places, each subject to endless pilgrimages: the sites of his birth, his enlightenment, his first sermon, and of his death. Born in Lumbini in Nepal, he had been enlightened in Bodh Gaya, preached his first sermon at Sarnath, and died at Kusinagarm in Uttar Pradesh, India. But, to the devout, the site of his enlightenment – some accounts claim it to have happened in 528BC – was the most special of all.

An eager-to-share Australian meditator told us of his discipline's predictions: that the spiritual centre of the world was shifting to the West; that the next enlightened man would be from the West; that he would study at Bodh Gaya; and that he would arise in our lifetime – which perhaps explained the popularity of the meditation courses and the grand reception afforded Westerners!

An American monk with a large, wandering moustache at odds with his saffron garb and shaven skull accosted me after noticing my copy of *Mein Kampf* and began a soliloquy on the "connections" between Hitler and Buddha. "Did you know Hitler had Tibetan bodyguards and became acquainted with Tibetan powers of the supernatural?" he asked authoritatively. He spoke of the Eastern origins of the swastika, emphasising the different directions of the symbols' points. In the eternal life balance of good and evil, the Asian direction was towards good; it was implicit that Hitler's motif highlighted evil. "The West is in a nadir of depravity characterised by excessive aggression from eating meat," he said. "But Buddhism doesn't forbid eating meat," I interrupted, "even the Dalai Lama originally ate meat." "Ah. At high altitudes, eating meat is acceptable for survival," he replied. He had an answer for everything.

Avoiding puddles

When a day arose with no sun and rain began falling dismally, Jim and I caught a bus to Rajgir, a stopover en route to Nalanda, home to arguably the world's oldest university.

We found lodgings at a grandly named Nature Cure Institute where, for the equivalent of about 5c, we spread out in a small room bordered by a beautiful rose garden. A sign outside depicted a "disease" tree, highlighting afflictions of "hatred", "obesity", "sclerosis" and "unnatural cravings". With access to a cooling communal well, even though our ablutions were clearly visible to other guests, it was easy to decide to remain for at least a few days.

We climbed Vaibhara, one of seven hills enclosing the town, before returning to the institute for one of its acclaimed "health" meals, this night a heady feast of cauliflower, eggplant and onion and, for dessert, "matha", a curd mixed with water. And as wonderful finale, I prepared a chillum, using some Bodh Gaya grass I had bought earlier at a Government Ganja and Bhang Shop. So it was town again, and sweets again ...

A morning walk took us out of town towards the Japanese-built "World Peace" Temple. But on the way we encountered the "Maniyar Math", a cylindrical brick temple dedicated to the worship of a snake god, and here I lit a pipe and World Peace was forgotten. An effortless walk home was followed by plate after plate of "gallajamu" (gulab jamun, a sweet dough ball), health meal to follow, then one more smoke. Incredible!

After moving to even cheaper dormitory accommodation, we climbed another hill, Vipula, surfacing above scrub to three small shrines near which workmen were studiously laying the foundations of a new temple.

This was the site where Jain prophet Vardhamana Mahavir, revered as the religion's founder, "re-expressed" its teachings in the 6th century BC.

The highest and most famous law of Jainism was that of "ahimsa" (non-injury), requiring of its adherents that no lifeform be harmed. So severely was the injunction followed, that some Jains avoided stepping in puddles lest microscopic life be inadvertently extinguished. Jainism also emphasised that divine law appeared in the form of death whenever human law engendered a miscarriage of justice. Actions done in one state of being or existence, found their fulfilment in inevitable consequences in another state of existence. Karma.

World's oldest university

After Jim moved on, I pampered myself at outside stalls, over-eating and reading. Life was a joy till one day, itching terribly, a shower inspection revealed I had lice. They were in my pubics and my armpits, dispelling any belief that sexual intercourse was the only manner of reception. I had not touched a woman in months! I felt depressed. To Indian villagers, lice were something to be continually plucked: there was no cure. I resigned myself that it might be a long time before I would be able to effect permanent relief – perhaps not till Calcutta. After crushing as many as I could, I ventured into the bazaar to console myself with food.

As I sat, I watched a Brahman bull making painful progress amid the vegetable stands, both its front legs broken above the hoof. But still the stall-keepers slapped its hindquarters to hurry its departure. This was one of the worst aspects of India. Men kicked animals or threw rocks at them, for no particular reason. A cart driver thrashed his horse with a stick. When it stumbled, skidding yards on its knees, he dismounted to examine it for injuries, then returned to his seat and resumed the whipping. Often, horses pulled carts containing 10 or more people, yet the drivers showed no mercy. There were worse cruelties, I thought, than the eating of animals.

One morning I received a visit from my hotel manager. My dormitory room had been booked and he would appreciate it if I departed. I knew this was snobbery. Higher caste Indians would not willingly share space with a "low" European. "Don't you mind," he said, hovering closely while I packed, in futile expectance of baksheesh.

Transferring to Nalanda, I found a resthouse with a proprietor in the depths of a hangover. After a tremendous effort, I took possession of a

181

large bedroom, and headed for the site of the university. According to some accounts originating in 427AD, to others', built by Buddhists in the 6th century BC, the university was notable for its subject range, from science and philosophy to religion and the arts. Pupils came from as far away as China and Sri Lanka. It must have been splendid to behold, great stone stupas and shrines leaning imperiously over open-air class-rooms, with placid lotus ponds encouraging study.

Sadly, some time after the 12th century AD, decline had set in, with some unlearned conqueror completing the fall with unsympathetic pillaging. Today, signposts of reconstruction abounded: "Site 13A" and "Temple", with painted arrows pointing in all directions and inscriptions providing constant instruction. But amid tall trees and flower gardens, the site was immaculate.

Eternal truth

With no spare seats on the Patna express, I found a wall to lean on. A bag of rice stabbed painfully against my side and, for good measure, three similarly disadvantaged Indians pressed hard against me, render-ing movement impossible. "Which caste do you belong to," one asked. After each topic discussed, he turned to his companions and relayed my answers. They shared with me a coarse tobacco called "khaini", which I wasn't to chew, but hold in my mouth. I felt a potent heat and a rush of saliva and was compelled to spit it out the window. Later, I would read medical advice: "It is more damaging than chewing tobacco, and causes serious gingival ulceration"!

When the train rattled into Patna Junction in darkness, I claimed a platform seat to await the dawn. A well-dressed man approached me and asked me in immaculate BBC English, "To which country do you belong?" My reply sparked a flurry of verbiage: "Ah, General Freyberg, double VC, a brave, brave man, Second World War, the New Zealanders are brave men, are they not?" He began a tirade about the "brave Indian soldiers" who had defeated (sic) the Chinese in the northern "border clashes" of 1962, saying one brave Indian was worth 40 Chinese. It might have amused me but for the large selection of books on display at a nearby platform stall: *Indian Martyrs; An Evaluation of India's Victory over China; Pakistan Cut to Size*, and others. Spiritual India, it seemed, was not averse to jingoism.

I became aware of a ragged youth standing riveted beside a "Weight and Fortune" machine. When a family compared cards, he jostled among them, only to be pushed aside. I slipped him a coin then moved to another part of the station. Minutes later he found me. Without speaking, he passed his fortune coupon to me, then left with a smile on his face.

Patna was home and parish to Govind Singh, the tenth and most famous of the Sikh gurus. The Sikh holy book, the *Adi Granth Sahib*, begins: "There is one God, Eternal Truth is his name", before continuing, much as other Eastern religions, to proclaim an everlasting nature, "not begotten" and "eternal". It appealed to me that Sikh founder Guru Nanak identified the existence of evil or sin without imposing detailed ethical rules. Who among Christians need attend the Ten Commandments if they but grasp the simple Corinthians' message, "love"? It was the same with Nanak – at first reading, quite simple, and beautifully expressed.

Boy falls in love with girl

Eager now to be back amid mountains, I plotted a path towards Darjeeling. Faced with a train not due to depart till 3am, I thought it safer to sleep in the station rather than risk a dubious wake-up. As I read Michener's *The Drifters* in the waiting room, a young student asked me what it was about. I told him it concerned youth and its attitudes. "Films are the medium for true philosophy," he said, and I did not argue, for that medium was revered here, almost irrationally.

He invited me to attend a film with him, which suited my long wait. The film was called *Bobby* and I had already heard talk of it as an epic warranting the accolade "great". As we were speaking of a product of the world's largest film industry, I was keen to judge for myself. Though it was in Hindi, I could understand nearly every proceeding, so obvious the plot directions: boy from wealthy family falls in love with girl from lower station; classic lovers' misunderstanding; a chase; reconciliation; parents contrive to keep them apart; elopement; reconciliation… The story was aridly sentimental but the audience was enthusiastic to an extreme. Directed by Raj Kapoor, *Bobby* would become one of the top-grossing films of the decade, revered as a trendsetter in a Bollywood genre of "teenage romance surmounting impossible disparities".

When the time came, I cheekily entered a "sleeper" carriage, climbed into an empty bunk, and fell asleep. Leaving the train at Siliguri, I crossed a bridge for an artist's view of laundrists below pounding their cloths mercilessly while a succession of colourful trucks sped passed, spattering them. There was no outrage. Without any visible reaction, the women simply began their washing again.

Indian trucks were works of art, with sides of varnished wood and painted cowlings, chrome mudguards sparkled, and even hubcaps were polished. At each driver's window there was invariably a shrine of Shiva, alongside driver mug shots and coloured streamer paper. These trucks were everywhere in South Asia. It was as if one company had extended its influence across a continent. My reveries were interrupted by a speeding truck that vomited parcels of oil all over me.

Back in the mountains

I left Siliguri with an argument. Well-to-do Indians, averse to struggle, hired "porters", professionals whose job it was to lay claim to their seating. When I boarded the Darjeeling bus, I found coats and jerseys spread across the entire passenger area, and moved them aside. There was a brief altercation but I managed to retrieve enough of the back seat for myself and a Japanese traveller, Kleoe, and, together, we withstood all abuse.

My permit for Darjeeling was for one week only but after just one glance at the town I knew that would be insufficient. Darjeeling lay at a precise 2134m, making it significantly higher than Kathmandu, and me grateful I was here in February rather than December. We arrived amid a dense, uncompromising mist, but it soon cleared, allowing wonderful glimpses of the Himalayas, notably of Kachenjunga, at 8580m, the world's third highest peak.

Darjeeling was at once Indian, Tibetan, Nepali, Sikkimese and Bhutanese. It was remote, yet modern, utterly strange and utterly beautiful. Dropping in layers, its narrow streets wound up and around, under and between three-storey mountain houses of stone. To get from Point A to Point B was never a simple matter. Colossal mountains to the north appeared sternly protective and the vast scale of it all filled me with awe. We were very close here to the "forbidden territories" of Sikkim and Bhutan; Tibet too was nearby, and troop movement in the area was noticeable. India was prepared for further border clashes, albeit with .303 rifles.

Kleoe and I settled in a small rooftop lodge that bestrode the city like a throne. We enjoyed a Chinese supper, before retiring after a fine session on the chillum. Kleoe carried good hash. We woke to a view of the whole mountain range: Kachenjunga bestriding a Himalayan chain that, under clear skies, did not seem quite so formidable. Too late to catch sunrise, we scrunched down stairs to the Chowk Bazaar where long rows of vegetable stands enticed us. Then, laden with tomatoes, onion, chillies, fresh lemons and bananas, we returned to our room for a gigantic salad breakfast.

Trekking in Nepal, I had met a photographer from Darjeeling and I decided to look him up. My timing was perfect, for his photographs of Everest were only newly developed. Remembering me, Mohan Das invited Kleoe and me to tea at his house where we met his family and other guests, including two huge German Shepherds and a Tibetan Mastiff. His human guests were owners of local tea estates, all friendly, despite our "hippie" appearances. Mohan showed no disdain. He told me he had travelled widely through Europe where his only disappointment had been England. "That is the sole country I was made aware of my colour," he said. "I was insulted there, and I am not a man grown up on colour differences."

The next morning, per arrangements, we were woken at 3am for a trip to Tiger Hill, a noted vantage point for viewing the Himalayas at sunrise. Unfortunately, the short night engendered a long price rise, enough to cause the gathered group to return to their beds and an irate American to abuse our driver: "Motherfucker!" On the plus side, one of the disappointed customers turned out to be Irish Jim and we arranged to catch up later in the day.

There is never a void in India. After breakfast, Kleoe and I followed a procession to a secluded monastery nestled in a grove of pines. Today was the last and most important day of the Tibetan New Year. Tibetan-style, the chang flowed and, in no time at all, we were accepted as family. A man introducing himself as Nawang and his friend Passang invited us to visit them the next day. Afterwards, a little hungover, we caught up with Irish Jim back at our hotel for a smoke. We ran short, but a little patient questioning soon revealed for us the whereabouts of the local Government Ganja and Bhang Shop, supplies were renewed, and all of us were soon happy.

I would like to introduce you to Tenzing Norgay

Kleoe and I rose early for what turned out to be a long hike to the Mountaineering Institute where Narwang and Passang were instructors. Narwang's room was decorated with mountain gear, and photographs of peaks cluttered all four walls. An accomplished mountaineer, he had scaled 8500m on Everest. Over the hearth, was a smiling picture of Everest co-conqueror Tenzing Norgay, and beside it, a large bookcase devoted to climbing books. These occupied most of our morning, for many were beautifully illustrated and, for me, evoked many memories of Everest and the Annapurnas.

A slim, debonair man with a thin, smiling moustache joined us. As I stepped forward to shake hands, Narwang said matter-of-factly, "I would like to introduce you to Tenzing Norgay!" Tenzing was, of course, Hillary's companion to the top of Everest, the first climbers to "knock the bastard off" back in 1953. It was akin to meeting royalty and, afterwards, I could remember little of our conversation. He spoke to us without any pretension, and before leaving, insisted on linking arms for a photograph. He left with a wave, followed by three chubby children.

The institute was a veritable museum, with displays of climbing gear, alpine techniques, and a roll-of-honour of the most accomplished Sherpas, known as the "Tigers". Unsurprisingly, Tenzing headed the list, but even his achievements were overshadowed by some of those following. Passang himself had reached 8000m on Everest – without oxygen. He shrugged this off as an everyday achievement. Also on display was an ancient telescope, marked clearly as a gift from one, Adolf Hitler. There may have been a germ of truth underlying the conspiracy theories!

Both Kleoe and I required visa extensions. We had been told the local office was refusing extensions, so were grateful when our two Nepalese friends offered to accompany us. My permit, because it was issued within the district, was readily extended, but Kleoe's, issued in Calcutta, was denied. After lengthy argument from Narwang it was agreed he could have his extension if he could produce a medical certificate. And of course, with Narwang's help, he could.

Narwang and Passang took us to a friend's house to drink a beer called "dongba". A tall Sherpa woman filled large bamboo mugs with fermented millet then, as we waited, poured on boiling water, leaving it to stand for about five minutes before drinking. We toasted each other, "tashi deleh", and, on leaving, were given "sangus", colourful double-ended bags to be worn slung over our shoulders.

Outside, Narwang gestured, "Over there, beyond that point, is Sikkim." It was a beautiful view. The hillside fell away sharply, with lengthening shadows over infinite pastures, houses on stilts dotted along the way. We visited a nearer version, a two-room cabin occupied by his sister and, once again, the hospitality was overwhelming. Laughing at our awkwardness, the sister taught us New Year greetings. We placed pinches of tsampa flour against her shoulder, then a pinch into our own mouths. She responded by pouring chang into our cupped hands, which we drank. This was enacted three times, we all cried, "tashi deleh" – and the drinking began in earnest.

Kleoe became ill, legitimately. After making him breakfast, I ventured to the bazaar for my own, to be joined by a man with a sign around his neck proclaiming: "Engraver of rings, pens, watches etc: Reasonable prices". He told me he had brought his family east from Varanasi after finding it difficult to earn a living. But Darjeeling had proved no easier. "Agriculture used to be at the heart of our lives and life was slow and manageable," he said. There used to be clear life directions: education followed by work, after which, having fulfilled family obligations, the man was free to enter a spiritual stage as a hermit seeking truth.

He sighed. Once, the caste system had had meaning. No stigmas were attached to life's stations: they were workable structures that fell into place naturally, "just as might families of doctors in the West". But the quiet lifestyle of rural India had been uprooted in an insane emulation of Western "progress", the emphasis on making money. "Why copy the West?" he asked. How much happier the man without goods! But today, it was impossible for him to retreat from society. "If I leave, it will be impossible for me to provide for my family." His seeking therefore had to be entirely within. Having felt the smear of misapplied caste, he saw a parallel with hippies – "the longhaired ones" – often despised without the chance to be judged fairly. "It is foolish to judge people by appearance," he said. He was a wise man, my engraver.

Take me to Ghoom!
Kleoe was even iller. Over ensuing days I operated as waiter, bringing him meals from the market some distance below. I also booked his onward travel for him, which brought the bonus of a conversation with the stationmaster, an educated man who called me into his office by the fire and grilled me on my opinions. Lesser beings were attended through a small window in the cold! The position of the railway official had from the time of the British been a highly respected one, engendering a remnant of elderly civil servants, often well-educated – and charmingly out of place in fast-paced 1974. The buying of a ticket was inevitably an experience.

The next day, Kleoe was much recovered so, after furnishing him with one last breakfast, I said my goodbyes and left. I liked Kleoe immensely. His English was not good but he was always "gentle", as the hotel manager described it, and sharing rooms with him was a great deal easier than with others on my travels. We made plans to meet up in Calcutta later in the month. But I had one last Darjeeling task. I walked purposefully to the landrover rank, jumped onto the back of an already overfull vehicle and shouted, "I want to go to Ghoom!" Ghoom was the starting point for the climb to the earlier aborted Tiger Hill, where I hoped to spend a couple of days at rest as well as enjoy famous views of the Himalayan pantheon. I had to stand against the backboard, clinging to a roof strut, and remained there for the journey, exposed to the winds and the cold.

Fog made views minimal but the overall effect was entrancing – swirling greys stretched in fingers about pines before disappearing mystically down long valleys of green. Arriving seemingly at nowhere, a shriek of wind had me sprinting to a solid stone tourist bungalow defying the elements some two kilometres below the summit. Immediately guided to hot tea and an electric heater, I began to wonder if I had been mistaken for royalty. The register provided the explanation: I was the sole guest. I booked a bunk in an outside dormitory – the only cheap beds available – with hot water, blankets *and* a heater. For the price I was paying, the facilities were ridiculous.

I began the next day with a hot shower – my first since Kathmandu after Everest. When my heater died, I made a dash for the bungalow where a working heater and an armchair were again at my disposal. And in glorious warmth I poured over David-Neal's *Magic and Mystery in Tibet*, New Age claptrap that was doing the traveller rounds. An Austrian couple arrived, and two English boys fresh out of school. We talked long into the evening before retiring with a request for a 4.30am wakeup. The Tiger Hill trek was on! Weather be damned!

At the start of the ascent, the sky was only half way clear. At about 2500m, foliage receded, though not the cold, so we were all relieved when the last star retreated. Just as we reached the peak, the sun made a semblance of an appearance. World-renowned views, however, were denied us: no Lhotse, no Makalu, and certainly no Chomolungma (Everest). As Tenzing forewarned in his autobiography, "You cannot see it for long from Tiger Hill. Soon the sun is up; the clouds come." So be it.

Daredevil antics

The railway line from Darjeeling to Siliguri spiralled presumptuously along slender hill ridges, turned full circle in its descents, before assuming its original direction, one level lower. When the train crossed the road, cars accelerated to avoid a collision, or braked desperately. Young daredevils in the villages we passed through leapt terrifyingly aboard side duckboards, waiting till the train entered a loop before sprinting hard to rejoin the carriage as it once again entered a straight.

I left the train in darkness at New Jalpaiguri, laying down my sleeping bag in the station's first-class waiting rooms. A German woman and her Icelandic husband joined me and, for the remaining hours, I politely feigned listening to their complaints about India and Indians.

In 1970 the Awami League, campaigners for East Pakistan's autonomy, won a crushing election victory, which West Pakistan refused to recognise. In 1971, an independent Bangladesh was declared and the states were at war. With India's backing, Pakistan was quickly defeated, however, and with socialism enshrined in the new constitution, PM Mujibur Rahman began nationalising key industries. 1974: severe flooding kills about 28,000, devastating crops and the economy. A year later, Rahman will be assassinated in a military coup.

XVIII

The inevitability of war

Bangladesh: an illegal entry; accused of being a journalist; told off for exposing too much leg; and the war of secession from Pakistan still hitting a very raw nerve.

The story of Bangladesh/ Is an ancient one again made fresh/ By blind men who carry out commands/ Which flow out of the laws upon which nation stands/ Which is to sacrifice a people for a land/ Bangladesh, Bangladesh; Bangladesh, Bangladesh/ When the sun sinks in the west/ Die a million people ...
(Joan Baez, *Song of Bangladesh*).

This is a restricted area

"This is a restricted area and you must immediately return from where you have come." At an Indian police border station, I was unprepared for the sharpness of the response to my query about crossing into Bangladesh. When I persisted, I was told I could cross from Haldibari, a town in another district. "Tell them I sent you and there should be no problems," the policeman lied. He then called a rickshaw and ordered the driver to escort me to the bus. My leaving his area of responsibility was not being left to chance!

At Haldibari I was directed to a local bus that took me 10kms into wilderness. A fellow passenger directed me across rice field dykes to an unpretentious check-post that might easily have been missed. Here a bare-chested official studiously examined my passport before announcing, "Fine, you may go. Follow the Peace Road to the border," he said, cryptically pointing to a path that disappeared into a padi field. The "border" was a bamboo pole between two dying palm trees. With no officials to be seen, I ducked under the pole and entered Bangladesh.

I walked for six or seven kilometres, passed housing of thatch and crumbled brick before discovering Chillihati where a villager led me to a police post and the fun began. "You've entered Bangladesh illegally," I was told sternly. The check-post I should have visited for an Indian exit stamp was in Haldibari. That wasn't all. Policeman: "Your passport is for the United Kingdom which requires a visa, which you do not have." Me (desperately): "Yes, you are right for the UK, but where's the mention of *Britain*?" Policeman: "I will look." Me (reading over his shoulder): "Look. New Zealanders have free entry. Look what it says under citizenship in my passport."

My "non-departure" from India was more serious, however, and his solution was unsurprising. "You will change your money with me now: one Indian rupee for one Bangladeshi taka." I knew elsewhere I could achieve 2 for 1, but had no option. He *suggested* I change 30rp and I did so. My passport was stamped and he smiled. "Atchaa!" He was cleverer than I had given him credit for.

At 7pm I boarded a train for Parbartapur, from where I hoped to catch a connection to Dacca. Bearded Muslim passengers provided a sharp contrast to India: rounded skullcaps, long jackets, and straggles of whiskers hinting at wisdom. At one of numerous stops all passengers bar me were ejected from the carriage to make way for a military regiment. They introduced themselves as "liberation forces". Those "liberated" filed meekly to other carriages.

At Parbartapur, I spread my sleeping bag in a waiting room, waking just in time to board the Dacca train sometime after 3am to be uncomfortably seated on hard, third class seating. Just before the train departed, an army officer briskly ordered me to follow him, delivering me to a first-class carriage that exactly resembled third class – except the seats were padded. For the first hour or so I practised Hindi with a military detachment. I declined to practise Bengali, only because I was getting thoroughly confused, which may have offended – their fight for liberation had ostensibly begun over the right to use their language. The

West Pakistan government had insisted the national language be Urdu and, in fact, Urdu was still the official language of the army.

When the soldiers departed, I was joined by an agricultural officer named Marzebar. "We are very poor," he began, and the train window provided plenty of illustrations of this. Not one man was engaged in hoeing, but 20 and, everywhere, long queues were at work where one man might have sufficed. It was a terrible paradox. Modern machinery might be the salvation of Bangladesh; it might also impoverish many of its people.

We grow very good betel

The train ground to a halt at the banks of the substantial Brahmaputra river where, with hundreds of others, I struggled through acres of silvery sand to a large bathtub ferry. It was so large, I might have been lost on board if Marzebar had not been on hand to guide me to the first-class deck. One could do rather well with a third-class ticket. An economics' professor joined us. "Ours is a poor country," he began, "over-population is the biggest problem." I nodded. There was a common belief – not always reduced to a joke – that God gave children to the poor as a comfort. The line became obscene when it was extended to, "the more children you have, the greater the chance of at least one being successful enough to be able to look after you when you grow old".

Both men agreed post-war problems could be solved after 10 years – the time seemed arbitrary – "provided the people work hard for the benefit of the state". Bangladesh's current problems, they said, owed to smuggling, wartime destruction of infrastructure, corruption, and the clandestine activities of "enemies of the state". Improving production lay within the agricultural officer's milieu. He cleared his throat. "Bangladesh is the world's largest producer of jute and has large numbers of sugar mills. And we grow very good betel."

They spoke about the war. Pakistan expenditure had been heavily weighted towards its west, but it was the language question that triggered the conflict: "beautiful Bengali" versus "raucous" Urdu. Bengali was ruthlessly repressed, until India joined the fray and the balance tilted. "Have you ever experienced war," I was asked. "Then how can you expect to understand what we have been through?" And I couldn't. But I understood that no country could operate for long, split geographically as had been East and West Pakistan.

A ship steward interrupted us, asking if I had lost my train ticket.

I had! The found ticket was handed to me, an unexpected display of honesty amid the poverty. When the boat finally cast off, I claimed space at a bow railing for good views of the Brahmaputra, one of the world's largest rivers. We shunted away from one endless shore of silver sand, found wide mid-channel, and ploughed upstream like an ocean liner.

The agricultural officer warned me to prepare for the landing and as soon as the boat hit the wharf, before the gangway was lowered, passengers were clambering over railings, through portholes, over shoulders and under feet. One of hundreds, I sprinted across the sands to a waiting train and defiantly spread over two seats. It was rather an anticlimax – there were enough seats for everyone.

Numerous beggars entered my carriage, each first questioned by an elder who listened patiently, weighed the facts, and made a decision. If he gave, everyone gave; if not, no one did. At a later stop, a religious official entered, pointed to the site of a new mosque, and was given a substantial amount of money. Two youngsters entered beating a drum: someone had lost some money and they were wishing to return this to the rightful owner. Presumably they hoped for a reward, but their honesty amazed me.

Brief excitement ensued when two armed policemen began rummaging through passenger suitcases but our compartment, perhaps in deference to me, was left unmolested. A neighbour whispered to me of a secret police department called D.A.B, muttering that the state had "many enemies". The police made two further incursions. Someone told me – in a whisper – that they were after smugglers. It seemed a likely answer. Then he added that it was guns being smuggled.

One of my neighbours was an engineering student, but his conversation was limited to sex. "Like you," he said, "Bengalis have sex before marriage. They force the girls and, afterwards, have to marry them." When his stop came, I stretched full length and fell asleep till the arrival of Dacca station where I stumbled into a waiting room and unwrapped my sleeping bag.

I awoke to find the room crowded. Central figure of a joyful mass was a man garbed in Islamic white, beautifully edged with gold brocade. "I have just married," he beamed, thrusting into my hand a thick sugar sweet between two slices of bread. He looked like a king. Looking around, I could see a huddle of well-wishers, all chatting inconsequentially. The bride was crying – she looked terrified. I guessed she was about 15 years old.

Are you a reporter?

Venturing outside, I discovered a New Dacca and an Old Dacca, the one broad and business oriented, the other narrow and crowded. The New suburbs were Sunday quiet; the Old shouted its presence. I walked both areas, stopping at many hotels, all with managers who could say "house full" in perfect English. I began to think there was a reason for my rejection, especially when the few who would speak to me began their conversations, "Are you a reporter?" It was taken for granted I was here to report the conflict. I eventually booked into a small hotel where my presence elicited stares.

The streets of Old Dacca had colonial linings but its pavements belonged to Bangladesh. Beggars lay on mats, their heads lying perilously across the street, and they all attracted attention, like sideshows at a circus. One boy had a tyre-sized growth issuing from his stomach with a deformed third foot attached: he did good business wriggling it. Three men without limbs pointed at their bared sores suppurating. At the end of the street, an abandoned, half-finished high-rise housed hundreds of semi-naked indigents in a squat. I hurried past.

I managed to change money, not well, but at a better rate than the miserly bank, and Bangladesh was now cheap for me. A stall owner, a wheedly character with bloodshot, betel lips, prevailed upon an English-speaking customer named Manjural to act as a translator while he questioned me. Both men were amazed that New Zealand was so small, that it had no snakes, and no enemies. "Ah, you live in a paradise," said the translator! I may have got carried away!

Manjural, a librarian, took me to his workplace. In a dusty room, with no books on display, he told me conditions were immeasurably worse than before the December 1971 war. "People are beginning to question the benefits of separation," he said. Foreign aid was not reaching the people, the government was corrupt, nepotism rife, and there were no strong leaders, civil or religious. Since the war it had been insisted the state be secular and, in consequence, people had no moral guidance, he said. Today's youth were not going to the mosque! He also bemoaned wage structures: teachers earned as little as rickshaw drivers, while government officials received exorbitant salaries. "The middle class is dying," he said.

The war still very much lingered in Dacca. Craving a good meal, I visited the upmarket Motizheel district where restaurant windows had curtains. I asked for an egg with my rice and vegetables and an omelette

194

was slapped in front of me with a, "sorry, no vegetables". Everywhere I stopped, I was asked, "are you a journalist" or, occasionally, "are you with Red Cross?"

One stallholder thrust a circular in my hands, begging me to have it published abroad. It was a text from the Koran. He could not understand why Arab countries were at war. "There is one God only and all religions, Islam, Christian, Judaism, Hindu, Buddhist, all point to that one God," he said. Two young men sidled up to me. "Journalist? Come with us!" – and tried to lead me down a dark alley. After convincing them I was a tourist, we all shook hands, and I was told, "not to mind". Later, a man who said he was an international wrestler, was fiercely critical of fighting between Arabs. "We are all one before God, even the Jews," he said.

Steered by the librarian, I discovered a riverboat to Khulna was scheduled to leave in two days' time, though its departure was dependant on the arrival of a shipment of coal from India. Come travel day, I set off early on foot for the Sadarghat terminal. Old Dacca was just rising. Market workers trotted along the street, their wares supported by swaying bamboo poles across their shoulders, slipping expertly through the congestion of rickshaws and pre-WWII taxicabs.

A motorcyclist accidentally slapped a woman in the face with his satchel, a careless VW buckled a rickshaw, and a potato carrier had his wares spread across the street after being knocked by a hurrying cyclist. In each case, abuse was showered on the participants and crowds quickly gathered, including pukka policemen under white pith helmets and sun parasols. Two women in purdah passed, veils across faces, and I marvelled at the scarcity of this phenomenon in Bangladesh. Then I looked around and realised how very few women of any description could be seen.

Presenting myself at the steamship's offices, I booked deck passage. "No second class is available," I was informed, "you must travel first." It took an argument, but I emerged with deck passage tickets, not winning me approval, but significantly cheaper.

An impossible war

The steamer, the *Mohmand*, was known as "the rocket", a fine irony. I climbed a cracked gangplank into a kind of oval tank enclosed by thick dodgem buffers. Amid a large passenger crowd, I squeezed a share of deck space against engine cowling from which an unbearable heat emanated. On one side of me, four ragged waifs had spread a sheet; on the other, a fifth lay almost naked, asleep. Eventually, they moved, relinquishing their spot for a fee to a serious young Customs officer. And shortly after midday, a gigantic blast of a hooter was repeated thrice, and the journey began.

Bangladesh the land of rivers, the journey encompassed a succession of river confluences, the more so as we approached the giant delta regions before the sea. Two airforcemen told me they had been in West Pakistan at the war's outbreak and been confined there for the duration. "We were not treated badly," they said generously. But when talk shifted to me, they revealed an overbearing morality. "Showing your legs in public [I was in shorts] is a crime," one said. "This can disturb the mind of a young girl and give her unclean thoughts." Masturbation too was a crime – it weakened men and "wickedly deprived" their wives.

I sneaked into second-class for my evening meal, where a family planning officer named Ali told me: "I did not want the war. I did not believe separation would be beneficial." Nevertheless, he had gone to India for military training and returned as an officer in the liberation forces. Once India entered the fray, he said, the West Pakistan forces were in an invidious position, deep in foreign territory with nowhere to retreat to. Their arms were inferior and, as the liberation forces – courtesy of India – gained access to Russian and American weaponry, the war's conclusion was inevitable.

India, however, was to be distrusted. Its reasons for intervention were not noble and many now felt Bangladesh was being ruled by Delhi. "India has benefited most from the war," he said. "It no longer has a hostile force on two fronts and Bangladesh, though 85 per cent Muslim, has been founded as a secular state." Ali put our journey in a terrible context. "On this bank I had a battle with the Pakistanis ... here a boat was blown up ...". He told me tales of rape and torture perpetrated by his opponents. "My side never killed prisoners," he said. "We just sent them to India."

Many passengers disembarked during the night. When I woke in the morning, those remaining were energetically changing from lungis into smart "pyjamas". As I wiped the soot from my short trousers, the Customs' officer asked me why I wore such clothes. "They are not seemly," he reiterated. I retreated to the second-class lounge, resuming conversation with Ali. I liked Ali. He was big for a Bengali, powerful looking, but gentle. He spoke of the war without glorification. "I killed men," he said. "But it was a war I did not want." He conceded it was an impossible situation for a state to be ruled from a country 2500km distant.

Ali showed me extraordinary views of ship wreckage along our way. Rusted remains bordered the banks for kilometres like ribboning and I sensed just how intense the fighting must have been. When we came across a large vessel leaning ingloriously, its side marked *SS Lightning*, Ali spat with contempt. "It was my detachment that sunk her," he said. "We warned the captain to leave the scene. He did not and suffered the consequences. We used limpets."

The end of the war had not improved the people's lot. Under "Father of the Nation" Sheik Mujib (Mujibur Rahman), an extended upper class had flourished but the people had starved. Ali accepted he was one of the lucky ones. The government was sending him to America for his work and, if the opportunity arose, he would stay there. As other Bangladeshi I had spoken to, he expressed feelings of helplessness. "Just what is the use?"

I took advantage of Ali's influence to have a second-class bath then donned long trousers and returned to the deck. "That is much better," said the Customs' officer. "How much did your trousers cost?" At not quite noon, the *Mohmand* arrived at Khulna, where I booked into a small teashop that had seen better days.

Men are not born equal

Two well-dressed men invited me to their home, saying, "New Zealand is a great friend to Bangladesh". The older of the two had superior features, and his dress confirmed his aristocracy; the younger, handsome in a South American sort of way, hung one pace behind, agreeing with his senior rather more than was necessary. They took me to a small alleyway and up several flights of stairs, where my host, introducing himself as Captain, sometimes Dr, Islam, knocked imperiously on a heavy wooden door. The stairway began from a dirty corner where the street urchins lounged. Inside was a mansion.

We entered a gigantic living room with large mirrors and cabinets dominating, the sense of size accentuated by vast pillars at each end. I followed the men through rooms of rugs and richly hued bedspreads, then sat, entertained by long-playing records of Indian poet Rabindranath Tagore's verse put to music. We listened in silence, occasionally interrupted by soft-footed servants.

Over a sumptuous lunch, I clumsily asserted New Zealand was "part-socialist". "There is a strong move towards socialism in this country," Dr Islam said dismissively. "It's a fashionable move, prompted by big-brother India. But it leads to the elimination of merit, to the destruction of men of nobility, of men of genius." Bengali was replacing English as the language of instruction. Yet the country's leaders sent their children to Oxford or Harrow who, upon their return, were immensely advanced to the home-schooled Bengali. The latter were relegated to "mere office boy". He was especially concerned at the continuing influence of India. Bangladesh was 85 per cent Muslim, yet its government strangely insisted on being a secular state. Islam was being "stunted", he said, to allay the fears of the larger country.

Insisting I sleep at his place, Captain Islam dispatched me to collect my bags from my lodgings. For the rest of the evening, we again listened to Tagore, including readings of his famous poem *Gita Govinda*. The younger man, Rashid, disapproved: "This is Hindu and sinful," he said. From the roof of the apartment, I could see a whole city at work: the beggar approaching his first shopkeeper of the day, the sari-dressed women pumping hard at the common well, the Muslim praying soberly towards Mecca, assorted bastard boating jostling the river calm... Many houses sported the new Bangladeshi flag, red circle on green, today waving in recognition of the birthday of Sheik Mujib.

Captain Islam was "Haji", having recently returned from a pilgrimage to Mecca, and entitled to wear the white cap that marked the holiest of the holy. He had returned with a present for his wife, a 31-piece wristwatch that had cost him more than US$500. He had three children, two boarding in Dacca. Left behind for the family adulation was a child called Peeti, spoilt, but loveable.

Son of a man of the "Gemanda" class (a baronetcy abolished in 1951), he had lived a cushioned life. Under Pakistan he had enjoyed a series of sinecures and, when war broke out, had enlisted in the Pakistani army. "They are our brothers". At war's end, he had been offered a post as head of Khulna Port, but recoiled at the workload, opting instead for the lucrative post of head of industry in the Khulna-Jessore districts. "Once or twice a month I visit the concerns under my care. I want the papers right," he said. "If they want to fiddle the books, okay, but I tell them to keep the papers right. Otherwise, I close down. Once a month, I draw a salary, sign my name and go home. I am happy!" What he really wanted, he confided, was an ambassadorial appointment: "Give me Bangkok or Tokyo."

He spoke of the knife-edge that was modern-day Bangladesh. "A man who speaks out publicly is in danger of his life," he said. Indeed, since I had arrived, there had been two train crashes caused by sabotage, with accompanying loss of life and looting. These were not isolated incidents. The earlier 1965 conflict had been a victory for Pakistan, he said. "We advanced 1200 miles in seven days. But 1971 was a humiliation and the Pakistani does not forget humiliations! There will again be war and, make no mistake, Bangladesh will enter as ally to Pakistan!"

Let them die!

We talked for several hours, with incredibly frank revelations. I believed his every word. I saw the respect he received on the street, his affluence, his confidence, and his inherent superiority. "Men are not born equal," he said. "Socialism!" He spat the term contemptuously. He also gave me a "man-to-man" talk. "Prostitution is legal in Bangladesh. At night, you can see queues along the waterfront, but business has to stop by 10pm." The workingwomen themselves, however, were impure and would never be accepted back by village or family.

At breakfast the family talked excitedly. Bangladesh's opposition National Socialist party had demonstrated and the police had opened fire. The papers reported five dead; the captain said 50 had in fact died, and about 300 were wounded, including party leader Abdur Rab. The response at the breakfast table was one of glee. From the balcony I viewed a noisy procession of red flags and clenched-fists. Captain Islam shrugged. "Let them not bother me, let them die!" Approaching midday, another procession appeared, a pro-government group, noisily blaming the incident on "enemies of the state" and "miscreants".

When the doctor was busy, Rashid kept me company. Just 23, he already held seniority over the town's captains of industry. We had many discussions but rarely agreed. He displayed an unquestioning acceptance of dogma: the Koran was the actual word of God, prayers were essential expressions of faith, all men would be paraded before the Lord and graded like cattle... I had cut two articles from the paper: one about the arrest of a poet who had criticised Buddha, Christ and Mohamed, the other, of the recent demonstration. These mysteriously disappeared and I was convinced he had removed them in the interests of Bangladesh's image.

By contrast, the captain was literate and rare for enjoying Hindu scripture. He was equally at home discussing Shakespeare and Milton. Once, he confessed to me he would like to be a sadhu – "no responsibilities but to God". He might be utterly corrupt, but he was also oddly likeable and generous. When guests arrived from his home village he sadly told me they wanted money. "I will give it of course, but it would be nice if people came to see me for friendship alone."

When I was ready to move on, he drove me to Jessore. On the way we were stopped by students wanting money, and by police who searched the car and compared the engine block number with registration details. The captain gave money to the students, but was contemptuous of them. We side-tracked to his Yusof Mills, where workers were on strike for higher wages. Bizarrely, I was invited to sit in on negotiations. While the workers spoke with their heads lowered, Dr Islam sat in silence, showing no emotion. The men agreed to return to work after being offered a mediocre wage rise.

Late afternoon, he deposited me at a small hotel. The doctor told me he understood my desire to live cheaply. "It is good. You are not known in this town – enjoy yourself." Evidently, he expected me to sample the local prostitutes and it occurred to me that when he had first spied my cheap rooms in Khulna, he had assumed desire, not frugality, had informed my choice.

In the morning I caught a bus to border town Benapole. Knowing my passport was not in order made me a little nervous, so I made a point of dressing well and allying myself with a distinguished-looking Bengali. As I approached Customs, I remembered I was in possession of some ganja. My companion came with me, distributed cigarettes among the officials, and my bags were not examined.

From the 1920s, the Sri Aurobindo ashram in Pondicherry taught a "mode of evolution into a spiritual divine". In 1968, co-founder Mirra Alfassa ("The Mother"), with UNESCO and Indian government support, founded Auroville, a utopian community aimed at "fulfilling" that path. But as the "city-in-the-making" took shape, rumours grew it was attempting to produce a superior race, with no place for locals, except as servants. 1974: a year after Alfassa's death, construction is well underway, including a school and houses.

XIX

No chillums in the new utopia

South India: a perpetually stoned beach settlement; a beach walk
that almost kills me; a Pondicherry spiritual retreat promises
a super race; and I miss my chance of sainthood.

*[Commercial enterprises] keep two-thirds of the profits and pay no tax. The locals
think it is not fair ... "I feel like a slave," one of them told me ... it's like being
back in the days of the British Raj," said another. "They are allowed to get away
with whatever they like, including paying our children to have sex with them"*
(BBC News, 24.5.2008, *Local concerns over Indian Utopia*).

Fakhir's house

Fakhir's House was a ruin. The Puri freak house may once have been luxurious; now it subsisted on bare concrete, broken windows and faded cobwebs. My room had no door and my bed was a half-decayed mat. But from the floor I could see the beach, and the crash of water on sand was ever the background.

My hosts were a large Hindu family. The eldest son's exposure to hippiedom had left him with a vocabulary created to impress: he greeted me saying he had had sex with an English girl, then asked if I agreed Nixon was stupid. The other guests comprised an Australian couple in freak attire; a Frenchman who smoked constantly; two quiet Americans and a third, loudly-know-it-all; and an Argentinian who invited tiresomely deep conversations. We ate together at a beach stall where we were trapped by a sudden onslaught of rain and jagged lightning flashes. Then someone produced a chillum and that was that. I had to run through the rain to reach my room, falling asleep on damp sleeping bag. The wind was too great to light a candle.

Next morning, I set out to explore the famed temple of "Lord of the Universe" Jagannath, but was denied entrance: its spectacular tower carried a sign barring entrance to "non-Hindus and untouchables". Neither street cleaners nor I were allowed inside, no matter how devout. A law change currently before parliament allowing all to enter, fulfilling the wishes of Mahatma Gandhi, could not come soon enough. A sadhu joined me on the beach, occasionally chanting the familiar, "Hari Krishna, Hari Ram". As larger than normal waves soaked my trousers and his lungi, we burst into laughter, jumping back towards the beach.

Back at the house, all guests were stoned, so I went straight to my room hoping to read quietly. It began to rain again and the entire sky was illuminated by a brilliant electrical storm. I could not escape the chillum. The loud American arrived with hashish, shouted, "Boom Shankar", and we were away. I was soon befuddled, but still managed to register my distaste as he brayed his contrived vocabulary: "Man I'm stoned!" "Wow, I'm like a motherless child!" I doubt he noticed.

One morning, a group of Filipinos from a floating Christian book exhibit arrived. They were taking their faith around the globe on the ship, the *MV Logos*, which was berthed further along the coast. Among them were a silent Finn who sat reading his bible and an Indian who insisted on telling me how he had been converted. Fakhir's son came over to me with a concerned look. "Hey, what they want?" I told him. "Bullshit, man!" He had learned his English well.

Another guest arrived, a tiny Scottish girl named Isobel, and that night I sheltered in her room when the rain became too heavy to reach mine safely. She carried a copy of the *Bhagavad Gita* with beautiful illustrations, but I had not much consciousness that evening. Not much consciousness at all!

Isobel, the Frenchman (Jackie) and I sat for a long time listening to music. We smoked a little, though had to supplement with bhang to fill the chillum. The rest of the gang joined us, and Fakhir. When the party broke down, the three of us somehow found the energy to seek out the town market. Along the way, we picked up a naive Australian girl and I began to feel protective as one shopkeeper after another contrived to cheat her. She showed me a white plastic ring she had bought as ivory.

Wearying of the community, the following day I headed to the beach where a Belgian asked me to watch his gear while he swam. He was far removed from my mode of travel, but it was pleasant for once to discuss something other than the quality of the local grass. Without a sliver of a boast, he told me he was one of Europe's leading artists, creating geometric patterns with car enamel paint – modulism. His work had been bought by Belgium's largest bank, a sign he had "made it", he said. His name was Philippe Decelle.

Bitten on the beach

I decided to walk to neighbouring Konark along the beach, a journey, I was told, of about 30km as opposed to 60km by road. My directions, in full, comprised, "head left till you arrive". I was advised not to walk in the heat of the day but disregarded this when a cool breeze blew up a little after noon. Contemptuous of a mere 30km, I carried my water in a small plastic soap container good for a mouthful or two at best.

My first stop was at a tiny fishing village where men in loincloths hauled their boats to the beach with fish to sell, swollen loads that drew crowds and their purses. The boats were little more than logs tied together by hemp, with gaps for seams, and it seemed a miracle they could travel out to sea. When the sun declined in affluent gold I lay on the beach where I was, hoping to spend the night in a semblance of comfort. Half of my water had spilled.

I awoke with a sharp pain in my big toe and, looking down, found a crab attached. At times I had woken during the night with a strange croaking noise in my ear. Perhaps I'd blocked its exit route! Under morning breeze, I walked hard. But when the wind dissipated, the sun hit me with a power I was unprepared for. After a long rest, I found that the last of my water was spread over the bottom of my pack. I had no choice but to continue. A river running parallel to the shore appeared and, foolishly, I drank a mouthful. It was salt.

At the wide river mouth, I was stuck, for it was impossible to carry my baggage across. I waved at some fishermen scrubbing boat hulls and eventually, one responded, ferrying me to a spit from where it was possible to wade ashore. Asked for money, I in return exacted vast quantities of water before continuing, tired, as the sun grew steadily hotter.

When I shouted "Konark" after two bronzed fishermen, they pointed inland. It had not occurred to me that Konark might not be on the sea.

The temperature seemingly in the vicinity of 40 degrees, my throat parched, my feet sore, and still with no idea where Konark was, I resolved to lie where I was till evening. But I spotted a track leading inland and found a bivouac and its owner, who satisfied my hoarse cries for water. After this it was easy. I found an abandoned stall and fell asleep outside on two benches I pulled together as a bed.

When I woke, I could hardly walk. I limped the few metres to a communal bathing pool and tried to look dignified as I washed in my lungi. A family of frogs scattered and even the Indians seemed surprised to see a Westerner bathing in such fashion. I emerged to see a large sign stating: "Puri – 84km"! The distance along the beach must have been similarly misrepresented me.

Nevertheless, I prodded myself to explore Konark's famous chariot of Surya temple. It took the form of a magnificent chariot drawn by seven horses, the tower the throne for the effulgent sun god. But the tower was more famous for its erotic figures, bared breasts, couples coupling, and I did due diligence, all the while harassed by a vendor of erotic photographs, whose services I declined.

A bad, bad man

The bus ride to Bhubaneswar was notable for having two books stolen from me and for a fight breaking out between a passenger and the bus conductor. Gandhi might be constantly on people's lips, but it was a myth the Indian was the most peaceful of races. Politics were smeared brutally across buildings in thick paint, and strident banners were always evident. Days could be spent reading the streets: "Indira is a liar and should resign!"; "Mr Devi is a liar and a cheat!"; "We demand longer lunch hours!" It did not take much to spark a quarrel in the name of honour or justice.

I had intended to stay longer, but, spotting a large blackboard outside the train station that proclaimed the Madras Express, two hours late, was about to depart, I impulsively jumped aboard. There had been changes recently to Indian rail. Before, the choice was of first class or third; now the latter had been abolished in lieu of a new second class. Thus, for the first time, I was travelling second class. Stops along the way were notable only for the disappearance of tea vendors for coffee. By day's end I had completed a *Study of Islam History* and C.P. Snow's *Corridors of*

Power, so was especially tired when we reached Madras sometime after 9pm. My usual late-night practice was to sleep in the station, but under a full moon, I took a rickshaw to a recommended hotel and booked into the last available bed in its dormitory.

Madras seen became just another big city. I decided to remain a few days because I was tired, and because of the facilities: each morning and night I enjoyed a protracted shower, between times, dodging the heat at drink stalls. It was too hot to eat more than one meal a day. A man accosted me, telling me he represented millions of Burmese refugees and would like to discuss New Zealand aid organisations that might help. "My family were once wealthy but were deported by the Ne Win government," he said. "My mother died on the way and I was left an orphan." Of course, he wanted money and I somewhat guiltily refused. If he wanted just a few rupees for a meal, did it matter that he had spun me a yarn?

Another man offered me "marijuana, opium, hash, change money, nice girl" and, upon my refusals for each, asked me to buy him a cup of tea. When I refused, he asked me to accompany him to a church for prayer, it being Good Friday. I responded I was not a Christian. He looked at me sternly and replied: "You must be a bad, bad man!" So much for the opium, the nice girl, and the black market!

I rediscovered the holy at seaside Mahabalipuram, joining a queue of orthodox Hindus walking along the beach towards the carved stone attractions of the area. This eastern coast of the sub-continent had to be one of the longest stretches of uninterrupted sand in the world: I could not see a peninsula, jut, isthmus, or even wharf out to sea! Occasionally, a triangular sail broke the monotony, a rare variance to the endless straight lines of southern India.

The men in the group – heads shaven, ash smears across their foreheads – after observing my brief swimming attire (underwear), likewise stripped. The women waded into the water, fully dressed in their ample silk saris. It was unusual to see Indians discard their dignity so readily. A sadhu took hold of my hands and cricking my fingers, beginning a sequence of massage that included wrenching my arms and my neck. He too wanted money.

I reject sainthood

The first thing I noticed in Pondicherry was the orderliness. French names abounded: Rue Saint Louis, Boulevard Sud, and the old men in the streets had wizened Simenon faces, worn lines about their foreheads suggestive of long sessions sipping vin ordinaire over the evening meal. The French had ruled this port for some 250 years, till 1954, and their presence was very much in evidence. Many women wore shorts – unheard of elsewhere – and the buildings all required translation.

I was drawn to a high, whitewashed wall with a large plaque proclaiming, "Sri Aurobindo Ashram". Peering into its gardens, I could see men relaxing in pyjamas and one of them welcomed me. When I told him I was looking for lodgings he led me to a rooftop apartment that I could share with an Indian worshipper. After registering as a "foreigner", I was presented with an admission card for all ashram activities – which included three daily meals. I had found my Nirvana!

The reception room was unashamedly commercial. A counter had goods for sale: bags, photographs of ashram founders Sri Aurobindo and Mirra Alfassa ("The Mother"), spiritually inclined books, and souvenir badges. Sri Aurobindo, heralded as one of the greatest of Indian philosophers, was long dead; Alfassa had died just last year.

In the evening, I walked with an American, Bob, past the pink and orange-blossomed Parc à Char Bon and the neighbouring governor's mansion, both lit up in rainbow fantasias, to the dining hall, which was marginally less ostentatious. We followed a queue to several big rooms where portions of rice, curry and curd were ladled generously. Pictures of The Mother and Sri Aurobindo overlooked us while we ate, their quotations to be read on blackboards beside, so that we might absorb their wisdom while eating. For the most part, people ate in silence. Afterwards, Bob and I sat above the beach where evening breezes afforded maximum comfort. It became our daily routine: retiring after breakfast to the seashore with a book. We made a point of attending lunch, showing our "passes" to a security-conscious official, taking our meals outside to a patch of lawn that was more comfortable than the hard wood dining hall benches. Outside, there was no one to disapprove when we talked a little loudly or laughed over-enthusiastically.

Needing a cholera vaccination, I sought out the public health office, finding it in a modest upstairs' room in a faded mansion signposted, "Hotel de Ville" and "Mairie". Half way up the stairs was the large Prud'hon painting, *Justice and the Divine Punishment Following the Crime*. It was in terrible disrepair, corners folded and decayed, with a clumsy attempt at restoration signed off by a scrawled workman's signature. A gift from the French government, the painting was inscribed: "Vive la Patrie, Vive la Republique"!

Worryingly, my vaccination was with an unsterilised needle. I became aware of this just as the needle was withdrawn from my arm, so complaint was pointless and I took consolation in two large cups of coffee in a picturesque restaurant propped right on the sea.

Bob's roommate had moved on, so I took his place, thus gaining a permanent bed for the rest of my stay. After dinner, we strolled the ocean promenade, the "Cours Chabrol", sitting for a long time looking at the stars and a lone cargo boat at sea that was lit up like a Christmas tree. Others were of the same mind: middle-aged couples held hands coyly as they walked and the atmosphere was more of a European resort than an Indian city.

An American named Wendy joined us for breakfast. On a spiritual path, she kept house and garden for her Indian guru, all the time maintaining an admirable level of humility. She told us her "master" had designed a type of electronic music that helped one "realise the infinite". She had noticed us sitting alone, though it was more probably Bob, for he was becomingly pious in white pyjamas and an abbreviated hairstyle. She asked why we had come to India.

Bob said he had followed a spiritual path to Beas, north of Amritsar, where he had won an audience with local saint, Maharaj Charan Singhji. "It was obvious this man was a saint so I requested initiation," he said. The swami being currently on tour, Bob was taking time off to explore the Sri Aurobindo library. His master had advised him, "finish your studies, explore other fields", but he was already convinced. I told Wendy I had come to enjoy the beaches. "I find it difficult to grasp the heart of this ashram," said Bob and Wendy flashed him a winning smile. "If it is God's will, you will be involved," she said. Ignored, I retired to the cool of the library to research the lives of Sri Aurobindo and The Mother.

Born in Calcutta in 1872, Aurobindo had been caught up in the nationalist turmoil aimed at dislodging the British. Unlike Gandhi, he had refused to rule out armed resistance and, as many of his contemporaries, had spent long periods incarcerated. In prison, he had taught himself yoga and undergone "spiritual experiences". In 1914, he had met French Jew and occultist Mirra Richard (nee Alfassa) and together they forged the movement and ashram that would become the largest in India. Their teachings followed broad precepts of Hinduism: "realisation of the divine within, realisation of the divine without, realisation through the transcendental". Their books covered a large proportion of the library's shelves.

Every Thursday and Sunday nights devotees gathered for group meditation at the "Playground", a sand-over-cement quadrangle behind high walls, and I joined a broad spectrum of meditators ranging from hippie to high society. When floodlights were doused, we stood in silence for a few minutes, then took positions cross-legged across the rectangle. After an hour, without direction, the compound was relit and we all went home. I couldn't help but feel a little disappointed.

Wendy again met us for breakfast. This time I was ignored completely as she enthusiastically broke her news to Bob. Her guru was interested in him. That very evening he was holding a recital for a select few to guide them towards the divine. He must first make a donation but she was sure he would find the rewards sufficient compensation. I had several times noticed in Bob a sharp inclination to depart from the spiritual plane when money was discussed, and this morning was no exception. Sorry, he had had some money stolen from him, he was adhering to a strict budget, he needed to conserve every penny he had…

Clearly believing their meeting to have been pre-destined, Wendy was briefly silent. Another possibility abruptly crossed her mind and she turned to me. She had been drawn to something spiritual and special in our company. If not Bob, I must be the one! "Well, Alan, perhaps you would like to enjoy the performance." I thanked her, but declined, without excuses. She looked disappointed.

In the evening, we were treated to Beethoven's *Violin Concerto* from a stereo system. Not many turned up for the performance, but the society fringe was there, and I conspicuously sat myself a little apart among the discarded sandals by the entrance steps. The music, I pondered, did more to induce spirituality than a dozen meditation courses. I walked back to my room in silence.

The next morning, I asked a pale American devotee about his routine and he told me he ate, slept, meditated and wrote. It was entirely up to him. An Indian joined us and in a pithy parable compared Bob's spiritual seeking to a man looking for a horse: he had mounted his steed and begun a search around the world, devoting his whole life to the endeavour. On reaching home an old man, it had suddenly occurred to him he had been on a horse the whole time! "Much valuable time can be wasted exploring new paths when the answer is close to home," he explained needlessly.

A super race in the making

On the outskirts of the city, a new settlement was in the making. Bizarrely named "Auroville", it was planned to be an avenue for the advancement of a "super race" of humans at high spiritual, cultural and physical levels.

In The Mother's words: "Life on earth, we consider, is not a passage or a means merely; it must become, through transformation, a goal, a realisation… a decisive choice has to be made between lending the body to Nature's ends in obedience to her demands to perpetuate the race as it is, and preparing this body to become a step towards the creation of the new race." She promised, "an exceptional movement that will liberate [chosen ones] from the ordinary human nature and its endless journey, enabling them to take part in the spiritual progress which will lead them along the quickest path towards the creation of the new race, the race that will express the supplemental truth upon earth."

Worth a look, Bob and I thought, and hired bicycles. Cycling a path through red-clay villages with yawning buffalo, we stopped to talk with an Englishman who had been living in Pondicherry for a year. He told us an American had initially proposed to the ashram a scheme whereby unmarried mothers would leave their babies in its care, shielding them from any "untoward influences". The plan was dropped, he said, but only after it was discovered it also involved his begetting children with the unmarried mothers.

But plans for the perfect society had endured. Believing that human evolution was not at an end and could be shaped, The Mother had decided Auroville would be the heart of an evolution, a universal town where people from around the world could live in harmony. In exchange for volunteering for a few hours weekly, Aurovillians received a small grant, partly funded by the government. The rest of their time was spent "seeking the divine".

Today the ashram owned more than 10,000 acres of good farmland, controlling production and distribution. "How many buildings have you seen carrying the names and pictures of Sri Aurobindo and The Mother?" our Englishman asked. "And where did the first rickshaw you encountered here offer to take you?" I remembered: "Ashram, mister? Sri Aurobindo?" Upon her death, the Holy Mother was found to be the richest woman in India and second globally only to Woolworths' heiress Barbara Hutton, he said, adding that Pondicherry business was controlled by the "Bombay mafia".

Auroville in 1974 was little more than desolate waste. Situated on a plateau, it had wide ocean views but no protection from the dry, reddish sand that forever hung in the air and appeared as ochre stains across all clothing. It had only a few buildings, prematurely placed in sparse surrounds. We came across an unfinished building cleverly designed in segments to keep the sun out and the cool breezes in. Inside, a school-teacher was dispatching his wisdom to three young children, one of them European.

A village was, however, taking shape. The few houses so far erected were modern, with well-thatched rooves and sliding partition walls. After finding a teashop where the proprietor tried to overcharge us, we toured the complex, observing factories for making paper, bread and paint, and an impressionist restaurant with floor seating for low tables. We also saw several European advisers, and assumed the complex was well funded. When finished, it was to be dominated by a gigantic obelisk dedicated to The Mother.

I wasn't impressed. From breakfast to bedtime, Auro children would be exposed only to Aurobindo thinking with no learning by experience. The one redeeming factor was that Sri Aurobindo and The Mother essentially taught good. They believed in love, and their philosophies included much common sense. Yet the control this community promised to exercise over minds was frightening. Bob booked travel back to his saint – through "Auro-Travels". I spent a few more days enjoying the sea and the scenery without any guidance at all.

In 1960 the world's first elected woman prime minister, Sirimavo Bandaranaike set out to make Ceylon a socialist state. In 1965, she was ousted by the United National Party which sought to reverse socialism. Returned to power, she in 1972 renamed the state Sri Lanka, proclaimed its religion Buddhism (antagonising the Tamil minority), and began an extensive programme of nationalisation. 1974: with rules breaking up large industry, severe shortages of key staples rice and bread ensue. Tensions simmer with independence-seeking Tamils, a precursor to decades of conflict.

XX

Shoot Mrs Yam!

Sri Lanka: a cholera outbreak; rediscovering the joys of the trek without drugs; the genesis of ethnic conflict in a fledgling socialist republic; and joining yet another pilgrimage.

The introduction of Buddhism ... did not however ensure peace, for during the reigns that followed that of Uttiya, the country was a constant prey to the invasions of the Tamils who came from the neighbouring coasts of India, or to civil wars among the different parties who contended for supremacy (Barthélemy Saint-Hillaire, T*he Buddha and His Religion*, 1895).

No one ever searches a tourist
My Christian neighbour on the train to Rameswaram lectured me for nearly seven hours on the glories of the Lord and his message – one that seemed to primarily concern the inferiority of other beliefs. We shared a seat row with a Muslim, but it was the Christian who held court. Just a few days earlier he had met a Kiwi girl who had horrified him with tales of loose living. "She paid for her trip working as a prostitute. Ah, the decadent West has much to learn from the spiritual East," he said.

The Muslim agreed. "For obvious reasons", neither man let his children see movies. A little rashly, I suggested that Calcutta was the world's most sinful city, and accused them of upholding a society where all things were tacitly permitted – if out of sight. Prostitution was common, but never admitted, and village life harboured many sexual dramas. If I had not said earlier that I loved my mother, I might have shocked these men.

Only the Christian continued all the way to Rameswaram. Despite my candour, he invited me to keep him company as he ran to view the temples of Hinduism's second most holy city in two frantic hours before catching the train back to his Madurai home. I agreed, but shocked him further by first finding accommodation in a derelict shack.

Rameswaram's religious appeal was detracted from somewhat by the pungent odour of drying fish. But the locals seemed not to notice. The island was deemed immensely holy for its connection to the Ramayana legend. It was from here the monkey god Hanuman had managed the epic's incredible boulder leap to "Lanka", the kingdom of Ravan or Rawana (evil), the abductor of Rama's bride, Sita. And it was here, Rama himself had retreated to pay homage to Lord Shiva, to free himself from the sin of killing Rawana.

Following the footsteps of the Christian's long, utilitarian strides I saw all the sights, from the high walls of the Sri Ramanathaswamy Temple to the famed Fishermen's Hindu Temple by the sea, then hastened to the railway station where, like a good friend, I made sure he caught his train.

My accommodation, "Bongi's", was a crumbling ruin. An Australian named Hans confided to me that Bongi was a smuggler who, twice a week, powered his boat to Sri Lanka for cloves, nutmegs and precious stones. Hans would wait for him, fill his pack to the brim with the smuggled goods, then deliver them to a Madurai address. "No one ever searches a tourist," he said. Hans cleared 500rp per trip, indicative of big profits higher up the chain. Bongi also dealt in black market currencies and, as he controlled distribution, all other dealers were subsidiary to him. Thus, while other black marketers offered me 1.2 Sri Lankan rupee for the one Indian, he gave 1.35. He liked hippies!

Hans was powerful, and aware of it. He showed me his knuckles, all deliberately broken, and boasted of the power that gave his punches. Yet he was a Buddhist. Five times daily he lit incense in accordance with Zen practice, and finished his routine with 2am prayers. I might have been impressed, but for his love of weed. Hans was famous here. He wandered the town with bare chest and a brief lungi and, at nearly 2m, presented an awesome figure.

I swam, but the water was hot and unpleasant, and the sudden appearance of numerous jellyfish did not make for enjoyment. The walk back under scorching sun soon destroyed all effects of the dip and I became horribly achy and sore. Dizzy and with a suppurating rash about my arms and back, I collapsed. Perhaps I had suffered a mild heatstroke.

Though weaker than ever, I persisted with my Sri Lankan timetable. I filled in forms, revealed finances, paid surcharges, offered up passport, then, after two hours of stoic endurance, hopped aboard one of three connected scows and waited for them to fill. A tug attached itself to the lead scow, and towed all three to the offshore berth of the ferry for Sri Lanka, which was apparently too large for the Rameswaram wharfs.

And then we departed, the Indian coastline disappeared, and the Indian tourists began strolling energetically about decks admiring the ocean. A lungi-clad German with long blond beard fell asleep above hatches and I relaxed nearby with some cheap literature perfect for an afternoon of boredom. Unfortunately, I finished the book in an hour and a half and there was nothing left to do but peer over the side at ever-increasing shadows.

It was dark when Wolfgang and I arrived at Talaimannar port and even darker before we were allowed ashore as the authorities competed with their Indian counterparts at bureaucracy. A loudspeaker boomed, "Once disembarked please confine your eating and drinking to the railway cafeteria. There has been a cholera outbreak. Do not drink the water. Do not eat local food." Crap! Fifteen hours later, after stopping at every conceivable station, we stumbled into the fierce mid-afternoon glare of Colombo, catching a bus to a youth hostel beautifully situated in a suburb full of mowed lawns and flower gardens. Wolfgang, wanting to be closer to town, stayed just one night.

The next day being May 1, I made an effort to view the May Day celebrations which, in newly-socialist, newly-named Sri Lanka, were massive. The Havelock Park bulged as worker hordes arranged themselves behind blue and red banners. Several times I was slapped across my shoulders and welcomed, each time made to promise I was not a capitalist. One government employee, however, was fiercely anti-communist, which made me wonder why he was there till he confided that attendance was compulsory. I did not stay long in Colombo.

Wrestling a turtle

"Hikkaduwa," said my neighbour as I stepped from my bus onto a foot-path of sand. I immediately headed for the beach where the sand was gold, the sea mottled green, and the bay protected by a prickly reef promising wonderfully safe bathing.

I found accommodation, and Wolfgang, who had also ferreted out the inexpensive. The one other guest, also German, kept to himself, though once I caught him with his arm around the proprietor's wife, who looked shy. Wolfgang of course had beer so, when I finally escaped out of doors, the seashore was hazy, sparkling but wobbly.

Early morning found me floundering about the coral with a borrowed snorkel admiring a strange diversity of fish in rainbow hues. Lying bliss-fully on the sand afterwards reading Patrick White's wonderful *Riders in the Chariot*, I felt all the aches of the trail drain from my body. Then pandemonium as Wolfgang emerged from the sea frantically struggling with a large turtle that thrashed in his arms, staring wetly sidewards in its desperation! He had found it just inside the reef. I held it while a camera was clicked and a salivating local imitated a knife slash across the neck. Thankfully, Wolfgang returned it to the sea. We watched for some time after in case a local mounted a pursuit.

For dinner, Wolfgang and I bought from the market cabbage, leaks, onions, and a fresh tuna. We gathered sticks and some wire grating for a barbecue, while the other German hovered, full of sudden goodwill. As flames spurted, we threw in the fish and vegetables – and the May monsoons chose precisely that moment to make their appearance.

Hundreds were trickling into Hikkaduwa. The full moon day of May represented "Vesak", a commemoration of Buddha's birth, enlightenment and death. It also meant a shortage of bread, milk and other staples. There was simply not enough to go around. That night a long procession wound along Hikkaduwa's single street, participants including an elephant, a platoon of elderly women in starched white dresses, a group of teenaged girls with clackers, and a truck overflowing with saffron-robed monks. The festival continued for three days, though the activities gradually subsided. I spent my days on the beach, regularly diving into the water to relieve the heat.

Wolfgang and I began a routine of tuna barbecues, followed by a homemade icecream using condensed and plain milk and topped with slices of banana. Excellent! As the days passed, I got lazier, not leaving my bed for the beach till mid-morning. Our hosts didn't know what to make of us. One girl in particular took every opportunity to sweep our front porch, to enable one more glance at those strange creatures inside.

One day an oil slick hit the beach. The ugly brown blotches rode the waves to shore, leaving greasy stains where the wet sand and the dry merged. The beach took on a dismal air and there were few swimmers for days after. Encouraged to move on, I chose my day, took one look at the rain thundering outside against helpless palms, and spent the morning in bed.

When we returned to our room after another sumptuous meal, Wolfgang discovered a small grass snake huddled under his bed, probably seeking protection from the rain. But the drinking of beer paid off and all three of us slept soundly. The strong rains, however, showed no signs of abating. One morning, Wolfgang heroically took off with near-zero visibility for the train station. I followed him at midday. The early train to our joint destination of Matara had not yet left but there was no sign of Wolfgang.

The "nonsense" of socialism

The awful weather propelled me faster than I had planned to Ratnapura where a round of cheap hotels proved fruitless, leaving me suspicious that travellers were being channelled into expensive resorts. Eventually, I slowed for tea, where I met a trade unionist recently returned from Russia. "I am a communist," he said, watching on silently as the shopkeeper tried to overcharge me.

A gem salesman rescued me. Careless of my disinterest in his wares, he bade me follow him. "Zahir will look after you," he said. Zahir, a prominent jeweller, was ill in bed but introductions were made and I was offered free stay in the attic of a brother's shop, also a jeweller's, right in the centre of town. Ratnapura was a city of gems: sapphires and rubies, onyx and alexandrite. Just getting to the shop required a determination to escape the hawkers, all immensely surprised I had no interest in their specialty.

Fellow guest Baskaralingam, a tall man with Omar Sharif features, welcomed me warmly. A pharmacist from Jaffna in the north, his work meant an almost permanent separation from his family. He was poorly paid and it was only possible to visit home during his annual vacation. Seven, all-male guests slept in the attic on camp stretchers. Downstairs, a concrete tank provided water for bathing, but it could only be refilled from city supplies for 50 minutes each morning, 30 each night. We had to be frugal. I had just enough to wash my trousers, dressing while they dried in a borrowed sarong.

Two men accosted me, telling me for the umpteenth time of the sad state of Sri Lanka's economy and the corruption of its government. But this pair had a solution. "We want to shoot Mrs Batalota!" Sri Lankan for "yam", Batalota was the contemptuous nickname for Prime Minister Sirimavo Bandaranaike, coined from the supposition her policies were impoverishing the population, that the national staple of rice had become too expensive, forcing the population to change diet to the more basic sweet potato.

They were serious about the shooting, becoming excited in their dissertation, and I couldn't help but reflect out loud that the outcome of violence would likely end with the rich becoming richer and the poor, poorer. To them it was all so simple. With her dead, the opposition party would sweep into power, the "nonsense of socialism" be removed, and the Sri Lankan people would live happily ever after.

Just one year after becoming a republic, the economy was in dire straits. There were shortages of sugar, rice, cloth and flour, together with a fuel crisis and a chronic cholera outbreak. The British had a lot to answer for. They had moulded the island to the production of tea neglecting all other crops, so that now Sri Lanka, self-sufficient in few things, had to increasingly rely on imports. Yet, looking about, one could only marvel at the land's fertility. The solution was obvious – shoot Mrs Batalota!

Trekking and peppermint

With trekking in mind, I caught a bus to Haputale, sitting next to an oil executive who embarrassed me by knowing more about New Zealand than I did. I arrived in mid-afternoon, booking in at a guesthouse where a white-haired man and a younger woman greeted me courteously, directing me to a bedroom that was a colonial relic, just as was their service. Oblivious to my distaste, two elderly servants persisted in calling me "master".

At 7am I was out of bed and walking energetically towards a lookout point from where it was reputedly possible to see five of the nine Sri Lankan provinces. I was not disappointed. For kilometre upon kilometre, the hills displayed the bright-bunched tea plant, minute splashes of white of the pickers above deep falls into plains of mist below. Everywhere, pickers were hard at work, baskets on backs, inching up the steep hillside in near-impeccable lines. All were women, while for each grouping, a couple of men stood by to supervise, which they did in time-honoured fashion. At Dambatenne, the settlement heart of the Lipton's group, I jumped on the back of a tractor headed out into the estate, up and over steep gorges till the pickers appeared in the most difficult of terrains.

These plants were not tea, but peppermint, an experiment in diversification compelled by the economic crisis. A smartly dressed supervisor decried colonial Britain's single-minded emphasis on tea whereby Sri Lanka had fallen so far from self-sufficiency. He was less than optimistic, however, about his company's experiment with diversification. Mrs Bandaranaike's interventionism had reached communist proportions, he said, especially in the enforced break up of land. A 50-acre maximum had been set for all landowners. "So far, tea estates are excluded, but nationalisation remains a constant threat and most companies are unwilling to risk money on experimental projects."

The next day I hiked to "World's End", a euphemism for the end point of an exhaustive daylong trek. After a ride to Ohiya in a miniature train with varnished walls and silver bulkheads, I began the trek with a party of Sri Lankans in neatly pressed shirts and office trousers. They were, they informed me, members of the Sri Lankan army boxing team: three were army champions and one, national. Most solicitous, they took turns to ask if I was tiring as we climbed steadily through forest, green and shadowy, while a thousand birds screamed abuse at us.

As the mist closed in, we stopped for tea at an unexpected hotel, the "Far Inn", old-fashioned colonial, before filing uncomfortably out of doors back into rain and dreariness. A signpost read: "World's End: 3 miles"! Briefly, things cleared to reveal a crystal river rustling lightly over moss and stone. Here the boxers decided to have their lunch and invited me to join them. "Don't you mind," they said as they dolloped noodles for me on a banana leaf. Then one of them jumped out of his clothes, delivered a vicious left hook to an imaginary opponent, and leapt into the icy stream. While the rest of us doubled up with laughter, he began a shuffling dance that we accompanied with a slow handclap.

Another clearing and we were at the clifftop marking World's End. Below us, was a terrifying drop, far below, a suggestion of red rooves, probably attached to a tea estate. The cliff was said to be 1220m high. Some boulders had been graffiti-ed: "Goodbye to Monika and Brito". My companions said this referred to a recent suicide. Again, the rains came, harder and more furious, and we began jogging. One of the boxers screamed a warning and pushed me aside as a small green grass snake slithered across where my foot had been just a second before. It lay for some time in the middle of the path where I admired its green leathery back with black patches, ink splotches on velvet. The boxer wanted to kill it, but I prevented him from doing so.

We parted at Haputale, firm friends, agreeing to meet the following day on the Colombo Express, they bound for the capital city, I for Nurawa Elya, yet another hill station. The express was on time, and the boxing team on cue hustled me aboard and demanded a seat for me. One of them presented me with a large bag of guavas for my journey. Just before I disembarked at Nanu Oya, a lunch pack was handed me. The other passengers might have mistaken me for royalty.

Serendipity

The bus to Nurawa Elya was over-booked so I was relieved to be serendipitously shouted at: "Come on. I've bought your ticket!" The term "serendipity", when something delightfully unexpected happens, had been proudly related to me as Sri Lankan. In fact, its origins owed to a *Persian* fairy tale about three questing princes from "Serendip" (old Persian for Sri Lanka) who enjoyed all sorts of wonderful, accidental discoveries. That the term entered the English lexicon was down to 18th century English statesman Horace Walpole – after his serendipitous discovery of the fairy tale. My entirely Sri Lankan benefactor was squeezed down the other end of the bus so I did not manage to thank him till we had arrived.

I found the youth hostel where, browsing through the register, I spotted the signature of Glenn with whom I had travelled in Nepal. He had made it! All night long, the rain thundered and, with morning, came no sign of abatement. I had planned to climb Pidurutalagala, at 2524m, the island's highest mountain. Instead, cold and dissatisfied, I bought a bus ticket for Kandy.

I was excited about Kandy, for the name was a famous one, with literary connotations, James Michener but the last of many to pen eulogies. When the bus stopped on a sloping embankment opposite a large fruit market, I began to get it. The town was engulfed in jungle, surrounded on all sides by hills. As I walked above the Kandy lake, beautiful and cool, I could hear monkeys screaming. Unsolicited, a car offered me a lift to *Mrs Peidris's*, delivering me to a mansion that took boarders, a palace hidden in a valley of its own. Wolfgang was here, so I quickly learned the price of Kandy beer.

Walking through town, I spotted a long line of people clutching loaves. I had been told it was impossible to buy bread. I tried, only to be rebuffed with: "no bread for tourists", "ration card system", and "sorry"! I eloquently argued my worthiness, however, and the result was one loaf, which I was told to hide under my shirt till well away from the vicinity. Bread was rationed all over Sri Lanka.

For the remaining daylight, I sat at the lakeside with a policeman. If anyone showed any interest in me, he waved them imperiously away with a long stick, rocking back on his heels with a slow, studied arrogance. Studying at the university, he anticipated a high rank upon graduation. He shook my hand and told me we were now firm friends.

The Socialist Republic turns two

The next morning, I made an effort to see the famous caves and frescoes of Sigiriya with a likeminded Sri Lankan and an Indian. Because of a cancelled bus, we didn't reach Sigiriya till 5pm, but continued to the high rock outcrop on which the nation's artistic reputation seemed to depend, a solitary rock rising smoothly for 200m, bringing to mind the leaping torso of a whale. Natural hollows pitted the surface, many of them hallowed as shrines. Fortunately, handrails aided the climb, which at times was near vertical. We found the most famous frescoes, those featuring semi-naked maidens, with artistic emphasis on the upward tilt of fingers or the delicate presentation of flower stems between forefinger and thumb. I could not remember seeing work of greater skill in Asia.

The last bus home having departed, we had no option but to begin hiking. But the Sri Lankan, Saheed, identified birds for us – ash doves, parakeets – and as we walked through jungle, the time passed quickly. Eventually we reached a junction and, an hour before midnight, we were able to catch a late bus back to Kandy.

I began the morning reading the Sunday papers. Initiations at a local university had shocked the nation, with girls forced to strip and kneel before their "gods"! In a week, all of this would be forgotten, and the people would be able to resume muttering about streakers in New York. May 22 was the second anniversary of the creation of the Socialist Republic of Sri Lanka. Under heavy rain, there were no celebrations to be seen in Kandy, though I later read of military parades, with pictures of grim marching through Colombo. Really, there was little cause for elation – the nation was worse off than ever. At least it was a nation, but it was hard to muster respect for Mrs Bandaranaike. Her solutions relied

219

on a levelling down process, when in such a small country there might surely be more effect in elevating the poor.

Holding on to power via an alliance with the communist Party, her survival depended on playing off one ethnic group against another, one party associated with the Sinhalese majority, the other with the Tamil minority. Small wonder the minority despaired of equality through democratic means. At times I longed for the low key, mediocre politics of home.

Buddhist pilgrimage

Anuradhapura had a New Town and a Sacred Area. I had met Wijesinghe and his young companion on the train from Kandy and they invited me to join them on their pilgrimage. Taking the direction of the Sacred Area, we walked across botanical bridges and forest glades to the aptly named Pilgrim's Rest House where we booked into a spacious double room. Adjacent floor space was cordoned-off for the poorer pilgrims; the ceiling above had been usurped by a band of silvery monkeys who stared insolently down on us.

Our pilgrimage began at the white-walled Sri Mahobodi Temple where we walked solemnly upstairs into a hallway guarded by a massive Buddha, placed a fresh white lotus flower on a front table, made prayer with our hands, then withdrew to meditate. At the back of the temple a gold-plated fence marked the home of the famous Bo tree, claimed to have grown from a sapling under which Buddha achieved his enlightenment near Gaya in India. I was told it was the oldest documented tree in the world, dating back to the 3rd century BC. It appeared to be little more than a propped-up stump. But we paid homage to it with further prayers.

Our next stop was a modest wood hut, reputedly on the site of a once-glorious structure built in the 2nd century BC, rebuilt in the 12th century AD. This was Lovamahapaya, translated for me as the "Brazen Palace", an odd name for the once nine-storey residence of the city's monks. We prayed, then continued along an avenue of lamps to the most imposing construction of all, the Ruwanweli Maha Chaitya, a dome-shaped shrine of immense proportions. Flowers in hand, we climbed up to a moat-shaped courtyard and began three clockwise circuits.

At a small temple beside, we made signs of prayer to another Buddha, and recommenced meditating. Wijesinghe urged me to concentrate on an image, such as a flower, till my eyes closed and the object "became transfixed as a picture in the conscious mind". All outward distractions eliminated, the path was then clear to reflect – on the "way". I was again first to rise. We stepped outside into darkness to begin even more meditation. Their appetite for purification was boundless! I tried hard for an hour then Wijesinghe, brimming with love, paid a fee in my name to the temple guardian and 2000 lights abruptly lit the structure. It felt strangely, if briefly, spiritual. Perhaps so, perhaps not!

Back at the Bo tree, Wijesinghe bade me sit one more time while he recited a special prayer to grant me sanctity in my travels and a safe return home. Next to us, a long railing of butter lamps flickered and cooling evening winds shuddered through the treetops. The monkeys were silent. There was no need to talk. We stopped once to remove a large beetle off the track lest it be hurt, then bed. It was nearly midnight.

Our pilgrimage was not quite over. In the still of early morning, we trudged stiffly to Sri Mahabodi, placed our incense sticks in their stand, our flowers to the altar, and again meditated. Aware of no wrongs needing righting, I reflected on my immature metaphysics, a muddle of Buddha and Spinoza but, mostly, just a form of self-reassurance. No revelations came but I stood up refreshed, having very briefly convinced myself of the good of mankind and in the right frame of mind to follow Wijesinghe in his search of further purification.

We circumnavigated the dome shrine Ruwanweli Maha Chaitya under an umbrella, then scuttled inside for prayer. Wijesinghe struck up a conversation with a blind man, informing me in whispers he had the power to consult with the gods. Money changed hands. The blind man passed into a trance before emerging to affirm that the power of Buddha was too great to proceed. We adjourned outside and the process was repeated. His chant began: "Sadhu, Sadhu, Sadhu". Wijesinghe handed over more money, wrapped in a betel leaf, and the medium carefully felt it. "Sadhu, Sadhu, Sadhu". Sadly, he again had to concede defeat. Nevertheless, he was paid well.

After breakfast we proceeded to one final temple, Thuparamaya, a modest relic of the 3rd century BC. We walked around a smallish stupa surrounded by pillars, placed our flowers, and again meditated. This routine was becoming taxing and I was somewhat relieved when my two companions abruptly announced they must return home. I saw them off at the station and moved to a secular resthouse in the heart of the satellite suburb, Jaffna Junction. Pilgrimage done.

Outbreak of cholera

For only the second time in Sri Lanka I found myself with a room to myself and made full use of the luxury. Finding some out-of-date newspapers, I learned of India's nuclear bomb test and Australia's dissolution of its government. The former did not surprise me. Entering the nuclear race was not out of kilter with its incredible overspending on defence; the poverty was accepted and ignored. Australia's dissolution, I could not fathom.

I bumped into Wolfgang, dressed as I had left him, in his brief, pink lungi. He greeted me, "Hi, man!" then, after a brief catch-up, disappeared in search of beer. I caught the early train to Talaimannar and, true to form, just as it was about to depart, Wolfgang jumped aboard clutching a pineapple and a huge bowl of cream curd. We made a picnic, spreading luxuriously over unoccupied seating.

Suddenly there were people. A man pushed roughly aboard with many others behind him and drew three cards from his pocket. Then the old trick was begun. A young couple placed a modest bet, won, and started betting more heavily. But they were poor and it became obvious we were the real targets. But we would have none of the idiocy and at the next stop the disgruntled card player made his exit. Strangely, a goodly proportion of the carriage disembarked with him.

At Talaimannar station, we made for the stale cafeteria we had arrived at, the thin line of restaurant stalls opposite perched disconcertingly on sand. The loudspeaker message had not changed: "Passengers are urged to confine their eating and drinking to the railway cafeteria. There has been an outbreak of cholera…"

Meditating on a rock at the confluence of the Bay of Bengal, Indian Ocean and the Arabian Sea, Swami Vivekananda dedicated his life to the dispossessed. Dismissing Hinduism's renunciation practices, he came up with a "Kanyakumari resolve" – that the poor need food before religion. But to many Indians, his saintliness jingoistically rests on a speech to the 1893 Parliament of the World's Religions in Chicago where he argued the worth of all creeds, "taking Hinduism to the world". 1974: thousands of pilgrims converge on the site where the swami meditated.

XXI

Cleansed of all sin

South India: purification from bathing at the confluence of the three southern oceans; the prostitute-seeking tourists of Kovalam; and an off-road dash through the Periyar Lake game reserve and the Cochin canals.

They looked awkward and a bit comic, too young to be wearing lipstick, nose jewels, earrings, and slipping bracelets ... they gave the impression of schoolgirls in their mothers' clothes. None could have been older than fifteen.
"Which one would you like?" (Paul Theroux, *The Great Railway Bazaar*).

Purifying souls

"How do you like India?" On a tiring network of trains to Cape Comorin and in no mood to be diplomatic, I voiced the opinion it was shortsighted to pursue military ends when people were starving. The man took immediate umbrage.

"China and Pakistan are poised at our borders and could attack without reason," he said. "They've done it before." I responded that any danger was slight. China had disagreed (rightly, I suggested) over a border delineation, attacked to prove its point, then withdrew; Pakistan had (rightly, I suggested) disputed India's moral right to a Muslim-heavy province and made its point. As he continued prattling about India's great social advances, thankfully, I fell asleep.

Cape Comorin was another of India's "most holy" towns. Early worshipers saw significance in its siting at "Land's End". Here projected the cape that projected into the Bay of Bengal, the Indian Ocean, and the Arabian Sea. So on three sides was water, a boundary counterpoint to the gigantic landmass far to the north, the Himalayas, home of the Gods.

It certainly had scriptural cred. Dividing India into nine parts, one for each of his nine children, legendary emperor Bharata had given the southernmost tip to his daughter, Kumari. Urged on by scriptures proclaiming that a dip in the sea at the point of confluence purified the soul, it was hardly surprising the town was beset by a constant stream of pilgrims:

Going to Kanya [the bathing ghat] with regulated diet and subdued mind, one reaches the region of Manu, the Lord of Creation; whatever gift is made at Kanya, the rishis [sages] of rigid vows say, is everlasting
(The Mahabharata).

But, more often than not, it was actual history that attracted the pilgrims. In 1892 Vivekananda, a key figure in India's emerging nationalism, swam 500m offshore to the Shripada Parai rocks to meditate, there formulating his philosophies before travelling to the West where he famously proclaimed the equivalence of all religions. Sadly, locals often translated this into a "Hinduism is best" primacy. Adding to the allure, Gandhi's ashes had *for a while* been stored here for viewing. By design, every October 2 (his birthday) the first rays of the sun illuminated the plinth where his remains *had* been housed – for the pilgrims, a must-see-nothing-see!

Much more impressively, on the eve of a full moon, I watched the sun rise from the Bay of Bengal and set over the Arabian Sea and the moon simultaneously rising in the east. As night fell, I was startled by a shouting procession transporting a tall effigy of a stag, with a fully tusked elephant walking beside. The next night I was woken by the screams of children chasing a temple "car" nearly four storeys high. The structure was towed by large numbers of pilgrims, using tree trunk levers to edge it forward, inch by inch. Each time it shifted, a great roar issued from the crowd and I wondered why the previous day's elephant had not been harnessed for the task.

Immersed in the devout, I visited an exposition of Hinduism, from early scriptures the *Vedas* and the *Upanishads*, to epics the *Ramayana* and the *Mahabharata*. It was an articulate account, bringing in Buddha, Mahavira (Jainism), Nanak (Sikhism), Kabir (Sufism) and other saints. The words of German philosopher Jürgen Habermas – "Hinduism is not at all a single religion with a creed to which everybody must subscribe, it is rather a federation of different kinds of approach to the reality that is behind life," – especially resonated. It was already apparent to me Hinduism was not a single religion, but *hundreds*.

But the heart of the tableau was Vivekananda, a "man of the people" who had responded to the oppression of the lowly. His international fame owed to his 1893 speech to the Parliament of Religions in Chicago in which he had said: "The Christian is not to become a Hindu or a Buddhist, nor a Hindu or a Buddhist to become a Christian. But each must assimilate the spirit of the others and yet reserve his individuality … if anybody dreams of the exclusive survival of his own religion and the destruction of the others, I pity him from the bottom of my heart". That too, resonated.

I decided to join the hundreds of pilgrims retracing Vivekananda's path, starting with the offshore "rock of meditation" with its memorial temple and an indentation revered as the footmark of the goddess Kanya. From shore, the complex appeared as a reflecting palace with the three oceans savagely pounding at its doors. To cross to the rock, required a brief ferry ride, with the sexes strictly separated. When I stood up on board for a better view, I was reprimanded. That was against the rules.

At the meditation site – Shripada Mandapam – I walked with everybody else around the "footstep", fruitlessly wondering why it was a protrusion not a hollow, then up to the Vivekananda Mandapam (temple), where a series of pillars, delicately engraved with white line designs, encircled a larger-than-life bronze statue of the swami. I followed the pilgrim queue, admired the view when they admired the view, then filed back down for the ferry without deviating from the line. The whole process was a masterpiece of organisation.

On the mainland, I visited the unostentatious Gandhi Mandir (temple), housing the plinth that had contained the Mahatma's ashes. And finally, I sought out the Kanya bathing ghat, the dipping point for purity at land's end. Most of the lungi and sari-clad bathers were amused when I entered the waves in red skants. Some glared. But I had the satisfaction of knowing my soul had been purified: bathing here, one is cleansed of all sins, the Mahabharata promised.

The moon rose almost full above the eastern ocean, but I missed the miracle of simultaneous sun fall into the western sea for the interference of cloud. As consolation, there was an effusive red slick splashed gloriously across heaven and ocean and a delicate rouge settled about the moon. I chose my seat on a rock extending into the Arabian Sea and allowed the now strong winds to whip at my body. I was alone, as once all mankind, with the sky and the oceans.

They're just kids!

On one side of me on my bus ride to Kerala state capital Trivandrum sat a member of the Sri Ramakrishna Mission who wanted to know if I took drugs; on the other, a straight Frenchman who was curious about the "life of a hippie". As we munched on roasted cashew nuts, my talk with the latter drifted from spiritualism to France's Mururoa nuclear testing. No world problem was beyond our reach as we raced through numerous southern villages, the more affluent identifiable by a prominent cinema.

Disembarking at Trivandrum (or Thiruvananthapuram) into a confused procession that included three heavily tusked elephants, I made a spur-of-the-moment decision and caught a bus to nearby Kovalam, beach resort for the gentry. An elegant, crescent-shaped beach, Kovalam was almost solitary but for a modern hotel that had a monopoly of the foreshore. A jumble of children converged on me with baskets of peanuts while, along the sand, strolled affluent day-trippers. I despaired of finding accommodation till three youngsters led me to the next bay along where their sand-floored house had an uninterrupted view of the Arabian Sea. For all the world, I was on a Pacific island, a feeling of solitude enhanced by enduring odours of jackfruit, coconut and banana.

The surf was strong but I lay for hours under its spell before being joined by an English teenager on a gap year before university, and an American freak with flowing hair, and we got stoned together, perfectly stoned, for the moon was the merest off full and the waves were illumined in bright phosphorous patches, ripples of light from sea to shore. Kerala grass had a deserved reputation!

By contrast, the tourist beach was earmarked for development. The hotel there had doorways marked "massage room", "recreation room", and the only villagers to be seen were the peanut sellers, the vendors of a miniature morning market that dispensed fish and mangoes, and a privileged few employed at sweeping the beach. Their village was once at the water's edge. The government had moved them a few hundred metres uphill where the sea was denied them.

Higher up the road, more hotels appeared, all expensive, with coconuts stacked on their verges, testimony to the fantasy setting. It was these "highland" hotels, though deprived of waterfront that did the best business, for they served also as brothels and the invitation was overt. Indian womanhood seemed to be entirely reserved for the men of white complexion. I met a portly, middle-aged Canadian who grew red in the face as he told me of his brothel experiences. "You could never have it this good at home," he said. "They are just kids!"

I did nothing to encourage the conversation, but guessed it was implicit I too was a brothel seeker. Why else would I be here? He was flying home the next day but first wanted to make maximum use of the amenities. He was excessively fat and sweated as he enthused about his pastime. Back at my private beach, I was blissfully alone. I bought a pineapple for my dinner and ate it under the moon with the Southern Cross clearly before me, reminding me of another, distant land, now in the dead of winter.

An Israeli emerged from nowhere wearing only baggy white under-pants, and stayed for the morning. I had not seen many Israelis on my travels. When military service was completed, the feeling seemed to be that no time could be wasted before forging a career. Odel was different. He had spent months travelling through Africa and Asia, though of course some countries were denied him. In Ethiopia when the Yom Kippur war broke out, he had flown immediately home, fought, then casually resumed his travels.

I listened avidly as he described Rome's airport overflowing with Israelis returning home to take part in the war. He surprised me, however, with his distaste for former Prime Minister Golda Meir and Defence Minister, Moshe Dayan: "Ours is a young country and needs young leaders," he said. I liked Odel. His stop, though, was brief and I was soon alone again, enjoying my lunch of pineapple and mango.

Angry elephants

On the train to Quilon (or Kollam), a passenger joked to me about India's rapid population growth – "we are hard workers" – and his disapproving neighbour piously urged me to pay him no heed. "Over-population is not a problem in India. Do we not have wars? Do we not need people?" The problem, he said, was solely one of distribution. There was plenty of food for everyone. The first speaker should not have discussed political issues with a foreigner!

He may have been partly right. Assuming India's population remained static, it was possible its many problems could be solved. But its population was not static, nor was stasis within hope or reason. I wondered, if the population reached 1 billion, if the nation would be doomed to starve. I had heard it estimated that figure would be reached within 20 or 25 years.

At the Quilon market I stumbled into an Englishwoman looking rather miserable for wont of a place to stay. It was logical she should move in with me, already successful in my seeking. We got on well, talking freely from the start, sitting cross-legged on the riverbank where the moon hovered and the lamp-lit launches darted. I made new decisions. Alice wanted to see a game reserve – I wanted to see a game reserve!

On her way home after two years in Australia Alice was excited, but also lonely. Immediately we were tangled in all sorts of strange discussions and it was flattering the regularity with which we agreed. Our stage was a lengthy bus ride into the heights of the Deccan Plateau, and we attracted a lot of attention for our earnestness. Meanwhile, the scene outside became steadily more beautiful as the forest thickened and an ascending road left civilisation behind.

Thekkady was the end of the road, but no township, just a too-expensive hotel that looked askance at our packs and directed us elsewhere. But I was in good form and obtained for us a room with a 20 per cent reduction in recognition of the off-season. A two-storey parabola of grey stone brick, the hotel was immersed in forest, with just sufficient clearing in front to show off a burst of pale white frangipane and a deep orange bougainvillea.

We set off on a long afternoon walk to neighbouring Kumili in the company of a game warden, who was "very pleased to meet foreigners". "Life is short enough," he told us. "We live and we die, so must make the best use of our time and as many friendships as possible." We detoured to his home, a clay hut with a camp stretcher, and sat on packing cases talking inconsequentially. Like many government employees this man was forced to live away from his family, but he accepted his lot stoically, for jobs were precious.

At dawn, we presented ourselves at Lake Periyar, hoping to find a boat for our game reserve exploration. We were dependant on meeting other tourists because, even for two, the costs were prohibitive. And we were lucky. A group of tie-and-collar Indians and their families arrived and agreed to split the fare. We saw our first elephants within minutes, but it was a tragic viewing: a cow with a broken foot with two smaller elephants leaning at her side as futile assistance. A larger bull eyed us angrily, making sporadic charges to the bank and trumpeting loudly. He knew who his enemies were.

We came across wild pigs and a fair smattering of white cattle, but it was elephants we saw most, bathing and changing colour according to the lake-edge soil. We reached a dam destination with some anticipation for a tiger had recently been sighted there, but had to be content with yet another herd of elephants. As we turned for home the Indian children on board began singing, "The Lord is my Shepherd".

Canal crazy

Our plan to rejoin the sea via the region's famous canal network, a confusing system of waterways from Quilon in the south to beyond Ernakulam (Cochin) in the north, Alice and I caught a riverboat to Alleppey. As the boat moved slowly along the narrow canal, with mud dykes acting as borders at each side, it began to rain, prompting crew to overcautiously throw sack curtaining across our window.

Fortunately, the squall soon passed and views were again allowed us: women touching toes at their washing, or picking lice from the hair of their young. At occasional stops, commuters sat patiently on isolated dykes, long distances from shops or facilities. We entered new canal zones and left others, each with its own launch services, and swollen barges that inched along guided by muscular boatmen. Alleppey arrived at mid-afternoon and, though Cochin could now be reached by road, we opted to continue on the water.

With eight hours before the next departure, however, we took a bus to a nearby beach where, sitting under palms, Alice dexterously elicited the gift of a coconut from an inquisitive band of villagers that encircled us. Then it was back to the Alleppey "terminal" where she befriended a shrivelled old woman for whom the embankment was home. "She's probably a thief," a man warned us. He had no justification, except that she was low caste – a sad testimony to the attitudes of socialist India. Alice gave her a Buckingham Palace postcard. By the way the card was clutched to her bosom, you could see it was appreciated.

Next, it was my attitudes in question. After boarding our boat in darkness, we joined an Indian student in making a joint payment to make things easier for the fare collector. But I was asleep when the collector returned with our change and in the morning the student reimbursed me at a lower level than I expected. Things became heated and he stalked off without repaying me. Instantly, I realised it was I who had miscalculated, engendering a red face but no one to apologise to. The amount of money involved was miniscule.

From Ernakulam, we gave up on canals for a bus to Fort Cochin, one of a trio of Cochins that took some unravelling. At Fort Cochin we found accommodation in an old tourist bungalow with rooms big enough to house 10, with large shuttered windows that opened out onto the sea. An obese Indian guest invited us to join him for drinks later. To fill in time, we caught a ferry to Bolghatty Island, former seat of the Cochin British resident, before being side-tracked to Mattancherry, a town noted for its Jewish community, with a "Jew Street" in a "Jew Town" – and of course forgot the invitation.

Irritatedly waiting for us on our very late return, he waved us imperiously into his room where an array of savouries, salads and fruits and a bottle of brandy awaited us. He was already a little drunk. Calling Alice "my dear sweet lady", he insisted on refilling our glasses with devastating regularity. He had a self-effacing nature, folding his hands and dropping his head in a way reminiscent of Uriah Heep. He told us he was a member of Christian Orthodox sect the "Jacobites", a branch of the Syrian-based Syriac Orthodox Church of Antioch for whom, clearly, alcohol was not an issue.

Alice resolved to move on. She was in a hurry to reach England, hardly compatible with my tortoise meanderings. I would have liked to accompany her at least as far as Bombay but, really, there was no sense to our continuing together, especially in view of the Australian boyfriend. Though I thought about it. I enjoyed her company immensely. She was intelligent and had a broad range of interests that included my present obsession with Hinduism. The boyfriend was due to visit her over Christmas. I, she said, was her last fling.

We both packed, for I planned to move to Ernakulam but, in the meantime, there was a morning to enjoy and the Cochin stillness made it desirable to "potter", as Alice would say. We farewelled our alcoholic friend (after eating his boiled eggs but refusing his brandy), and set out for stroll in a park where we talked about nothing in particular for quite some time. Stumbling upon the 16th century St Francis church, the first church built by Europeans in India, we played tourists, poring over sombre antiquities including a gold-engraved edition of the Lord's Prayer and the tombstone of Portuguese explorer Vasco da Gama. We wasted more time reading old baptismal records, one annotated, "converted from heathenism". Walking out ahead of Alice, I turned to see her at prayer. A couple of years later, a letter from her reached me telling me the boyfriend had moved on and she would love to hear from me. But my health at the time precluded a response and we lost touch.

Alone again. The rain began just as I reached the railway station for Coimbatore, but had little effect on a large band of chanting Indians carrying a large flag emblazoned with the hammer and the sickle. A collection box was rattled under my nose. Kerala State had earlier elected a communist government but terrible pressures had soon restored the status quo. Nevertheless, they remained a power to be reckoned with.

I felt strangely emotional. Rural India had laid claim to my soul. Everything was possessed of a fairy-tale quality anomalous to this century, Mrs Gandhi and the bomb. The farmer still ploughed with oxen and the bullock cart was still the best way of transporting product to market. The women dressed in saris, the men in dhotis, just as they had for centuries. The same old thatched straw huts grouped protectively about the same old communal wells and one could still recognise the house of the village elder for its firmer clay construction.

No fertiliser being available, the people squatted in mid-paddock and the cow was encouraged to excrete where most needed, for its production was vitally important to village income. Along the road, the bullock driver fell asleep but his charges carried him along the same path they had taken the previous day, and the day before too. At the village, a tiny shop dispensed rice, corn flour for the chapatti, as well as small luxuries like matches, cheap women's finery, and tea.

Bangalore Beggars' Association
I caught an early bus to Ootacamund, a hill station more commonly known as "Ooty". We climbed, spectacularly at times, valleys unfolding into forest and, eventually, plantations of tea. Ooty was a rambling collection of stone houses dotted at some 2300m, mixed in with modern-built schools and supermarkets. Collar and tie were the order of the day and, as reflection of another era, there was a large party of visiting

English schoolchildren in khaki short pants, taking furious notes at the direction of their form master.

There was of course another side to the town, tattered jackets thrown vainly about bare feet and legs, small boys crossing arms and jumping to keep out the cold. "Paise, mister? Paise?" Men squatted close to the warmth of the tea stalls and, occasionally, they too asked for money. There was a large settlement of Tibetans here, perhaps reflective of the good sense of government resettling programmes, and most maintained their national dress – the long, black skirts and bodices, and the red patched aprons. None looked askance at the weather.

I was summoned to a hotel via a shout from a second storey window. The storeowner had formed upstairs' partitions with cardboard, but I was happy enough at the price, unexpectedly cheap in a tourist centre. Then I explored. Winding above the main street were sombre law courts, where manacled prisoners could be seen enjoying the sun in an open courtyard. It became very cold and I began to regret having posted my sleeping bag home. I climbed up narrow stairs to my room and there on my bed was a thick woollen blanket. My dilemma had been appreciated.

When the next morning offered only rain and more cold, I presented myself at the bus station, only to be told that the bus to Mysore was fully booked. Suddenly a spritely old man seized my luggage crying, "Quick, direct bus to Mysore" and I leapt aboard an old vehicle gathering momentum on the street. Only when the collector asked twice the expected fare, did it dawn that I was aboard a pirate bus.

Mysore hummed. I found accommodation in a cheap penthouse cell overlooking the incredible Maharaja's palace, which spread for acres just a block or two away. The whole city seemed to explode with red-tinged domes, minarets, temple towers and mosques. Daydreaming cattle were sworn at but tolerated; jaywalking humans were sworn at, and not. My good mood was dented when a young girl, perhaps eight years old, pursued me. She had learned the art of clinging to one's legs in abject obeisance. Unable to escape, I picked her up and placed her on a seat beside some women nearby, but she immediately returned, throwing her arms around me. People were beginning to stare. Why couldn't that rich Westerner spare a few paise?

An organisation calling itself the "Bangalore Beggars' Association" had recently made a plea for an end to one and two paise coins, which were now almost worthless but still given to beggars, thus degrading their income. Beggars' union? *Seven Years in Tibet* author Heinrich Harrer recounted how, after the Tibetan government had employed beggars for public works, the work had quickly been crippled by absenteeism. So what was the answer?

Vivekananda aside, it was deemed honourable here to renounce society, and people did give. I rationalised that, the minute the government extended its socialist doctrine to pensions for the poor, I would donate generously. My Mysore incident was ended when a storekeeper came to my rescue with a piece of boxwood, which the girl felt about her legs. Of course, that wasn't the answer either and I guiltily endured terrible looks from a partisan populace.

On my final night in Mysore, I treated myself to a biryani and a mango. Soon I would be north again, among Westerners again, re-entering that well-worn path of the northern trail-ers: Amritsar to Delhi to Calcutta, with Southeast Asia before them. Apart from Alice and Hans, I hadn't spoken to a Westerner since Kovalam Beach and was quite happy at this state of affairs.

> 1960: Bombay state, after fierce lobbying from two ethno-linguistic groups, was split in two: in the north, Gujarat (capital, Ahmedabad), in the south, Maharashtra (Bombay). A tipping point was violent Marathi protests in which police killed more than 100. As new Bombay's heavy and manufacturing industries flourished, so too did its population, mushrooming from 4.5 million in 1960 to 6.5 million in 1970. 1974: with a population now of about 7.5 million, Bombay profits hugely from its regenerated film industry, its massive tourism and sex industries – and its crime.

XXII

If it sounds too good to be true

Goa, Bombay, Agra and Delhi: well and truly back on the hippie trail; stuck on a train for two days and two nights a few hundred metres from Bombay; falling for a scam that shames and impoverishes me; and a rickshaw driver takes pity on me.

I care not whether a man is Good or Evil; all that I care Is whether he is a Wise man or a Fool. Go! Put off Holiness, And put on Intellect; or my thund'rous hammer shall drive thee To wrath, which thou condemnest, till thou obey my voice (William Blake, *The Cry of Los*).

Freaks out of season

Goa state capital Panaji was smaller than I expected. Government buildings were mostly of utilitarian stone and I was struck by the Portuguese inscriptions: every word seemed to end in "cao", and the connecting word was invariably "das". Panaji had no skyscrapers, no sparkling office blocks, but it had a certain stylishness. Perhaps that was an illusion fostered by the predominant Western dress – even the women seemed to have dispensed with saris. There were liquor stores here too, patronised civilly with snacks and conversation. No one hurried you. And tea was served in cups.

Amid monsoonal torrent, I saw no travellers. But, spluttering in the rain, I was accosted by a scholarly-looking man with a neatly trimmed beard and became his lodger, in a tiny room overlooking the river. If I opened my door I stepped into the middle of a busy restaurant, acutely embarrassing when I was dressed for the bathroom.

The restaurant owner's son told me the Portuguese, who had quit the state as recently as 1961, had destroyed key buildings as they left, "a meaningless gesture". Portuguese was still widely spoken – a newspaper in that tongue persisted – but had largely been superseded by English, though the local Konkani dialect was most common. "The change-over was not difficult," he said, "but we miss many of the luxuries we enjoyed." He was talking about the "levelling" process that had brought Goa in line with the rest of India. Three disjointed Portuguese colonies had been retained as one state: Goa, Daman and Diu. Clearly familiar with hippies, he told me: "Indians are too proud. They judge people by what they have, not what they are." Our conversation did not last long – a cricket test against England was in progress.

I caught a bus to old Goa, dropped off at a statue of Gandhi surrounded by a few rickety stalls. Sitting at one to escape the rain, I was interrupted by a Bombay pair who introduced themselves as "Children of God, here to work among the hippies"! Expectedly, boringly, the man began telling me why he chose Christ, and I was pleased when the rain thickened and they moved on. On the bus back to Panaji, a man asked me if it made me angry to be called a hippie. I laughed at his seriousness but reflected how lately I *had* been annoyed at prejudgements. It was a timely nudge I should live as I wanted, ignoring ill-informed criticism.

India lost the second test, all out in their final innings for 42. Over dinner, I contrived to look suitably miserable.

Sex and revolution

Heading for Calangute beach, hippie territory, was a bitter affair: my bus trundled through furious rain and I was hardly able to see out the window. But occasionally I caught glimpses of rice pickers still at work beneath umbrellas. At Calangute village the ticket collector advised me to remain on board till we had reached the beach: "You will meet friends there," he said knowingly.

He dropped me just off the shoreline and it took but a short walk to find two or three "bar 'n restaurants", all of which had seen better days. I chose one, sitting on an old aluminium chair till a group of freaks appeared and, with their guidance, found accommodation at a thatch hut on the sand within sound of the sea. Then we all adjourned to a stall where we became embroiled in a political debate of anarchist disposition.

Two Englishmen and a Belgian in the group had left Europe just a few weeks earlier; a fourth man, Australian, had been here for months. One of the Englishmen, Eddy, was disturbingly dominant. He had a powerful, gymnasium-frame, and spoke with a deep voice that brooked no interruption. He was fiercely critical of present British governance but modestly esteemed the English who, he said, were "200 years ahead" of other cultures.

The discussion continued at the "Epicure" restaurant where others joined us, including a spaced out American and a mature Goan woman hyped on mandrax. We moved to a beach hut where chillums were produced and, pretty soon, we were all on another plane. Out of the blue, Eddy walked over to the Goan woman, Clara, and had sex with her, in front of everyone. She seemed a willing participant. Perhaps it was the mandrax.

Calangute was the largest of the freak settlements. In season, hundreds would camp about its beaches – I had heard many tales of thefts and orgies. All of which had not entirely gone over well with the normally placid Goans. Now, in fact, was the best time to be here. It rained a great deal but, with few freaks left, a measure of calm was possible.

After breakfast, the Australian (another Alan) and I set out along the seashore to Anjuna, home of the most famous freak settlement of all. At the end of Calangute beach a deep stream forbade crossing. Fortunately a boatman appeared and, for a modest fee, we were able to cross and climb to a half-ruined church at the top of a spur. Waves crashed below over flat slate rocks, reflecting across its stained-glass windows. We descended onto golden sand – the beautiful, compact, framed picture that was Anjuna. We read awhile, passed once by a naked hippie flopping up and down the shoreline. But, otherwise, Anjuna was empty.

Back at Calangute we headed to the Epicure, where everyone from the day before had gathered. The owner, a Ugandan immigrant, had installed a stereo system with a collection that included *Pink Floyd* and the *Beatles*. Everybody was stoned though I remained reasonably straight, side-tracked into a conversation with a middle-aged Englishman who had "given up LSD for meditation". Eddy and friends had moved on so Alan and I now had our house to ourselves.

There was an atmosphere to Calangute Beach. Houses might appear to be of matted twigs, but they had strong, clay walls and ceilings of half-pipe tiles that *almost* kept out the rain. My room even had tile flooring, wooden doors, and a "photograph" of Christ blessing the owner's daughter hanging by the window. We had access to a shared well. Each family maintained its own bucket and rope, to be removed after use. A pine grove by the sea was the toilet, with an army of pigs on hand to fulfil cleaning duties. Each morning, I brandished a large stick. Then I bathed. This was the best part of the day, for the neighbours came down to draw water and there was time to talk, which was always interesting, for most of the locals were from Africa.

"I had to leave Tanzania," one woman lamented. "Under new government laws my children would not be educated. There would be no choice for them." But after nine years in Goa, India too, was becoming intolerable and her current priority was to get passports for her children. These "African" Indians seemed more worldly than their homegrown counterparts, though one man shook his head sadly and muttered, "The whites in Africa were never like this. They didn't take drugs there!" I thought if he went back he might be surprised. Yet most were kind and tolerant. Where I stayed, prayers were chanted before every meal, so I was unsure whether it was the Good Book or the extra income that made hippies so welcome.

At the weekly market I met Don Juan, a local legend known for his perpetual tripping. A Canadian, he had been living in Goa for years, reputedly supported by an aged mother who sent cheques with commendable regularity. He had been claimed by the "Devil's Weed" ("Datura" or "Jimson Weed"), the pod of which, when dried, could be smoked in a chillum. It had a mildly paralytic effect and could prompt hallucinations, though I never experienced the latter. Occasionally, Don Juan said, "Hi". More often he muttered to himself and moved on. Among other characters, was an Irishman named Ted, a softly-spoken man who took his opium orally – one quick gulp to avoid the bitter taste. When stoned, the pupils of his eyes were lost high in his head. He was famous for having fallen off the Bombay to Goa steamer, treading water for an hour before being rescued. He too had been in India "for years".

Alan left for Bombay. With a raging storm outside, I remained in bed with Karel Čapek's *The War with the Newts*. A nearby hut crumpled under the strain of the wind and there was a struggle to retie the wavering poles and reassemble the rocks on patches of sheet iron that served as a roof. Though it was still raining when I awoke, I walked into town for a samosa breakfast and sat for a long time reading. Ted said hello before leaving for Mapsa, Don Juan passed dreaming, and a Frenchman cadged a rupee off me for breakfast. I attempted to swim, but this was the wrong season, for the tides had carved caverns and a vicious undertow made enjoyment impossible.

Clara sought me out. She told me she had become "known" to the freak population and that her name had been unfairly sullied. She left soon after, unsure whether I was "on her side" or agin but, as we parted, I was passed a none-too-subtle scrap of paper with her address pencilled thereon! I thought of her, of my situation and, in the end, moving on was not a hard decision.

Bombay deluge

My train had reached Nira before I realised how heavy the monsoons had become. As rain surged into the carriage, passengers rushed to the windows to shore up ineffective shutters. At Pune (Poona), I could barely make out the industrial outskirts. The rain was now savage and I braced myself for Bombay.

At the Greater Bombay station, we stopped: the tracks ahead were submerged and we were going nowhere. No information was made available, just gossip, and no one seemed to know whether the delay was for 20 minutes or hours. When asked, train workers looked dramatically to the heavens. With no sign of abatement, just half an hour from our destination, passengers spread out and made beds. Outside, a street wallah shouted, "chai!"

Later newspaper articles revealed just how seriously Bombay had been hit. "Rains force city bandh [standstill]" screamed the *Times of India*. "Several hours after the heaviest spell of rainfall in 100 years, which battered and bruised Bombay, the city on Friday night was still reeling under the impact. In a 15-hour continuous downpour starting at 5.30pm on Thursday as much as [20 inches] of rainfall was recorded … the exceptionally heavy rainfall [22.15in] during the 24 hours ended 8.30am broke all previous records. The nearest figure recorded earlier was on September 10, 1930 with 21.58in."

Meanwhile, trains kept rolling into the station from the outer suburbs before halting bitterly when onward passage was impossible. The crowds grew, the confusion grew, and the rumours too. "The sea has cut Bombay off from the mainland!" "Boats are taking passengers along the railway lines!" "Hundreds are dying!" "Bombay is doomed". All this was relayed to me with authority, and not always calmly.

The true situation was better judged from the appearance of taxi drivers who told us they were "prepared to run great risks" to transport passengers – at a price! Their fee to the central Bombay station was nearly five times as great as the "luxury" carriage, first-class express. The rain did ease, transforming into a thick mist, and eventually I could see big international jets roar overhead towards the Santa Cruz airport. To my right I could make out a shanty railway compound, immersed, and just beyond, a small temple. A neighbour told me that at the heart of the shanty block was a brothel, which seemed an anomaly, squeezed as it was against the temple. There would be no business this day.

At about 3pm, we began moving – cautiously – and I forgave Indian Rail. For long stretches, the track was not visible: a lake existed across all yards and, at parts, one could see sea water gushing in through the overflow piping, leading under the roadway from the harbour beyond. People ran after the train, some sprinting to board, and there were many accidents, with screams of laughter when a white shirt or tie were involved.

We stopped. We started. Once, loud shouting indicated a train approaching from Bombay central and, later, there was another. At Currey Road our progress halted. Here hundreds lay asleep across the platform and many passengers exited to seek places to spend the night. Yet an hour or so later we began again, inching through the lakes, passed the flooded cobbles of Bombay suburbia, till eventually we arrived at the large station Dadar, where many more disembarked.

It was raining heavily again, but it was clear we had won our way through. Beggars came on board here with hands outstretched. I escaped to the doorway where I looked out on high-rise apartments on all sides and people waving. I waved back. I had been parked at the Bombay outskirts for two full days. In darkness and with the rain still thundering, it was essential I find accommodation quickly. I had heard terrible stories about the expense of this city. But a helpful local directed me to a back street where I found a rooftop dormitory with a 5rp tariff.

If it sounds too good to be true

I shared the dormitory with a New York Jew, two locals and the hotel receptionist. New Yorker Eddy looked emaciated, his thinness accentuated by a two-day facial hair growth and a ragged lungi that hung loosely about his waist. After being robbed, he had slept for a week in the streets till money came through from home.

One effect of the monsoons had been to cut off water supplies and now even washing was a luxury. But after queuing for a rationed bucket, I rid myself of railway grime. Worried glances from the hotel staff were a constant reproval – I must not waste a drop! It was raining again but no one collected it. Rainwater was considered dirty.

Outside the huge, mosque-like Taj Mahal Hotel the next morning, I was approached by a well-presented Sikh who wanted to exchange dollars for my travellers' cheques to help him set up a business abroad. For some reason cash was less manoeuvrable for him and, wanting all the cheques I could provide, he promised me an exchange of US$115 cash for every US$100 in cheques. After a year and a half of travel, I considered myself worldly-wise, indeed, had rejected a similar approach in Rangoon as an obvious scam. But this was a lovely man…

A Ugandan joined us, saying he had already done the business and was extremely satisfied. After a long discussion that confirmed our friendship, I snapped at the chance of easy profit and the Sikh escorted me back to my hotel in a taxi to prepare for the swap. Fate almost saved me. My travel-soiled stack, barely recognisable for banana stains, was unacceptable to him but he kindly agreed to return after the weekend to escort me to my cheque provider for new bills.

Warning signs? I convinced myself I could not envisage a conman going to such lengths and, anyway, I would not allow my money to leave my sight till the exchange was complete! In a rare break from the rain, Eddy and I adjourned to a park, which quickly filled as the stallholders resumed their trades. One man earned his money from body massages, another cleaned wax out of people's ears, and a youngster cleaned toenails with a piece of broken porcelain. Everyone was friendly, including a naval officer who had just wed a New Yorker in an arranged marriage, had had to resign his commission, and was now about to move to America. He was terrified.

My benefactor arrived early, sauntered into my dormitory where he sat talking to fellow guests while I gathered my finances. We walked to a waiting taxi and drove to the plush Ambassador Hotel, where a plush breakfast – and the Ugandan, who had decided to change more – awaited us. After scraping my plate, I caught another paid-for taxi to my cheque provider where my stained cheques were replaced with crisp, new $100 bills. I left with a shining pocket book tucked inside my passport pouch, to rejoin my benefactor outside the Income Tax building from where a relative was earmarked to bring over the cash.

And, of course, that's where things turned sour. The Sikh asked me – and the Ugandan – to hand him the cheques outside while he sought out his relative. Determined not to lose sight of the transaction, I tried to insist that I walk inside with him. He replied: "You know what we're doing is illegal, don't you? I don't want to go to jail!" So I cast reason to the wind and handed over my notes, and the Ugandan passed over his. My last comment was, "don't fuck me, man". He entered the Tax building, a conglomeration of offices spread over multi-storeys. And, surprise, surprise, that was the last I saw of him.

The Ugandan grew impatient before me, running inside the building to explore its ground floor. Re-emerging, he brokenly told me he was going to the police, which I dissuaded him from till we had our stories straight. I advised him instead to first report his loss to his cheque provider – with a prepared narrative. After a few days, I would do the same. I felt surprisingly calm, especially when my recent exchange was barely credible. Ignoring my advice, shouting "police", the Ugandan abruptly leapt into a cab and disappeared. With hindsight, it was obvious he and the Sikh were in league. For him to have been on the level, required accepting he had profited from his earlier exchange. A conman did not prolong risks by prolonging deals.

That truth having hit home, I decided to immediately report my loss. So within an hour of leaving the cheque provider's office clutching clean new notes, I returned looking shocked, desperately trying to keep control of myself. I had carried my new notes in a back pocket as I made my way through a busy underpass! When I broke through at the other end, they had gone! The cashier looked unbelieving but accepted my urgency and directed me to a desk higher in the hierarchy where I repeated my tale.

The new man, equally suspicious, gave me long forms to fill out, then sent me out in the rain to a notary public where I paid nine rupees to have my affidavit decorated with seals and stamps. My signature guaranteed I had not lost my money in an illegal transaction, and that my description of circumstances was true. An American girl was in a similar predicament. I asked her how she had lost her cheques and she whispered, "You know!" "Hustled?" "Yes." My receipt for the notes had disappeared with the theft, so I had to return to the provider for the cheques' identifying numbers. Running back, I was able to learn what I required minutes before the office closed for the day. I was now soaking wet and faced further immersion in the dash back to my hotel room. A required report to the police could wait till the morning.

Fortunately, the police accepted my story without question, recording it in flowing ink over a page in a thick records' book. It was obvious they intended no investigation. I left the building with a certificate stating that, at such and such a time, I had reported a theft and, this time carrying an umbrella, returned to my provider's.

They were sorry, but they were not empowered to give me money without first telexing America, which would take time – "three weeks, four, who knows?" I pleaded, I cajoled, and was eventually led to the manager. "There are bad points in your case," he said. "People are usually too aware of the dangers to keep cheques in their back pockets and the fact you have just changed to higher denomination notes is not in your favour." He also queried my accommodation. "I don't know this Modern Guest House, but certain hotels are black-listed, known hunting grounds of confidence tricksters. People are engaging in illegal transactions."

After a sideways glance, he suggested I telex a New Zealand lawyer to have a bank reference sent to the American head office. This would speed proceedings, he said. My lawyer being unlisted in the telex directory, I instead sent an urgent telegram. I asked that my money be paid in Delhi, then left, heart pumping. Now I could do nothing but wait. I was fortunate in still having 350rp in my wallet.

At night Eddy and I broke open a packet of grass I had bought in Kerala. We were joined by a house guest, Ragu, tall and urbane and, when the grass was gone, we adjourned to his room for a fruit spirit that took quick effect. Ragu taught me how to shoot an elephant – which didn't seem at all unusual.

I was depressed. It was easy to think of the conman as the criminal. But I too was dishonest. All had arisen out of greed. Throughout the night, beggars wailed from the street below what sounded like: "Ek ye paise dega, Allah dega" – if you give a paise, Allah will give two. From my window, I could see a blind man with his hand extended; a spastic clumped his way to doorways with the aid of a pole; a seemingly healthy woman thrust her baby at people; and a mutilated body towed by a child on a crude cart rang a bell. How badly off was I?

Eddy and I had many deep, on-trend conversations, from the *I Ching* to women's liberation, from Hesse to Thoreau. I often felt slightly the

242

pupil but there was no insult in this, for he never feigned superiority. On our last night, he gave me a present of two LSD dots, recommending I find a "safe place" to enjoy them.

Delhi on 350 rupees

At the Victoria station I struggled my way through a heaving crowd onto the Delhi Express. "You want a seat? Give me three rupees!" I found half a seat where my neighbour, "engineer and ex-service", talked to me of his experiences in the war against the Chinese. "We were taken from sea level to 20,000ft (6000m) and expected to wield a shovel," he said. "Others were expected to fight."

Knowing I would have to fill in time till my money would become available, I risked side trips to the famous Ellora and Ajanta caves. And luck accompanied me. One bus ticket collector neglected to charge me. I also had a nervous encounter with police who ordered me into a "blue" Maria, but it was just for conversation. They gave me a lift part of my way.

At Jhansi, two boys on a bicycle somehow delivered me on their carrier to a "dharamshala", a Hindu institution providing free accommodation for up to three nights. My room smelled of urine and my rope bed sagged in the middle, but the manager, delighted to learn I knew about Vivekananda, the *Mahabharata* and the *Ramayana*, took a shine to me. He looked disapprovingly at a gaggle of listeners. "*He* knows (indicating me); *you* don't (indicating them)!" I was very much in favour. I was saddened, however, at his common interpretation, "Vivekenanda showed the world that Hinduism is the best religion", when he had in fact emphasised all were as one.

Still I was lucky. My remaining money took me to the Khajuraho temples – more famous erotic carvings. To me they seemed flat and unexciting, but perhaps it was my circumstances. And a couple of days later I was in Agra where a full tourist bungalow allowed me to stay for free in a storage hall I shared with overflow furniture.

Despite my lack of money, Agra could not be glossed over. Even the tourist puffery outdid itself:

What shall I say of Agra for my heart is full … stand in the moonlit shadow of the Taj Mahal and you may understand, as Shah Jahan did, how after many ages of wandering the heart will sink to rest at last in the arms of the Beloved.

I was fearful of anti-climax but that was quickly dispelled with the first, famous views of glittering white marble at the end of the long carpet lake and yew tree avenue.

Almost out of money, I caught the late passenger train to Delhi. On a slow train, I could sleep and would be spared the cost of a night's accommodation – an old traveller trick. Setting off for the station, a rickshaw driver asked me why I did not like rickshaws and I told him I had been robbed and was broke. In response, this man in ragged shorts, his shirt half torn from his back, offered me money. Of course I refused, but conditionally accepted a free ride, my condition that I pedal while he sat, a role reversal that attracted much attention.

In the old part of Delhi, forewarned, I walked purposefully to the main bazaar, Pahar Ganj, a long market line that bought and sold everything imaginable and by repute contained the only cheap accommodation available. I found a clean if crowded dormitory offering a much cheaper rate than I expected and, at 7am, showered and went to bed.

Arriving early the next day at the office of my cheques' provider, a rolled-down door reminded me that *New* Delhi did not open till at least till 10.30am. So I sat on a ledge where other travellers joined me. Most of them were recent arrivals, looking confused: "God, this city is expensive, I couldn't get a hotel under 60rp!" Cheaper places, seen for 20, were described as "brothels". I didn't mention I was paying three – that would have been beyond comprehension.

My money had arrived but, frustratingly, no small denomination notes were available. I had better luck at the post office where a letter from home began, "Dear 'Uncle' Alan, It's a girl!" The news was well out-of-date, but I felt terribly homesick, cried a little, and lay for a long time on the post office lawns, reading and re-reading: "7lb 9oz, lots of dark brown hair, and beautiful big blue eyes, and it looked at me!" With the last of his rupees, Uncle Alan celebrated with a gigantic mango lassi.

Later in the day, after smaller notes became available, I spent half an hour signing them, then stumbled out of doors, free and clear, only to be assailed by Children of God proselytisers. I was passed a pamphlet enti-tled, *The Green Paper Pig*, which argued the intangibility of money. "Say 'poof' and it will cease to exist". The pamphlet had a price, however: 50 paise! The author, self-termed prophet Moses David, foretold a coming persecution of the devout. "But our faith will save us and after $3\frac{1}{2}$ years … Christ will come and rescue us."

In my dormitory, mature Indian student Johnson had more grounded economic concerns. "When a girl's parents interview a prospective bridegroom, the first question asked is, 'how much money does he earn', the second, 'how much is his under-the-table income'," he said. "Under-the-table" was destroying India. As he talked, he looked embarrassed.

In a nearby cul-de-sac, I watched on as women in elegant saris dispensed food to the poor, sparking a near riot when hundreds rocked their car. Till the police intervened, beating them viciously with long bamboo lathi (truncheons). I carried on through the central Connaught Place, eying the graffiti: "India has no place for violence. Help us fight Communalism, Linguism, Casteism!" Someone had scratched a fourth demand – "Injustice!" There was no mention of corruption. Or greed.

Early research suggested LSD could aid learning, combat mental illness and aid religious experiences. There ensued exaggerated reports of murders and rapes, and Harvard University dismissed two faculty members, one being Dr Timothy Leary. His response? "LSD is more important than Harvard." In 1965, *Beatles* John, George and Ringo famously tried the drug; a year later, Leary received a 30-year sentence after being caught at the Mexican border with half an ounce of marijuana. 1974: LSD and other hallucinogens are easily available throughout Southeast Asia.

XXIII

In the footsteps of Leary

Manali: I find in my pocket Bombay Eddy's gift of
two dots of LSD, take undue risks, and wax lyrical.

*You ask yourself, 'How do you come back from it? How do you then lead
a normal life after that?' And the answer is, you don't. After that you've
got to get trepanned or you've got to meditate for the rest of your life ...
It was a good trip. It was great but I wanted to go to bed after a while*
(Paul McCartney, cited in B. Miles, *Many Years From Now*).

Putting India behind

A traveller joined me on the walk from Chandigarh station into the city. If I remember him less than affectionately, my disgruntlement was partly – but not only – because his presence cut the effectiveness of my umbrella by half. "The world is nothing," he said suddenly. "People come and people go." The words were repeated with an increasing air of profundity. He was high, of course. "Ah," I sympathised, "so they do."

Chandigarh was a created-from-scratch city, designed by French architect Le Corbusier to be the new capital of East Punjab after the 1947 carve up of India. Lahore, the old capital, had gone to Pakistan.

Indians were very proud of their "perfect" city. Nehru said at the time: "Let this be a new town, symbolic of the freedom of India, unfettered by the traditions of the past." It was a famous if not fabulous city and one constantly heard of its great beauty, its aesthetic qualities. I was keen to see for myself – in silence!

Truth is, Chandigarh was the most un-Indian city one could wish to encounter. I lost my acquaintance with only a modicum of rudeness and began walking the streets: Western block suburb after Western block suburb over what seemed to my tired bones like a vast area, each block self-sufficient for the basic necessities of general store and tea shop. What Le Corbusier may have forgotten, was that this was not Europe. Without typical Indian hustle and bustle the locals seemed lost in strangely broad horizons. Bus stops were sparse and the locals had few cars to cut their community down to size. Perhaps you had to be high. I decided not to stay.

Catching the bus to Kulu was a good decision. As my bus churned through countryside lusher than I had been used to for some time, I was quickly asleep. When I awoke, I was among high hills and I felt the thrill keenly. I inhaled fresh mountain air through the bus window and big city bustle was easily forgotten. There were Tibetans on the road – the familiar black skirts, the plaited hair, the smiles – many seemingly living in carelessly pitched tent camps. Road labourers. We encountered vast shingle works and dam projects, but soon lost these to forest foothills. I watched a young Tibetan girl chasing a man across a paddock, playfully hitting him and laughing, and I thought that India was surely behind me when dignity was of such little importance.

Then abruptly we were in Kulu, a collection of stone chalets at the neck of a valley. It had grown suddenly dark. Finding a small house that took boarders, I lit a pipe. I didn't wake till midday, stumbling outside to bathe icily at the common well, then bought a bus ticket to Manali and the winding fairy tale continued. Manali, smaller than Kulu, began as a bazaar, climbing uphill to where the shops appeared more permanent. It was not hard to find accommodation: a tout led me slightly out of town through pungent fields of marijuana, redolent orchards and vegetable gardens, across a Madam Butterfly bridge to a solitary, stone homestead engulfed by fruit trees.

In the village, there were freaks aplenty, standing in ganja fields rubbing their product or sitting in a popular café discussing dope or clothes. But in my homestead, all was quiet. I bought bread and peanut butter and retired to my room in search of solitude. The next day I woke late. Then, at approximately midday, I took acid.

An acid notebook

I swallowed two purple dots, miniscule tablets the size of a fibreglass pinhead, the type used for tacking dresses. I had planned to take one but when one felt good ... I fell asleep 10 or 12 hours later ...

In those 10 or 12 hours, chasing insights, I took notes. Occasionally the script lapses into pompous jargon. In hindsight, I think I must have been trying to experience my maker – and write the great poem! The following (a selection) was scribbled during the trip, followed by a few summary thoughts – without judgement.

LSD poem: Truly a nice man...

248

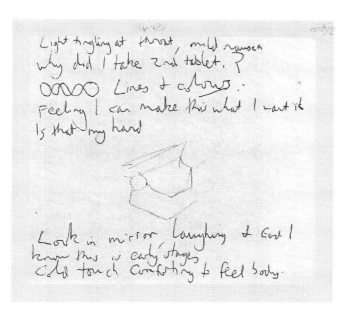

LSD poem:
Light
tingling…

LSD poem:
Concentrate…

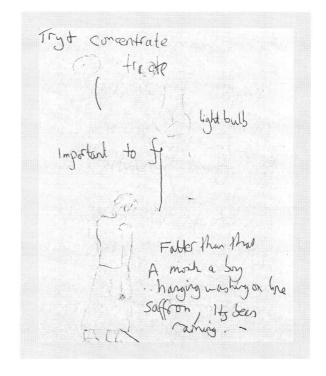

LSD poem:
Why shut out…

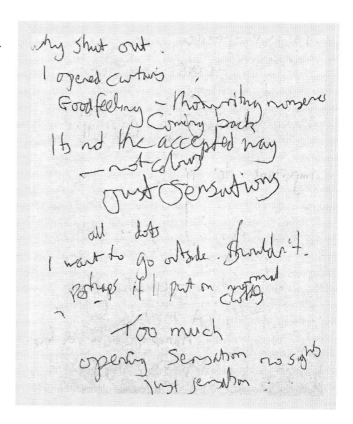

Recovered, I think

Sometime on the Sunday afternoon, still a little stoned, I wrote:

Recovered, I think? Sitting on my bed trying to recreate the day, the night before. Mr Freud, let me begin …

When I finally found the courage to go outside, scenes of heightened beauty awaited me. I became aware of what seemed to be a realisation of the diversity of nature, the minute parts that make up the whole. Everything was strangely alive and vivid to the touch: the sight, the taste, the everything. Then the Bengali arrived – the nice man – and began talking about thefts that had taken place in the area recently. It was too much to handle. But I remember him also showing me the full moon, which I couldn't see. He said it was the weather …

The garden, the veranda about me, became etched in my memory. I tried to recreate, drawing the trees and the washing line, and that

250

absurd cow that wouldn't keep still. Yet I felt I could see everything precisely: the pole, the washing, the clothes, the apple trees, the delicate growth markings about the bark, a tiny purple flower, the boxes with the awning on top, the people coming and going ... Then I wandered down to the garden bridge and the same sorts of feelings were again engendered.

I walked to town – and this was the most beautiful time of all. I was aware of an incredible sensation of colours and detail that would normally be beyond me. I was vaguely aware of faces and I reckoned I could read them! I could see the shopkeeper chattering away, shrewd, the smiling lines about monks' faces, and the wisdom of the old men. I believed I could sense trickery and small mindedness in some, but that didn't matter. I also convinced myself I could recognise a "continuum" between all men, all life. I philosophised about "being" and the absence of evil.

Entering a restaurant, my senses seemed even more heightened. Two Frenchmen sat at my table. They looked absurdly young and comical in their movements. I was aware of their clothes – long skirt, freak trousers, tassels but, more importantly, faces. Their every movement struck me as funny – "pops-a-daisy". I saw cunning in their faces too, but thought that too didn't matter. It was, I reflected, part of the overall scheme of things. "Here too, I felt a strong sense of past. I was totally familiar with my surroundings and the happenings. The meal too – the samosa and curries – the colours – the beans ...

I scribbled what I saw: shops with men working, piled sacks, seeing a late-night scribbler, the light. Colours were perfect. Chinese faces. Red-garbed monks. A child free-wheeling who I tried to save but wasn't needed. A monastery. Prayer flags – the whiteness – the greenness – avenues of grass. And mountains. How vivid that experience. I recalled mist and division, sloping fir pines ...

Attached to all this I felt a sensation of rare beauty and wanted to cry for the exquisiteness. I did cry! Returning to the garden stream, I found I could look clear across the valley and see people climbing tortuous paths. I thought I could discern detail where previously I had seen little but a mass of forest: the little monk in red with "gangly" arms; a kindly Bengali with a pigtail and a smile; restaurant Frenchmen; a boy in pyjamas who gave me an apple – I vividly remembered liquid dripping divinely about my face and knew that he knew, dribbling apple – and a cow who smiled at me; and roosters that had more important business on hand. So much more important!

At some time I became aware of rain, delicate drops slipping about my shoulders. Then I saw people reacting with urgency and, by conscious effort convinced myself that I should be inside. I felt no wet. I felt no cold. Yet I was aware of feeling good about myself and the situation. Inside my room I became very aware of my surroundings and began sketching – the items on my bed, my body as I sat there, looking down. It was important to be naked. I looked at myself in the mirror, touched myself all over – felt intensely childish and hunched myself into infantile poses.

I turned the light off and lay on my bed. My perception was of two centres of vision, as it were: the window, seen through languorously, and the movie-screen white wall across from me. This was either the most meaningful part of the trip, or the silliest. On the wall I could see faces, seemingly beautiful, seemingly stern, but they changed shape and form too often for description.

As foil to this, was the window. Here there was complete continuity. The apple tree outside my window had become glass crystal, shimmering and reflecting in psychedelic colours and patterns. Yes, patterns. For when I looked closely it was more like an elaborate glass ornament – that tinkled! Rain had a beautiful effect on glass crystal. These two centres briefly became my world: the one constant and reassuring, the other flickering back and forth from what appeared to be wisdom to revolting images that tended, more than a little, to induce panic.

At one stage I felt inordinately pleased with myself. As I absorbed what I perceived to be a fact of oneness, I began laughing absurdly. I began to enjoy the show – sitting up suddenly to admire pop art and Jesus Christ then, when things became too serious, flinging myself down on the bed and sighing at the crystal.

Then came disappointment. I shouted at the images, suddenly doubting what I had thought to be supreme experiences. But when I thought of the village, the sensations absorbed, what mockery it would be to demand even more from a god! It was the sideshow I doubted, the closed-in, unnatural surroundings. The vision of nature, the infinite senses – this was surely true. But awareness of this, the sole good?

Downhill to the monastery – square and white – colourful flags limp – a woman looking at me sadly as I pissed on a rock. Which welcomed the meeting. To the right, there was a huge tree, almost ruined, alone, yet impressively dignified in its solitude. And the mists, fragrant about the hill spurs and the people, moving softly about like benign parasites on some vast, greater being. All-seeing, all-knowing. The glimpses kept coming back to me! Yet at the end, lying upon my bed, I was confronted only with imagery. Was it imagery? I only know how I tired of the Solomons, the array of despair.

On reflection, I entered the experience with book knowledge of the drug and with predetermined questions to be considered – sexuality, metaphysics. So how much of what I saw was created by me? Sufficient that the sensory awareness, the tingling beauty, the feelings of love, the tears – at least in some sense – long remained. If nothing else, the degree of perception – the colour, the detail – indicated for me a greater capacity of mind than I could have believed possible.

The next day, trip ostensibly over, I walked into town. Nothing of course was as vivid as the previous day, yet there were occasional flashes of colour, surprise at beauty in the insignificant. I smiled at everyone. I could hear them talking. I felt I could appreciate every minute sound. I drank tea slowly, shyly, looking out on the rain, and took pleasure in the life passing meaningfully outside. I felt like eating a curd but for a long time was too embarrassed to call the man serving. I didn't want to trouble him. Then he divined my attention and served me. Ha!

In a kind of daze, I walked out of town to where the river thrashed its course impatiently along valley cleft. Two wide-fronted mountain lodges were perched above the high banks; below, cobble paving led to a pontoon bridge that crossed over to a road far on the other side. Rice paper prayer flags waved shrilly in the breeze from half a dozen wood poles sticking out of rock piles.

To the north, the river seemed to flow upwards, into rocky crevices and, higher still, a mountain appeared with snow in worried lines. To the south, the waters gushed frantically towards warmer climates. The pine trees, the cypresses, hung everywhere, sprouting out of boulder banks and scaling the very mountaintops. I climbed down to the water with a book but found it difficult to read. Others came down to bathe; I moved closer to the bridge and let the roar of the water overtake me. It was difficult to concentrate.

Possibly because of the lingering LSD I was in especial awe of my surroundings. The tapering, sloping valley surrounds seemed like Canadian high-country wilderness. High above me, a permanent mist swirled about formidable escarpments. Looking closely, I could just make out remote washing lines of Tibetan flags where mortal reach seemed out of the question. It occurred to me in LSD aftermath that as never before I now *wanted* to appreciate the nature about me. I was making an effort to look at hills, and the lines on faces.

During the trip, I had noticed people climbing high paths on the other side of the valley. This day I tried to look across the same view but nothing was visible except forest. This puzzled me for a long time. Then I looked closer to home and saw a mild hill path just a few dozen yards from the garden bridge – was this what I had seen? Clear across the valley? It was possible perceptions of space and time were blurred – I still did not know whether it was morning or afternoon.

None of my drawings were particularly imaginative – which disappointed me. A self-portrait took me a little by surprise, if at least for an appreciation of form I did not know I possessed. I was a horrible drawer! I was delighted too to capture at least partially, the lines of livestock. The rest was but repetitive copying. I drew a longhaired Nixon because precisely that picture appeared on the cover of a book I was reading and the couple on a horse was copied from a postcard. Other scenes were simply drawings of my body, garden scenes or chattels about my room.

Obviously, when I said I *saw* Jesus Christ, I meant I saw images that looked *like* him. There was no spiritual experience. I also saw what resembled a Buddha, a rabbi, and many other pseudo-religious features. Here in the east, religion was a constant exposure. And that was LSD. Was? Is! I was dazed the entire following day. I found it difficult to relate to people, difficult to think. I ate little and, after an evening meal, felt terrible. My belly distended and I was immensely tired. It was not cliché, however, to say that this was the most profound happening to date in my young life. I felt I had been "made aware". This would surely wear off, but the experience was mine.

Not wanting to spoil this, I threw my bag of marijuana away – though later replaced it! But at that moment I decided dulling the body was no abiding pleasure. I would consider taking LSD again, but only if I could be free of care and movement – that is, if others were aware, not disapproving, and provide for me a sympathetic background. I would have liked to have made love under the influence – but, I told myself, it would have to be sincere. How idealistic, this experience had made me!

The book I was reading at the time was Charles A. Reich's *Greening of America*. Reich saw of this age "a new and enduring wholeness and beauty – a renewed relationship of man to himself … a life that is more liberated and more beautiful than any man has known". Fully revitalised a few days later, I decided Reich was an idiot. He saw a "betrayal and loss of the American dream", but nothing of any betrayal or loss among the beautiful counter-culture, a generation that was in no way nobler than the one that preceded it. The beautiful people still stole, still behaved selfishly. And LSD would not change that.

Without taking up cudgels, there seemed to be evidence LSD could be beneficial. But timorous governments had stopped all research and the drug had gone underground. Now – unsupervised – perhaps it was dangerous. My ramblings were not intended as a defence of drugs or drug culture. Over the years since, plenty of evidence emerged that even marijuana could be harmful, especially for the young. At the time of my experiment, I could at least conclude that life was often hard, its meaning elusive, and be loath to judge anyone over-harshly.

The road is closed

Ready to move on to Dharamsala, I visited the bus station only to be told that slips had made 15km of road impassable. How wonderful that turned out to be! Three days after popping two small pills, I lay paralysed on my bed, weary beyond weary. I spoke to no one and no one spoke to me.

I contrived to make positive moves. I visited the market where I saw a donkey limp passed, one of its legs gangrenous and stiff, oozing a thick, white puss. I watched some bright fellow tie a small dog to a large one. When the latter took off, clattering agonisingly into traffic, the small dog screaming, restaurants emptied to laugh. When another dog came too close to a stall, the shopkeeper hammered it with an iron pipe that caused an agonised scream that lasted for at least a minute.

But some monks were now staying in my hotel, walking passed my room each morning to hang their washing, their movements deliberate and slow, and they smiled. It was "namaste" from me and "good morning" from them. They were the other side of Manali, a sincerity and warmth that might in time be appreciated. But after two days, I could only be the hippie. The Indian who had scared me with talk of theft during my acid trip stopped to talk. He was selling hashish but I was not buying. Still, he sat for a while and was good company. Then a Spaniard from the next room visited. He, two days previously, had had all his travellers' cheques and his passport stolen.

There was good news that afternoon. The road had been cleared and the bus company – for baksheesh – was taking reservations for the morrow. Clearer of head, I polished off Reich by the river and saturated myself one last time in the mountains, the prayer flags, the river, the valley... "People come, people go," I remembered. So did places. I reflected on the mountains, the prayer flags and the impressive military signposts: "Project Dee Pak", and "Manali to Leh, Highest Mountain Road in World". How the development of these Himalayan regions had benefited from the Chinese and Pakistani confrontations! Highest mountain road in the world? It might be so. Manali in its socks stood at not quite 2200m and Leh (Ladakh) almost straddled the 3500m mark. Between, towered a series of awesome passes, the largest of which was some 4300m high. And on this road, there were buses plying for hire! Buses, and a great deal of military.

I caught the Dharamsala bus with Jim, a tall Californian. As the road wound timorously in low gear, the extent of the blockages became clear. Road gangs huddled about slippages, throwing boulders, one at a time, over the slope and out of sight. Some worked with shovels, one pushing at the handle, another pulling at a rope tied to the blade. The Pandoh Dam lake area was worst. Here seal had crumbled to non-existence and sheer valley walls of shale hung dangerously about us, the Beas disintegrating some hundred feet below. All now was serpentine, ponderous gear changes and dangerous U-turns, and I was in constant prayer that no opposition traffic would materialise forward. And, fortunately, none did.

Vipassana meditation became popular with Westerners from the early 1970s owing to the teachings of S.N. Goenka, pupil of Burmese master U Ba Khin. When U Ba Khin died in 1971, Goenka began teaching the discipline in India in intensive 10-day retreats. He took his practice on tour, especially around the Buddhist holy centres in the state of Himachal Pradesh. 1974: to thousands of (mainly) Western followers, Goenka eschews proselytising, proclaiming: "The Buddha never taught a sectarian religion; he taught Dhamma – the way to liberation – which is universal".

XXIV

Another sort of high

Dalhousie: A week spent cross-legged; and a new favourite saying.

All things pass; What always changes? Earth ... sky ...
thunder ... mountain ... water ... wind ... fire ... lake ...
These change; And if these do not last; Do man's visions last?
Do man's illusions? During the session; Take things as they
come; All things pass (Timothy Leary, *Psychedelic Prayers*).

Day One

Goenka's Vipassana meditation course in Dalhousie came with a warning: once underway, there could be no escape to the outside world. The course's 10 days were to be a "total experience". And no distractions meant no distractions!

The double-storeyed Grand View Hotel seemed magnificently stately, high on hillside above an eternally flowing valley. Monkeys clattered across our rooftop while loose-lipped crows soared aimlessly overhead. Deafening crickets signalled first light in the predawn hours of the meditation, and at dusk, the evening lectures. At times the chants of monks echoed from a monastery somewhere downhill. For the last time in 10 days, I escaped outside to ice cream and papers. Gerald Ford the new US president!

By 7pm all meditators were back in the hotel, nervously scanning the timetable: 4.00am, wake-up; 4.30am to 6.30am, meditation by beds; 6.30am to 8.00am, breakfast; 8.00am to 9.00am, group meditation; 9.00am to 11.00am, meditation by beds; 11.00am to 1.00pm, lunch; 1.00pm to 2.30pm, meditation by beds; 2.30pm to 3.30pm, group meditation; 3.30pm to 5.00pm, meditation by beds; 5.00pm to 6.00pm, tea; 6.00pm to 9.00pm, group meditation and discourse; 9pm, milk and fruit; 10pm, lights out and rest. Yoi!

Posters exhorted work, discipline, and encouraged, "Be Happy!" They also, however, prohibited "dancing, singing, small talk and all intoxicants" and warned against "killing, stealing, sexual misconduct and lying". These contributed to "loss of mindfulness" and mindfulness was "one thing we really work for".

Inside the meditation hall the lights were turned off and there was immediate silence. Towards the back, I had a smudged view of a plump, greying figure, lotus-seated on a white couch. To his right sat a weary-looking woman in a sari; to his left, a stout Westerner in grey flannels and a green cardigan. The woman was Goenka's wife, the man an American, John Coleman, intended soon to be instructing courses in the West.

The greying figure at front – Goenka – began a slow intonation that drifted into a chant:

> *Rag-a dwesh-a or moh-a dur-a ho; Jagey shil-a samadhi gyan-a; Jana mana key dukhadey mit-a jayey; Phir sey jag-a uthey muskan-a;Phir-a sey jagey dharma-a jagat-a me; Phir sey hovey jan-a kalyan-a* (may clinging, aversions, delusions, disappear; may morality, awareness, wisdom, reappear; may suffering disappear; may the smiles on faces reappear; may the dharma arise in the world again; may the people attain welfare again).

We repeated the vows of the "Triple Gem" – promises to take refuge in the Buddha, the Dharma (the natural law) and the Sangha (the teachers). We were to learn "Anapana" meditation, which required concentration on the breath, from the upper lip, the flow, to the sensation felt on the upper area of the nostrils. Hopeless cross-legged, I shuffled every five minutes and there was no lack of movement from the rest of the hall. It was a relief when, at 9pm, we were dismissed to hot milk and fresh fruit while Goenkaji and Coleman took questions.

I introduced myself to my roommates. As well as Californian Jim, there was a smiling Frenchman called Marcel, a head-shaven Australian, Jeff, and a talkative American, Alfred. Except for Alfred, who fell ill and quit, these remained my companions throughout the 10 days. And I was lucky, for – mostly – they remained thoughtful and I was able to give to the course – mostly – the attention it warranted.

Day Two

4am! I tried. I struggled with my legs, cross-seated with no discipline but a determination to remain at my post and frequent half-glances at my neighbours who somehow always seemed to be alert at precisely that moment! A routine evolved: breakfasts of wheaten porridge and curd, lunches of rice, chapatti and curries, and teas, and suppers of fresh apples, bananas and pears. And, in between, long hours of excruciating meditation.

Goenka began each session with a hypnotic, singsong chant, before introducing the exercises to be engaged in. The meditation was to comprise three stages: "Shila", "Samadhi" and "Panya". We began with Shila (morality), accepting five precepts necessary for progress: no killing, stealing, lying, sexual misconduct or intoxicants. We got it!

Intermittently came the urging: "Concentrate on the nostrils, breathe normally, one nostril then the other". It was still hard for me to sit, but there was less noise from the group and I was anxious to keep up. I felt the promised sensations in the nostrils, but constant attention seemed impossible, my mind wandering haplessly. So the day went: periods in the hall, periods in my room, and I thought, frequently, how useless the practice! At 10pm, after a tortuous "hour of concentration", Goenka began what was to become a regular discourse, a nightly lecture that would always salvage my enthusiasm.

The object of our meditation, he said, was to purify our minds. The method involved concentrating on our breathing, and the reason for this was simple. To purify required utmost concentration, which in turn required the chaining of the mind to the present. Our breath being always present, our concentration on it was always in the "here and the now". Our breath reflected our mental state: it was hard and fast when we were angry, slow and smooth when we were happy. But we could also exercise control over it.

My legs screaming their approval, the evening closed with a comforting chant that exalted the Dharma and wished us peace. We learned to cry back: "Sadhu, Sadhu, Sadhu" – peace be upon Goenka too!

Day Three

I found myself enduring longer. Slightly longer. I was concentrating better too. Slightly better. But I was unsure about the instruction, for I found it difficult to equate breathing with purification, and pain in my legs was hardly conducive to peace of mind. As the evening lecture unfolded, I took refuge against a mid-hall pillar that provided admirable support for unscheduled rests.

We were on a path for liberation, said Goenka, beginning the first of many parables that he introduced with the chant, "story, story". "A man who commuted between two towns asked the Buddha, 'why are only some liberated? Can you not help all'? Replied the Buddha: "Do you help people who seek directions to your neighbouring city?" "Of course." "Well, if they follow your directions exactly, they will find their way. But the *work* remains theirs."

Story! A simple woman asked, without a great mind, how could she achieve liberation? "Abstain from all wrongful actions – any action that does harm," the Buddha told her. "Perform all rightful actions – any action that does good". The Buddha's "Noble Eightfold Path" could guide one to liberation, but equally to just live good lives. Its eight elements could be understood in categories: "Right view" and "right resolve", were the basis of panya (wisdom or insight); "right speech", "right conduct" and "right livelihood" came under shila (morality); and "right effort", "right mindfulness" and "right concentration" comprised samadhi (concentration), our starting meditation technique.

These paths, Goenka said, simply provided a way of good: if we hurt someone, a hell would be created in us. What hatred must someone have to perpetrate a murder, for instance! Heavens and hells were always within the person, never external.

Day Four

A laxness crept in. Jim still strove hard but Marcel returned to his bed, Jeff left the hall early, and Alfred was in the breakfast queue a good 15 minutes before time. Despite working hard, my concentration was not good and my legs gave me constant pain, requiring continual rests. It was only the prospect of the nightly lecture that kept me to task.

Shila (morality) and Samadhi (concentration), were beneficial to our practice, Goenka began, but neither contained an ultimate truth. Tomorrow we would begin practising "Panya", insight, but this was but a path towards the liberation sought. He spoke cleverly, concisely and with humour. His eyes danced and his shoulders shook, a handsome picture in a patterned green sarong and white tennis shoes. He gave examples of the flaws in our "insights": we admire a woman's hair, "how beautiful!" A hair falls in our food. "Beautiful? Then eat it!" "Peel off your skin! How much of us is beautiful? Turn us inside out and see!"

He spoke about illusoriness, the impermanence of all things. Our atomic nature was such that every minute portion of our body was constantly vanishing and being replaced. The only truth was of change and impermanence, which we would experience by exploring our bodies. A light bulb appeared to give off a single, static aura. But the reality was a continual flow of electricity and a quite different light every moment. It was the same with our bodies.

We needed to see things *as they were*. Learning to deal always with reality, a man could have love for a woman even when she was old and wrinkled. By understanding the *true* nature of things, we would see beyond the surface of the skin. Among three types of wisdom – learned, deduced by intellect, and experienced – it was the last that was most relevant in our search for the truth. Panya would give us a foothold on the path towards truth.

Day Five

Day five was "Vipassana day". "Today you will learn Panya, the highest stage towards liberation," Goenka intoned. "Now shift your attention … to the top of your head!" My awareness sprang as instructed and I had no trouble concentrating. "Move your awareness to the back of your head, the front, now feel all over … do not analyse or attempt to describe, just observe the sensation as it actually is at that precise moment … look at reality."

We swung our awareness about our bodies, aware of minute tinglings in a methodical sweep from the eyes, the ears, the lips, to the feet and the toes. The stage had been well set. People had been talking and thinking Vipassana since the course began. Goenka had asked for two hours of "utmost determination" and, indeed, it seemed easier than before to focus attention on such diverse areas. Yet it was exhausting too, and it was easy to forget his advice to neither try too hard, nor too little.

The evening discourse dwelt on Dharma, the underlying flux governing all things. Story! "A man mourning the death of his father asked the Buddha to ensure his ascension. The Buddha had him place two bowls in a lake, one filled with stones, the other with ghee. He then had the man break the bowls and, unsurprisingly, the stones sank, the ghee rose. "Now," said the Buddha, "find a priest to make the stones rise and the ghee sink," which brought scorn from the man. "Impossible! Stones sink, ghee floats! It is the nature of things." Exactly!

Each tingle, each throb felt, represented the reality of impermanence, Goenka said. This too was the nature of things. The seed determined the fruit, the cause led to the effect, which led to the cause, which led to the effect. "But if the seed of a bitter fruit is planted, no amount of good nourishment can turn it sweet. It is the planting within us that is important." We could observe impermanence in our practice: "Annicha, Annicha" ("Change, Change", everything passes). It was perhaps more appropriate we be called human *becomings* than beings, he concluded, for we were never the same from one moment to the next.

Goenka described four types of awareness: consciousness, perception, feeling and reaction. The sum total of these, he termed "Sankaras". A bad Sankara resulting from a bad seed necessarily led to Hell within. It was not just evil action that caused this Hell, he said, but the rotten process hitherto.

At death our "karma" – past actions and intentions – gave the deciding "push" of our life force towards its next body. The nature of its influence on that next body depended on our Sankaras. We did not have to believe this. What was important was that we could get benefits in *this* life. Bad Sankaras generated inner Hell, good Sankaras, inner Heaven. Bed!

Day Six

I had a good morning, changing my posture only once in the first hour. Later, Goenka invited people to report their progress and we all listened carefully, anxious to compare others' experiences with our own. Goenka warned against this. "Doing this you are dealing with illusion and your mind has wandered from the relevant – that which is occurring in the here and the now."

I quickly warmed to Goenka. His eyes were warm and intelligent, and he was inclined to laugh with his whole body as he uttered his assurances, shoulders shaking, head bobbing. I learned to anticipate his answers. A meditator might go into great detail describing a sensation and the rejoinder would lightly admonish for wasting time in analysis. Better we experience, deal with reality.

The day deteriorated, slackness appearing everywhere, and a noticeable increase in chatter during break. Jim and I broke silence over lunch to air our doubts. We could accept that external happiness could be achieved by removing the cause of our cravings. But we could not understand how maintaining bodily disinterest could resolve life's larger problems.

Goenka came through with his nightly discourse, in which he introduced Buddha's "four noble truths": the truth of suffering, the truth of the cause of suffering, the truth of the end of suffering, and the truth of the path that leads to the end of suffering.

How beautiful everything was to the Buddha, how graceful the birds, for instance, yet they still fought incessantly over a twig or a worm! Suffering! Man spent his life seeking material possessions, envying his neighbour, buying a house, then a larger one, yet was never really happy. Suffering! The old man dying in pain begged death to claim him but when death was pronounced imminent, the plea shifted. "Please, just a few more days." He had this to do and that to do, grandchildren to see one more time. Suffering! Craving!

Story! Upon the death of his wife, a man could not get beyond his grief. "Would you have mourned her before you knew her?" asked the Buddha. "Thousands die in this city daily. Did you mourn those deaths?" Of course not! The man was not mourning his wife but, rather, his loss. "All our lives comprise desires or aversions," Goenka said. "We desire something pleasant, cling to it, or desire to be rid of something bad, repel it. Yet suffering – Dukka – is Dharma! We cry being born, *desiring* oxygen, and from then onwards our bodies are changing, every second, adapting, flexing, becoming. Dukka is Dharma. Suffering is Dharma. Disease is Dharma. Dying is Dharma. We are born, we grow, we decay, and we die. Annicha."

If we could be rid of the root cause of suffering, the Buddha had realised, we could be happy. This root cause was our clingings and desires. Thus we must look at everything objectively, examining only reality, *as things were*. Desires and aversions could only be associated with the past or the future, hence the rationale for learning to concentrate on the present.

I was not entirely satisfied, but the final hour's meditation went well. On impulse, I later returned to the meditation hall where Goenka, still holding court, had just been asked if god existed? "All conjecture about whether there is a god is pointless," he said. "If a man shoots you with an arrow and someone offers to pull it out to save you, would you reply, 'Wait! Before you pull it out, kindly explain to me what it is made of?' It is necessary to deal first with the sufferings." It seemed the perfect answer.

Day Seven

Though this day was to be conducted in "Noble Silence", a general relaxation was again apparent, especially downstairs where breaks became the occasion of courtyard sunbathing. Upstairs a more sombre aura remained and I found it possible to remain objective.

The evening lecture exhorted work. It did not matter whether we believed in the transmigration of a life force, or not. We were not working to accrue benefits for a next life, but dealing with the reality that good results would arise in this one. By keeping indifferent, by observing, not clinging to or showing aversion to, we could prevent the arising of new Sankaras. And as our old Sankaras reached the surface of consciousness, they would gradually be peeled away.

Doubts were the appropriate subject of the nightly lecture. We were not learning a creed or a religion but it was important we understand what we were doing, Goenka said. "I apologise for not having long, matted hair, for not being able to divine your thoughts and for not walking on water. You must do the work yourselves. There will be no miracles."

Emphasising our atomic nature, he described eight constituents within us: feelings of heaviness or lightness (earth); heat and cold (fire); clinging and binding (water); and movement and throbbing (air). The skill was to experience each sensation dispassionately, to examine the reality of that particular moment.

In the final hour, he suggested we not only move our perceptions from body part to body part in methodical sweeping, but to try and experience our multitude of divergent sensations at once. This hour was electric. My mind was alive, my body dancing uncontrollably, jabs and flushes of heat. Impermanence! Change!

Day Eight

At the 4am bell, Jim and I made use of the half hour interval to walk about the courtyard. Abruptly, a satellite appeared, moving across the clear sky in the footsteps of the fading Orion. Good omen? I became zealous in my early morning meditation, putting in hours of hard work. But by mid-morning, I had faded badly. Doubts! Jim too, usually the most stoic of our party, lay down and rested.

Our concerns related to the link between meditation and life. How did a process that seemed purely physical (no thoughts allowed during meditation), purify the mind? Granted, the idea was to eliminate the cause of our physical suffering, desires and aversions, which paralleled the aim of eliminating the cause of all our suffering. But how was the meditation a path towards the latter?

Goenka was a mind reader. There was, he said, a clear connection between mind and matter. Breathing, for instance, was directly linked to our state of calm at a particular moment. Hard breathing, for example, reflected anger. The habit we were developing of looking at, of being aware of, our bodily sensations, would be forever beneficial when, in future, stress arose. If we became angry, we would recognise the symptoms and immediately become disinterested observers.

Just as there were enemies to our progress (clinging, drowsiness), there were also friends. Devotion and faith were important – as long as these were tempered with understanding. Blind faith was worthless. There was no point in praying or prostrating ourselves, then returning home and hating our brother, Goenka said. It was fine to worship Rama, for he had wonderful qualities – as did Krishna, Nanak and Christ. But our aim should be to incorporate their qualities within us. If we did not do so, then our worship was meaningless.

Story! "Hearing people were gaining peace of mind from the Buddha, a musician joined his throng. The Buddha had him walk in a circle meditating then left him to it. A few days later he returned to find the man still walking furiously, his feet bleeding. He had not stopped! The Buddha asked him about his sitar playing: if he tightened the strings too much, could he play? If he allowed the strings to become too loose, could he play? Panya!

After this last hour my mind felt clear, my awareness of body sensations, strong. I felt pain stabs, clinging feelings, warmth, cold, heaviness, lightness – I felt it all! I dimly heard the bell and the hall empty. My breathing became regular and smooth, but short and decisive. I must have sat cross-legged for an hour before becoming vaguely aware of Goenka holding his informal audience.

I could hear him with crystalline clarity. He was talking of marriage. "A man cannot possess a woman," he said. "For that would be indicative of the *I* and the *my*. "Sexual licence is evil, even in the context of the marriage. Harmony should be the rule. In traditional Burma the man and the woman often just move in together. The marriage ceremony *in itself* is meaningless." Unnoticed at the back, I fell on my side. In a trance, my mind seemed to be the only organ functioning. It seemed hours, but possibly only minutes later, I forced myself to move and stumbled down empty corridors to my room.

Day Nine

The morning session was sensational. From wake-up to bell I remained motionless. I had a smooth, clean feeling all over and found it unnecessary to progress through the chain to Vipassana. I was straight there. I continued meditating in the hall where Goenka and Coleman were meditating, through to the evening lecture without a glimmer of physical resistance.

"If a fire meets with a pile of dry grass, where does the fault for its subsequent spread lie," Goenka asked. "With the fire or the foliage? Within the family we hold up rules of conduct for our child. When these rules are broken, we bewail the wickedness of the child. Yet the responsibility, the suffering, the Hell we experience is due to us. One hundred per cent!

"We may dislike a man. If the basis of that dislike lies with our enemy, it would be reasonable to expect he would generate a similar reaction in everybody; that is, if it is his projections causing my hatred. But of course he doesn't. The fault is with us. We see everything through coloured spectacles. I have a viewpoint and I refuse to understand conflicting viewpoints and perspectives. Reality! Understand things as they are!"

There were various ways of reacting to pain, Goenka said: we could suppress it, ignore it, or observe it dispassionately. By suppressing the pain, we were in fact only delaying the problem, for the negativities remained. Ignoring it, we were merely slipping to illusion.

We were introduced to one more aspect of meditation, "Mettapana" or "Love Consciousness". The idea was, while relaxed in Vipassana, to generate love, compassion and "sympathetic joy" to all beings. Thus, after a long Vipassana session we could spend a few minutes engendering good feelings about others. For me this was stretching things, but it made me feel good. In the final hour, I again fell in a trance. Again, the hall emptied and I was alone. Mildly apprehensive at the prospect of spending a night by myself in the hall, I rolled onto my side and stumbled back to my room. Jim later told me he had considered putting a bag over my head to prevent hyperventilation.

Day Ten

This second trance shook me. I ignored the starting bell and slept through till breakfast but a good morning followed and I glided effortlessly through the hours, instantly clear of irritations. My heart slowed to a point where it appeared to sway, as if out of tune with a pendulum. Afterwards, I sought out Goenka who reassured me with an allusion to a tree being uprooted. There was bound to be turmoil in its wake, but this was temporary and a good thing. In future I should lie where I was. "No harm will come to you. There are only friends here," he said.

At night we had the final of our evening lectures. Story! "After the Buddha became enlightened, the first to come across him were two Burmese merchants who, overwhelmed by his radiance, begged strands from his hair as a keepsake. These were subsequently stored at the top of the Shwe Dagon temple in Rangoon, then a small temple perhaps 20ft high. "Today this temple has been raised by devotion [pilgrims attaching gold leaf] to over 350ft," Goenka said. "But these merchants wasted their opportunity. Wiser men would have begged knowledge of the Buddha's way."

At his last session, Goenka was asked whether plants had consciousness. "Yes." How then could we eat plants? "We must not go to extremes! Use Panya!" Could a plant become enlightened, the questioner persisted? "No! Panya!" When someone opined that, back home, it would be impossible to find a job where one could live up to the ideals of Vipassana, Goenka again advised we temper our actions with Panya. We should do our best and give guidance to others by our example. Could force ever be legitimately used? "Yes! Love force!"

Goenka also repeated a prediction that the Vipassana method would become an open secret 25 centuries after its conception and spread to the West. Those 25 centuries had just elapsed. His final words were: "Be happy!" And most of us were.

Day Eleven

Settling down for a last meditation, my pain returned! But I had stamina now and achieved a certain state of calm, the unravelling of tensions occurring quickly. We practised mettapana, projecting our love towards all beings with the familiar chant: "May all beings be happy; may all beings be peaceful; may all beings be free from hatred; may all beings be liberated …" It was traditional for grateful pupils to give their Guru a parting present. Goenka was delighted when someone turned in his hashish and his chillum. From the rest of us he asked only that we continue our practice and occasionally send our love – via mettapana – in his direction. It was not necessary to remember him personally for, after all, he was included in the words, "May all beings ..."

He had one final piece of advice. "Do not see life in terms of a Hare Krishna trip," he said, "nor a drug trip, nor a Taj Mahal trip, or even a Goenka trip. Your purpose in life is not to collect experiences. Vipassana offers you a way. No more. Be happy!" He recommended we should meditate one hour each morning, one hour each night, as well as about five minutes before bed. It would be "helpful" to meet up with another meditator for at least one hour every week.

No small concession

Back in the outside world, Jim and I agreed that much that Goenka taught was valid. It was possible to be sceptical about transmigration or enlightenment but these beliefs were not essential. It was easy to accept that, though not responsible for others' behaviour, I was responsible for the suffering such behaviour induced in me. This was no small concession.

And once I had accepted a relationship between the harmony of the body and the harmony of the mind, I had gone a long way towards putting an effective case for Vipassana meditation. Comparison with Freud seemed to support the benefits of exposing old negativities into the range of our conscious minds, and it did not seem far-fetched to see harm in their stockpiling by constant wrong action. The aspiration of the meditation, to purify the mind, was hard to criticise. It might fail, but no harm could arise from a discipline aimed at achieving good. If we could learn to view all tribulations in life with equanimity, we would surely be better for the experience.

An immediate outcome was to encourage me to meditate. It might also have converted me to Buddhism were it not for its implicit disparagement of creed. I could, however, content myself with accepting many of its precepts, in particular, the pivotal Middle Way. Moderation seemed to be the rationalisation I was seeking. There would be difficulties. If I were devout, I should give up liquor and weed and, probably, meat. None of this would be hard in Asia. But it might be infinitely more difficult back home. Goenka said we were changed people. I would wait and see.

Upset at India's troop build-up in disputed areas and its asylum for the Dalai Lama, China in 1962 invaded Ladakh, before withdrawing to its preferred line of "actual control". It also built roads from Tibet towards Pakistan. In conflict with Pakistan over Jammu and Kashmir, India built a Srinagar-Leh highway, slashing troop travel time to the disputed areas. In 1965 and 1971, India clashed with Pakistan in Ladakh. 1974: India maintains a big military presence in the north; Pakistan still claims Kashmir on the basis of its mainly Muslim population; and India begins nuclear testing.

XXV

Disputed territories

Kashmir, Ladakh and Amritsar: a houseboat startled by Barry Crump; a mountain pilgrimage to an icy lingam; Ladakh opens up for the first time since 1947; and I farewell India at the Golden Temple.

The Chinese say that they've always enjoyed dominion over Tibet, and that Tibet has enjoyed similar dominion over Ladakh … But the Indians say that between 1834 and 1841 Maharaja Gulab Singh, of Jammu, conquered Ladakh and annexed it to his state. But the Chinese say that Gulab Singh's advance in Ladakh was checked by their forces … But the Indians say … (Ved Mehta, *Portrait of India*).

In the footsteps of Crump

"From New Zealand? Ah, Barry Crump!" Having just arrived at the Srinagar bus station, the words were startling. The *A Good Keen Man* author, reportedly on a spiritual journey for his Baha'i faith, had arrived on an old Indian motorcycle, spellbinding the houseboat fraternity, smoking acres of hash and telling stories.

Jim and I followed houseboat owner Ramon to his triad of boats on Dal Lake: *Cherry Stone*, *Young Cherry Stone* and *New Australia*. The first was "luxury", the last, "semi-luxury", the one in the middle, humbly out of sight from the road, was our sort of economical. It was still occupied so we had to spend our first night on the *New Australia*. We did not complain!

Under a cloudless sky, we basked as the local shekara (gondoliers) plied for hire at our front door. We came to an agreement with one. For a rupee a day he would ferry us back and forth to land as often as we required it. We were moored in a section of the lake designated "canal", a confusing approach of waterweed overflowing with houseboats. Our views were of triangled rooves, latticed verandas, rooftop balconies, fortresses and palaces – but also of hovels, old amid the new. The names of the boats came straight off the Mississippi: *Paris, Hong Kong, Suffering Moses*, many with suffixes like *Palace* and *Queen*.

An English couple just returned from Ladakh joined us. The region had been closed since 1947 and their news that the route had just opened was thrilling. Few Europeans had seen Ladakh, at least in recent years. We had to go there! But when we attempted to book, we found the route was sold out for the next fortnight. Too impatient to wait, we bought tickets for two days hence from Sonamarg, a high glacier town part way down the line; we had discovered another bus company that provided regular rides from Srinagar to Sonamarg.

Meantime, we relaxed. We passed time over chai with a Muslim whose wonderful command of English included, "Bloody India" and, "Bloody Abdullah", the latter a reference to Sheikh Mohammed Abdullah (Sher-e-Kashmir, the "Lion of Kashmir"), a leading advocate for Kashmiri self-rule. Our man wanted all Kashmir to be part of Pakistan. Sheikh Abdullah was beneath contempt. And we slept. Sole disturbances came from hawkers, their canoes inching under our awnings and bombarding us with their products. An apple salesman pushed a container of mandrax at me. Two weeks earlier, I might have bought. Goenka!

A heavenly lingam

Sonamarg had been taken over by the army. A handful of chai stands hugged the roadway while, opposite, were a few tents as well as the more permanent stone of a Dak bungalow where we hoped to gain accommodation.

The bungalow sat against a mountain of rock, behind which lay China; further east, lay Pakistan or, more accurately, Pakistan-occupied Kashmir, and their closeness added to an atmosphere of tension. Crows cawed incessantly, fast-moving armoured cars patrolled the highway and, at odd intervals, bands of ragged horsemen galloped animatedly in an unreal perspective. We were at some 2500m but snow was only to be seen in patches upon distant peaks.

We came to an agreement with the bungalow manager. We could sleep on the floor for a reduced price, but were only welcome during sleeping hours. To fill in time we hired horses then tethered them when our walk was blocked first by rock fall, then a charge across our bows from about 100 horsemen, resplendent in dark brown woollen jackets and loosely flung turbans. Cries of "salaam" penetrated the dust screen created and the earth shook before they disappeared and we were left wondering if we had been dreaming.

The next day was wet and cold. An Australian couple arrived on a motorbike, then a European pair in a house truck, and an army helicopter landed outside our door. Each brought pandemonium, attracting welcoming committees from bungalow staff to goatherders – and their herds. When the helicopter arrived, even my waiter – at that moment fetching my chai – jumped over the fence and disappeared.

With a couple of days to wait till our onward bus, we settled outside with our books. But when somebody mentioned it was possible to reach Amarnath from here, we leapt to the road with our thumbs outstretched. Amarnath was a legendary alpine cave in which a "miraculous" lingam of ice formed each year. The "miracle" was the annual object of one of Hinduism's more difficult pilgrimages.

At the start of this month, some 40,000 devotees had embarked from Pahalgam – a different valley approach – on a four-day horse trek to reach their high destination on the month's first full moon. Now we were told the cave was also reachable from the Sonamarg side, indeed, with a trek of but a single day. We were warned that the walk from this side was a hard one – hence the pilgrim preference for Pahalgam. We were also told that within a couple of weeks the route would be closed, whether by army or snowfall. Thumbs outstretched!

The soldiers who stopped for us were deep-tanned men at the peak of their fitness. They carried us just a few kilometres, turning into a hilltop encampment signposted, "High Altitude Warfare School", leaving us to walk the high road above the Sindh Valley, ignorant of direction. Fortunately, a military policeman joined us, and a truck soon stopped for us. We were dropped off, however, on a barren spur with no sign of Baltal, the trek starting point. The provost pointed down. Far below, the valley floor was smothered in khaki tents. "That is Baltal."

It was already dark. We slithered to the bottom down a shingle slide where a goatherd rescued us, leading us to a compound with a sleeping tent annex, and introduced ourselves to a smattering of pilgrims. A "houseboat owner and guide" leading a group from New Delhi already had a fire lit and matting was spread for us inside the tent. Herdsmen squatting around the compound fire shared their water pipe of sweetened tobacco. Beside, a young woman cuddled her baby, naked but for a necklace of leather pouches containing auspicious messages for his life ahead. Meanwhile, an elderly woman dictated the cooking, her face wrinkled and strangely jaundiced. We dined on rice and chillied potato.

Our hike began behind an ill-assorted pilgrim queue dressed in suits and saris, with ears all pleasantly warm under fur caps from New Delhi emporiums. The ladies were eased onto docile ponies – no improprieties – while the men stationed themselves nobly to fore. They straightened their ties, the guide gave a wave, and we all began walking. Jim and I were soon far in the lead and we liked it that way, our exertions in our own time, our weak moments private. It was a stiff climb, with spirals and cutbacks on a mountain of shale, and Jim weakened. By the time we reached a refreshing glade of bluebells and daises, he was white and dizzy. A corner, and we had our first breathtaking view of the mountains – three oblong peaks leaning aslant as a fan, while at front cascaded a bucket slide of thick, glorious snow.

Reaching a high pass soon after, we savoured a signpost indicating 3km more: left to Amarnath, right to Pahalgam and in sudden, severe cold, began a final climb over shingle, glacier and scrub. We could now see the cave, a brown rectangle in a precipice of stark, pink rock. All about us were high escarpments and many pilgrims could be seen ahead on the narrow gravel path, a winding line to an aperture at valley's end. A helicopter landed just beyond us, leaving behind a platoon of soldiers who had a camp here.

The cave entrance was almost obscured by pilgrim mementos. In deathly cold, I removed my shoes, entering slowly into a plain cell where iron railings enclosed the Siva lingam, now ingloriously revealed as a melting blob. A sadhu made intonations then, beckoning me inside, gave me holy water to drink, oil for my hair, and smeared red dye upon the centre of my forehead. While Jim took his turn, I waited outside, jumping to resist the cold then, for the first time for me in India, it began to snow. A bell rang and the valley echoed. An exiting Calcutta pilgrim, radiant, uttered, "how magnificent"! He had seen what I had not.

Wooden chapatti we had saved from our breakfast sufficed for our lunch. But we did not hesitate long. It was much too cold and we set off, jolting downhill. It was overcast now, threatening rain, but the soft snow slopes and the hard rock protrusions provided rare beauty as they merged and changed shape under accumulating storm shroud. We marked our progress by the growing thunder of the river below before turning into familiar valley plain where we collapsed exhausted in the now unoccupied camp. We had walked 30km.

We found a canteen in the army camp – tea – then reluctantly tackled the harsh climb to the roadway where we sat breathlessly awaiting a ride. Baltal, at more than 2700m, had led us to a cave climax at higher than 3600m and we were exhausted. A high-ranking landrover stopped for us, squeezed us among baggage, and left us in darkness right at the door of the Sonamarg Dak bungalow.

Forbidden territory

Ladakh had been closed to tourists since India's partition, its capital, Leh, a forbidden city. Then, on July 15, 1974, someone in authority decided to open the area for tourism and foreign passengers were at last admitted on the Srinagar-Leh bus run. This was despite the fact that the troops of two unfriendly nations lay within easy trekking distance of each other: Pakistan-occupied Kashmir was to the northeast, Chinese-occupied Kashmir, to the northwest.

The latter's army was a mere 20km beyond the hill range behind Leh. In his book *Portrait of India*, Ved Mehta paints a tortuous existence for the Indian soldiers. Long service there reportedly caused hair to grow grey, hearts to swell, memories to fail, and sexual impotency. Wives were not allowed to accompany their men and there was little likelihood of Tibetan women becoming overly friendly with foreigner Indians!

A tiny American woman named Annie greeted us as we boarded the Leh bus. "Hello. Do you know where I can get some water? I've peed on my skirt." Seated over a rear wheel hub, the first few kilometres were of considerable discomfort. On a climb along a series of cutbacks that took us higher and higher up the Zojila Pass, the only vehicles to be seen were military, though they were many. Villages were few and far between and all had a strong military presence.

As we entered Dras at the end of a long valley, I felt the cold intensely, futilely hunching my arms as our vehicle halted at a thin line of bazaar. Dras was reputedly the second coldest town in the world, the coldest outside Russia. Temperatures as low as minus 60 degrees Celsius had been recorded here, though this day was a summery plus 3. We stopped for the night at Kargil, a predominantly Muslim town where all Westerners on board were herded to a Dak bungalow. It fell on me to negotiate a reasonable rate for floor space, which we shared with Annie and a Swiss couple.

Off again at 4.30am, we crossed many ravine bridges, each marked with lists of the fallen, illustrating graphically the sacrifices involved in such unlikely road building. Memorials read, "Died on Convoy Duty" or, simply, "Died". Namikala Pass at 3700m, delivered us to new plateaus, each seemingly more desolate. The ride became progressively more uncomfortable and, with long falls edging close to the roadsides, frequently treacherous. The ascents were especially frustrating, hot in one valley, icy cold in the next. A summit sign read: "Highest Point, Srinagar-Leh road: Fatula Pass, 13,479ft" (4100m)!

It was late when we turned into Leh (3500m), at first sighting, one long bazaar street. Groups of smartly dressed Sikhs could be seen, government employees, a large number of monks in long ochre robes, and the occasional freak, looking alarmingly well settled, despite a 21-day limit for tourists. Finding all hotels and the Dak bungalow filled with long-term government lodgers, we teamed up with tiny Annie and a big American (Phil) to rent a second-storey room in a Tibetan house with a clear view of the mountains. To the north, a volcano-shaped hill gave birth to the moon, a little past full, and a cloudless sky reflected the galaxy. Behind *that* hill, we were several times reminded, were the Chinese.

The morning's first port of call had to be the Leh Palace, a half-ruined 17th century structure built in imitation of the more famous Potala in Lhasa, one-time Tibetan home of the Dalai Lama. To reach it, we edged our way around sand slides above a sheer fall. Our reward was views overlooking all Leh. Because of our altitude, the mountain range to the south appeared strangely small, though I knew there were peaks of up to 7300m. Above us, the sky was peculiarly intense, a radiant blue that I recognised instantly from the paintings of Russian artist Nicholas Roerich.

Annie was a super-enthusiast: "Wow! Did you see that? Far out." She was in love with everything and everybody, especially the dzos and the Tibetans. "Jullay! Jullay!" She carried a cane with a metal spike on the end, to evoke sympathy or fear as the occasion demanded. Her desire was to learn Tibetan – one more "trip" for a girl grown up on "happenings". But she was nice.

We came across some drunken soldiers, one of whom shouted, "Piss on that!" in impressive English as we passed. Small children called out, "hippie"! When did that word arrive here? We tried not to stare at the women in their elegant velvets, neat pleats at the back and long black pigtails falling behind. An Indian monk who had been studying in Sri Lanka told us Leh was an awful place after lush tropical forests and coral beaches. He took us to a Tibetan restaurant, where we dined on thukpa, a thick noodle soup with vegetables and meat chunks. It became our favourite meal.

One morning, we caught a bus for Hemis, a noted monastery. Our ride along a still-forbidden section of the Leh-Manali road was halted at a series of incomplete canal walls that a soldier said, when finished, would supply regular water to Leh and the area's other settlements. But the harsh climate meant work was only possible for three months in the year. At present, he said, just five taps serviced the whole of Leh, a town with a population of 7500.

The monastery appeared abruptly over a high rock wall. In its courtyard, a group of monks squatted at prayer and, reluctant to disturb them, we wandered an inner sanctum overflowing with ancient thangkas and Bodhisattva frescoes surrounding a large, golden Buddha. The walk back to the roadway was a long one, and we were too late for a bus. So it was outstretched thumb again and almost immediately we were aboard a jolting army truck, crashing painfully the 35kms back to town.

The next morning, we set off on foot for another monastery, Spituk, taking an unauthorised shortcut through the middle of the military's airport, a field protected by high wire fencing. We entered through a tear. Sentries gestured furiously at us but, before things got out of hand, we were safe on the other side. "No photographs," screamed the signposts, as we struggled manfully up the slope towards the gompa.

A monk introducing himself as Lama Nawong Lobsang directed us down a passage to a platform where he and two other monks shared tea with us. They were just as interested in our attire as we in their bracelets, their bells and their dorjes (thunderbolt symbols of enlightenment). He showed us a collection of fearsome masks, faded thangkas, and a large statue of Hindu deity Kali. A thangka featuring laughing skeletons was more than 1000 years old, he said, though the claim seemed unlikely. The gompa was 550 years old.

Catching our stares, Lama Nawong pointed to a terrible welt running just above his hairline and a deep scar that cut across his neck. The welt, he said, was the result of a blow with a staff, the scar, from a bullet that had nearly taken his life. Both, he said, were courtesy of the Chinese in the fleeing of Tibet. He gave to Annie a gift of a silver bracelet – Annie, whose hair was shaved short, "just like a lama's".

After a hitch home with the ever-agreeable army, Jim and I wandered the streets till we stumbled on a "chang" house. In a veritable museum of old brassware, a tall woman in black waved us to a long, low bench where, sitting alongside a noisy group of befuddled Ladakhis and Indian soldiers, we drank chang. Quite a bit of it – the bottle was left behind for self-replenishments. New for me, a bowl of tsampa was passed round, with the indication we should float its contents on the liquor, and the evening quickly mellowed. Back at our lodgings, Annie was holding court with an elderly Tibetan from Lhasa. She was showing him photographs of the Forbidden City featured in Harrer's *Seven Years in Tibet* and he was enthralled, punctuating his page turns with unintelligible comment. But he did not remember Harrer.

They are a great delicacy, he said

Our bus back to Srinagar was beset with some curious ailment causing lack of power, but we stop-started out into desert, secure in a long line of military convoy. Each time we faltered, the driver and the ticket collector took turns at manually pumping the petrol valve. After Khalsi, we attempted the towering Fatula Pass, from this side, especially formidable. The bus inched upwards via an agonising series of cutbacks till we ground to a standstill just short of the summit.

It was bitterly cold and there was no escape as hours were wasted with mechanical fiddling. As cutting winds swept across us, a young Ladakhi girl impatiently left us, sprinting down a perilous goat track with no apparent destination. Dark now, our driver had the passengers push the bus around for us to head back the way we had come. Free falling, the engine weakly responded. As we re-crossed the bridge before Khalsi, a soldier challenged us and it was only after a long argument he allowed us to continue. All traffic was restricted to prearranged convoy timings. If you reached a point too early, you must wait; if you reached a point too late, again, you must wait! Fortunately, reason prevailed and Jim and I booked into the last available room in the local Dak bungalow.

Of course, we had to share. Our group included an Italian and a

Swiss couple, and an American boutique owner. An argument began over beds that I avoided, finding a place on the floor and falling immediately asleep. Next day, the Swiss woman said to me, "God, I admire you, being able to sleep like that!" But I had the feeling she disapproved. She had observed with distaste the smoking of hash in Leh and perhaps I looked like a smoker of hash!

Waiting for the bus next morning, I sat overlooking the river with an Afghani who had been in Leh selling questionable medical products. I indicated the beauty of some small doves nesting in the cliffs, and he nodded his agreement. "They are a great delicacy," he said. The American, Sue, told me later he had accosted her as she toileted! After a good two hours of toil, we at last crossed Fatula, revving as we reached the high-level plateaus, the drops behind us. Still faltering, we tackled one more high pass, Namikala, entering Kargil in mid-afternoon. We had hoped for a late run to Srinagar but the army would have none of it.

Our previous bungalow stay here was notable for giving us fleabites so, with Sue, we ferreted out a room in a tent, no charge. My smattering of Hindi had me nominated to search out the evening meal, which I did abominably, ordering a plain rice dish with but a sparse chutney covering. I was the only one to finish their plate! We left on time, but the old engine issues returned. Yet we made reasonable time, reaching Dras in morning warmth, happy in the knowledge there was just one more pass before the home stretch of Sonamarg and the Sindh valley.

No one wanted to spend the night in "the coldest valley outside Russia", so there was general horror when the engine cut. We were on the point of despair when three army trucks pulled up and their leader took over the repairs. He was a tall, confident man in a turban and when he insisted on driving the bus, there was no argument. He wasted no time, leaving his own trucks far behind before halting at the top of the Zojila Pass. From there, our old driver back in charge, we crossed the 3600m summit and began the slow drive home.

Ordering tea at a lunch stop, I sought to pay first in case the bus left quickly, but when the price named was suspiciously high, I attempted to walk away. The Sikh proprietor, blind in one eye, grabbed me by the shoulder exhorting me, "Pay"! I handed across what I believed to be the correct price then demanded to see the menu, which confirmed my understanding. Having lost face before a gathering crowd, he walked from sight.

We reached Srinagar in early afternoon, giving us ample time to buy icecreams in celebration of our completed journey. We rebuffed a houseboat owner who echoed earlier greetings of, "Do you know Barry Crump" and refound Ramon. Our shekara driver recognised us with glee – we had not yet paid him – and we were soon again aboard the *Young Cherry Stone*.

For our last day in Kashmir, Jim and I arranged a special evening. We were both leaving India soon and wanted a memorable last meal in celebration. Inviting Sue to join us, we chose "Ahdoo's", a palatial affair overlooking the river, with starched waiter service and cool outdoor terraces. With no liquor served, I made an illicit run around the block, purchasing three bottles of beer and hiding them under our table. My sleight of hand did not escape the attention of our waiter. He urged me not to be too blatant.

We talked of India till the restaurant had emptied, recalling the floods in Assam and Kerala, the droughts in Andhra Pradesh and Rajasthan, the cholera in Tamil Nadu, the smallpox in Bihar, the riots in Patna, the streams of platitudes out of the Lok Sabha (parliament) in Delhi, as well as the poverty, the starvation and the desperation of millions. We also debated the religion, which had affected all of us. Sue wisely argued the importance in our lives of retaining spirit, "oomph", and, as we left, presciently gave us each an Alan Watts' book as a present. We escorted her to her lodgings then returned to our boat in silence. India was nearly done!

God of eternal truth

Amritsar was hot, damnably so. Nevertheless, immediately upon arrival, we set out for the famous Golden Temple of the Sikhs, Harmandir Sahib, "the temple of God".

We were welcomed by an elderly man in a flowing white turban who explained it was his duty to assist because God was one for all people. On his advice, we passed over our shoes, took possession of cloths for head cover, then followed a fast-growing congregation to an auditorium for meditation. This done, we walked a long red jute path, washing our feet at assigned troughs, to a mausoleum bedecked with spires and domes of gold at the centre of a large water tank lake, which we circled. And at precisely 10pm, we watched Sikh bible, the *Holy Granth Sahib*, being transported from the mausoleum in a magnificent gold sedan chair.

Tall Sikh guardians wandered among us in flowing gowns with long, curving swords hung from their hips, familiar bamboo swagger sticks held at the ready. The Golden Temple was dedicated to the blood of Sikh martyrs and these temple policemen served as a reminder of the warrior orientation. It was a tremendous atmosphere: a religion alive in the practice, where poor and rich seemed truly on an equal footing. When Jim and I slept on the jute pathway, no one looked askance. For meals, we attended the temple's huge kitchen hall, where an army of cooks fashioned acres of chapatti in cavernous clay ovens, and sizzling dhal on giant wok fry pans. Twice daily, the temple offered free meals for all. It mattered not whether you were rich or starving. It was a simple meal but a good one, and I wondered why similar couldn't be done in other Indian cities. I had seen a crude soup kitchen in Varanasi, but elsewhere the beggars seemed to be left to their own devices. The honour of renunciation!

When Jim decided to move on, we had one final cup of tea, shook hands and parted – after two months of travel together. I shared a meal with an Irishman and a Frenchman who dithered over whether it was advisable to eat the Indian food and looked forward to being alone.

Progressive Afghan prime minister Daoud Khan (he allowed women to work, study and dispense with purdah) in 1963 ceded power for a "constitutional monarchy". In 1973, however, he overthrew the king – his brother-in-law – to set up a republic that was closely tied to the USSR. 1974: he modernises the army and engages in border actions inside Pakistan. In a few years he will be assassinated, factions of the ruling Afghan Communist Party will fall to infighting, presaging USSR's 1979 invasion, ostensibly to shore up a communist regime. The Khyber Pass is open, though this is short-lived.

XXVI

Sickness in Chicken Street

Pakistan and Afghanistan: collapsed in a Peshawar dosshouse; even iller crossing the Khyber Pass; hepatitis is diagnosed in Kabul; and I endure an appropriate hippie trail ending – spat on in Sydney.

In 1955 Iran banned poppy cultivation and the country's large addict community turned to Afghan opium to fill the gap ... it was only when thousands of Westerners arrived along the hippie trail in the late 1960s and early 1970s that Afghanistan became a major producer (Gemie and Ireland, *The Hippie Trail: A History*).

Out of sight, out of mind

The no-man's land at the Wagah border separating India and Pakistan was frenetic. Continuing hostilities had not halted trade and goods were being transported the length of the kilometre by an army of coolies to waiting trucks at each end.

I caught the bus to Lahore with Englishman, Ian, who was returning home after a month in India. Rural Pakistan at first looked just like rural India, at least in terms of the heat, the rice fields, and the dull, clay villages. Cows and goats wandered unconcernedly among heavy traffic, women carried water pots, and the men drank tea. It slowly dawned that the women were all in purdah.

At the first village we stopped at, a shouting crowd frog-marched a youth across the road. He was shaking convulsively. As it passed from view, I saw another group around another man, sitting in the back of a tonga with blood pouring from his leg, bright red against his white pyjamas, and it was evident he had been stabbed. Welcome to 1974 Pakistan!

Lahore was as I expected: big, dusty, dirty, modern and old, white-washed mosques with loudspeakers, cattle on the streets, occasional glimpses of women peeking from behind doors or under thick black cloth, handsome boys leering, old men staring. It seemed even hotter than Amritsar, which was disturbing, and I was happy to be guided by Ian who knew of a cheap hotel.

The hotel had no water. To bathe it was necessary to walk in our lungis to a nearby barber's shop that had little washroom cubicles in the back. Miniature tanks above had to be filled at the turn of a tap, with a second tap to release water to bodies. The next day was even hotter. The hotel manager assured me that a fortnight more should see a temperature drop, but I was not prepared to linger that long on a promise. One could not eat in this heat, just drink, and drink and drink! The streets were unbearable.

I grew accustomed to comments – "Hello my dear! What is your name?" – but it was difficult to adjust to the grabbing of hands, or the aiming of bicycles in private wars of nerve. Sometimes cars powered towards me, forcing me to leap smartly out of the way. Perhaps I was over-imagining things, but what was certainly not imagined was the hatred of India. Whenever I mentioned I had stayed in India for more than six months, I was looked at with suspicion. "Why?" Equally common questions were, "Have you been to Kashmir? Is there much army there?" But this was just my second day. Pakistan had just won hockey gold at the Asian Games so, for now, there could be no question where superiority lay. Ian was more self-conscious than I, constantly feeling hidden hands and reading contempt on people's faces. "What have *I* done?" he asked. He thought people reacted differently with me. They smiled. I might have mentioned that first I smiled at people! I rarely encountered bad reactions – just occasionally, games.

The hotel manager talked the usual tosh. He did not approve of "free love". When I asked him what that meant, he replied: "Western people change partners every second day." I vainly argued that inner discipline was better than having one's personal life controlled. Vainly in part because I sometimes doubted that myself! I thought of the young women travelling alone who dangerously took "support" as it was offered. But the Oriental so often assumed a polarity: Eastern women were pure, Western, slatternly. It was a simplistic belief that appeared wherever I travelled. And the accusation was always about the women.

There was, however, a point to his moralising. It was the first day of Ramadan, the month of fast, holiest day in the Islamic year. Many of the most memorable events in Mohammed's life had occurred during this period but, rather than a commemoration, Ramadan was intended to be a self-discipline to draw practitioners closer to God. The rich were to learn what it was like to be poor and the cleansing process of a lower food intake was to benefit all. In theory. Excesses during the permitted hours of darkness were legendary!

Ian and I endured the midday sun walking along the city mall. Here stood the inevitable showpiece of a futuristic hotel, a Secretariat, and a long avenue of European-style shopping, with policemen directing traffic and small boys disrupting it. Directed to a room out of sight of religious spoilers, we ate and, later, had all our worries removed as we spied locals eating and drinking heartily, similarly hidden behind canvas awnings. Out of sight, out of mind.

Ian accompanied me to the station – his train was leaving soon after mine – before becoming paranoid upon finding a souvenir he had bought was missing and sprinting back to the hotel. I ate a kebab. It was impossible to be vegetarian here for meat was the staple of the Arab world. "It gives you strength," said the Pakistani. "It gives you unnatural aggressiveness," said the Indian. And it did seem that the Wagah border divide of people the same ethnically, signified a change from the passive. But I was brought up a meat eater too and, as I had discovered, there were more myths extant about Indian spirituality than facts.

Courtesy of my railway concession, I rode second-class for the price of third, which meant padded seats and almost no fellow passengers. The journey progressed slowly and uninterestingly through lowland plains, then changed to a series of tablelands, strangely cut out as if archaeological digs. At each station we halted at there were fewer and fewer vendors, as if the potency of Ramadan was strengthening towards the Pakistan heartland.

As night approached, the police entered my carriage, smiling men with long swagger sticks who asked if I carried "charas". "No sir! I don't smoke! Don't drink! Good Christian – prophet Ysus. Like Muslim." You could win many friends with such a dialogue. One policeman became concerned for my welfare, explaining that there were many bad people about and that I should take care.

House arrest

On the policeman's advice I disembarked at Peshawar's cantonment station rather than the main city stop, because the former had a waiting room where I could sleep the night. The waiting room was closed. But I met Povich here, a short, strongly built man with determined blue eyes, close-cropped fair hair and a mild Cossack beard. He wore baggy Muslim trousers tapered at the ankle and drawn tight about his waist. He told me he was from the German Democratic Republic. He had escaped to West Berlin "in the 50s, when it was easy".

Povich was just one week free after three and a half months in a Peshawar prison. But I gratefully accepted his offer to share the night at his Dak bungalow where he remained under effective house arrest, for all his possessions – car, television, camera and stereo – remained impounded. His room was like a home. He had a typewriter, an over-flowing bookcase, a high frequency transistor, and photos of his girl-friend and child, who had flown home at the onset of his troubles. But he did not have his freedom, and this showed in his face.

Povich's problems had begun in Afghanistan after being persuaded by a fellow German to smuggle cloth into Pakistan. Pakistani Customs had unerringly gone to the precise section of his luggage where he had stored it, and he had been arrested. Cloth? It was almost certainly a euphemism, but I did not press him. He had begun his sentence with 20 days' solitary before being confined to the "hospital ward". It was not thought fitting he mix with the general prisoners. Among the inmates were the abject poor, the old and the decrepit, men long forgotten who would live out the rest of their lives behind walls. They smoked hashish all day, life's sole pleasure, and he had had no one he could talk to. Parts of his story sounded fantastic: his embassy had been lukewarm; he was accused of having CIA affiliations; when an officer hit him, he hit him back… Eventually a friendly Pakistani lawyer had paid his bail – 1500rp – "but I am still a prisoner," he said.

Povich helped me find cheap accommodation at the National Hotel, a three-storey building with a rooftop of cell-like rooms, each with a solitary string bed – no shelf, no window, no ventilation. This was a hotel for freaks, the largest gathering I had seen. On the bottom floor, a black and white television held the attention of bored Germans, French, English, Austrians, Italians, Australians, Americans, beyond number. And Kiwis.

The discussion was almost entirely of travel or of dope, and hash was openly enjoyed. Europe was transferred to Asia behind the doors of a dirty, stone hotel. At intervals, groups of three or four would venture into the adjacent Khyber bazaar and return clutching cornflakes or fresh grapes. And, by stages, the Europeans became more interesting than the locals, sparkling in gypsy gowns, gold earrings, mysterious silks, long flowing beards, curving toe shoes. Small wonder the amazed Pakistanis gathered by the hotel doors and stared!

At 6.30pm, an approximate conclusion of the day's Ramadan fast, I explored the bazaar, a wondrous network of double-storey stalls, part stone, part wood balcony and wood veranda. Beginning right outside the hotel, shops offered curds, meats, fine leather sandals, and exotic bronzeware. It extended like a maze, widening into main streets and narrowing into back alleys, concluding with sprawling arenas of fruit, or the sombre white walls of a mosque.

Everywhere, people were eating. As if a bell had been rung, the plates had been flung down, and now there was a race to force bread and mince down digestive tracts. So I joined in, gulping water between mouthfuls from an old can that was serviced from a garden bucket. Ramadan! We saw sparrows for sale – for food, of course – but we ate pomegranates, guavas and dates. Abruptly, I realised I had not seen a woman – other than Westerners – since arriving, not even in purdah. I was eternally surrounded by virile red beards and fresh-faced boys. In the hotel, I was among an equally bizarre universe of freakish Europeans speaking half a dozen languages – hardly of this life at all.

Very sick indeed

Feeling ill, I slept throughout the afternoon, though later managed to surface at the television hall where WWII spy movie *A Night Train to Paris* was showing. Two Muslim doctors interrogated me ceaselessly about drugs and morality. "Do you know that LSD causes insanity and Parkinson's Disease?" "These men and women, are they married? At night, what do they do?" I saw little of *A Night Train to Paris*!

One of the doctors took umbrage with New Zealand for not opening its borders for Pakistanis and I carelessly snapped that that was a good thing. Then, up to my cell, I pulled the string bed outside into the open air where a bearded German strummed his guitar and the wind blew Europe. I felt very sick now, physically and mentally, and lay motionless. Reading was impossible.

I didn't waken till midday, stumbled to toilet, then bed again. I was very sick indeed. At the Ramadan day's end, I surfaced once more and forced myself to the first stretch of bazaar to eat – one chapatti, one small plate of mince – then returned to the television hall where the fans were turned in on the audience. I soon gave up, climbed slowly upstairs, tried once to vomit and, to prevent myself from fainting, took rest on a concrete ventilation cover. Mid-morning, and I was still sick. Therefore still observing Ramadan! I made it downstairs where I was heartened by a visit from Povich and I managed to walk to the bazaar with him, admiring old Russian samovars and Persian plates with designs like pen strokes. But feeling terribly weak, I soon had to return to the hotel.

The hotel staff included two men who other guests called mad. One was tall and quiet, with a peaceful face; the other, dwarfish and fat, but chirrupy and mischievous. The former visited me in my room, talking with his hands, for he was mute. The latter frequented the downstairs' area, eating all day long, but sharing all he had with the people about him. He teased the girls by throwing garlands of flowers about their necks, offered the men incense sticks and, occasionally, begged. I liked them both. But this morning I heard a German shout, "Get him out of here or I kill him!" and in the afternoon a garland thrown about a neck elicited a gesture of disgust, the flowers thrown to the floor. Not everyone was happy. So I watched television out of which a quivering beard recited the Koran. So I went to bed.

I was barely asleep when a rude knock awakened me and a face appeared demanding money. I had not paid for my room – true – but now was not the time to deal with finances. There was an argument culminating in my slamming the door, which in turn brought the hotel strongman. Being no match for the hotel strongman, I paid, protesting vehemently while making the usual threats to leave! I was far from well.

With a Kiwi and an Englishman, I risked another bazaar visit. Some-where, we parted and, by chance, I found myself outside a bus company selling tickets to Kabul and, on impulse, bought a seat for the day after next. There were many places I had hoped to visit from Peshawar: the famous Swath Valley; the ancient cultures of Chitral; even Gilgit, in Pakistan-occupied Kashmir where the Chinese road entered friendly territory on its way to the Arabian Sea. But all these required an energy I did not possess.

My usual dinner sufficed – a dollop of mince, one roti – then I drowned myself in lassis, drank tea with Povich, and watched television amid the crowd, this night a fantastic mixture of highland villagers and European travellers. Next to me, a bearded German was doing tattoos to earn his fare home. His customers were all Pakistani, delighting in having their names etched across their forearms. His wife contributed to their income by selling books left behind by departing guests – *D-Day* and *The Hound of the Baskervilles*. In the midst of the chaos the manager came across to me and apologised for the last night's unpleasantness: "Ah! Ramadan! Too much water, you understand?" I understood!

I managed somehow to watch a documentary on Afghanistan, showing guns in the possession of everybody, riots where policemen turned a blind eye to violence, and a final scene of a monk's immolation. The country was portrayed in horrible terms. According to the narrative – China excepted – Pakistan was surrounded by enemies. A newsreel showed thousands of Chinese road workers cheering President Bhutto as the Chinese road was opened through to Pakistan. It occurred to me that one might feel a little afraid, knowing 800 million Maoists now had access to the Arabian Sea.

No visa, no police permission

Tuesday, September 24, 1974, the day before I was to leave for Kabul, was my last diary entry. I was now very, very sick, only able much later to piece together snippets of my onward travel from memory. Certainly, the day was lost to me. I remembered only that, exhausted, I was unable to leave my rooftop cell, unable even to walk outside to eat. I experienced feelings of panic that there was nobody to help me. Among desolate freaks, the worst of them perpetually drugged out, I was one of them. Even my allies among the hotel staff had started looking at me with disgust. Or so it seemed.

Peshawar to Kabul was a mere 290km. Travelling at a reasonable speed on a good road, the trip might have taken under three hours. Of course, even before the incredibly dangerous times that would follow, a small thing like the Khyber Pass required a more cautious passage. Crossing the Spin Ghar mountains (Safed Koh) and part of the larger

Hindu Kush ("Hindu Killer" range), the road crossed elevations of more than 1070m. The crossover from Pakistan to Afghanistan, the pass had for centuries been of immense strategic value – including as pathway for invasions of the Indian sub-continent. Subsequent to my travels, the pass opened and closed several times but, more often, it was closed. When a bus service became available in 2015, for the first time in 30 years, it was quickly closed again. In the post-2010 years of renewed Taliban influence, nothing would be as simple as my spur-of-the-moment hopping on a bus.

Terrorists aside, the pass was a tribal area – mainly Mulagori, of Pashtun or Pathan ethnicity – in recent years, impossible to travel without a permit and a special guard assigned for your safety. With a permit to clutch on the Pakistani side, one has had to submit to being driven by tribal police to the border at Torkham, paying – and tipping – for the policeman's return to Peshawar.

A recent online advice reads: "avoid travelling at night, do not accept food from other travellers (lest you be drugged and robbed), ensure you are dressed in Afghan clothes and, at all times, avoid crowds – the focus of bombings or attacks." Such advice of course followed more than 40 turbulent years that included Soviet invasion, civil war among anti-Soviet mujahedin, and post-9/11 American-led wars against the Taliban and its allies.

How did I make such a trip? I have no memory of obtaining police permission or visa for travel. I simply made my own way to border town Torkham, and beyond, by bus. In my parlous state, I would not have taken precautions to look Afghani. But perhaps that came naturally!

I know I successfully crossed into Afghanistan and guess from my earlier mountain travel in the sub-continent that the road up to and through the Khyber Pass, geographically speaking, would have been tortuous, particularly so, for the area's wildness. The bus would probably have stopped for lunch at Jalalabad and certainly again at Surobi, the last big town before Kabul, neither of which I can visualise. My hazy recollection is that I ate nothing during the ride and that I fought a losing battle trying to stay awake for the views or the experience. I had terrible headaches and considerable abdominal pains. That much I know.

An abiding recollection of the pass is of desolation, of high, humped hills and river gorges through cliffs, of shale and limestone. Across the Khyber Gorge, the heart of the pass, there were glimpses of abandoned forts and what I thought were caves, and I wondered at the capacity of the Afghani to overthrow all invaders. This was wild country indeed.

Arrived at Kabul, I struggled to stand outside the bus. My immediate destination was the vicinity of Share Naw and the Central Bazaar, known to travellers as "Kuchi Murgha" – "Chicken Street". How I got there and found accommodation, I have no recollection. Without planning, I am unlikely to have held the name of a freak hotel and can only presume I submitted to a market tout. I vaguely remember a street-level, tiny cell of a room, filled by a single rope-mattressed bed. I also remember a growing sense of despair at finding no friendly face to talk to. Freaks no longer cut it.

The weekend bringing no relief, I forced myself to eat, probably the ubiquitous local naan bread, and little else. If I was of a state of mind to respond sensibly, I might have sought strength in the region's more sustaining "kabuli pulao" (steamed rice with pieces of lamb) or its famous kofta meatballs. I know I drank chai, copiously. I vaguely remember wandering Chicken Street, the very heart of the Hippie Trail. I have since learned that after endless war and colourless rebuilding, the appeal of the street has vanished. I would not have appreciated it but, in the 1970s, this was by all accounts a glorious carnival bazaar selling everything from Afghan carpets to lapis lazuli, saffron, intermixed with colourful fresh fruits and vegetables. Beggars were here, and the street vendors of good Afghan hashish beloved of the "trailers", but I know I was in no mood for drugs and could have out-beggared any beggar.

I was well aware I needed medical treatment, but Fridays were part of the weekend in Afghanistan. Most of my days, I know I spent in bed. Did I think clearly? Clearly not! At some point I shared my plight with my hotel manager but was not referred to a doctor, instead directed to the local public hospital. It is probable that, regardless of actual working days, I perceived the local weekend as my own – Saturdays and Sundays – and stayed close to my bed.

The weekend, however, brought an alarming discovery – I had become extremely jaundiced. A clue? I was at the nadir of a very low ebb, still isolated, still devoid of any sort of comfort. Kafka came to mind, or Dostoevsky's Raskolnikov at his most destitute! Years later, I still had nightmares of my panic and helplessness. I was hardly eating, was gaunt, and had lost a great deal of weight.

Hepatitis A *and* B

Probably on the Monday, I sought out the local hospital. Part of this experience I remember clearly. It involved a walk of somewhere between five and 10km out of town – give or take! But the walk there and back, together with a brief examination, took most of the day. It was a desperate walk, akin in my mind to climbing Mt Everest without oxygen or a marathon without training! I was given tests at the hospital. I know, because I had to return in a few days' time for the results, when my progress to and from was even more tortuous.

My jaundice was obvious and it was no surprise when, on my return to the hospital, I was informed I had hepatitis. They didn't tell me which type and, in a perpetual haze, I didn't ask. But much later, back home, it was confirmed I had contracted both Hep A and Hep B. I'd never used needles in my drug taking, was 99 per cent sure I hadn't contracted it from a sexual partner, but there had been enough examples of sufferers among the freaks from Kathmandu to Goa to here in Kabul, for me to be unsurprised. What shattered me now, however, was what came next – absolutely nothing. I was handed a piece of paper. The doctor disappeared. I was dispensed with.

The document, from the Ministry of Republic (sic) Health, National Medical Health, Republic of Afghanistan, was confusingly headed "Parasitological report". Next to a box inscribed "Date received", scrawled numerals seemed to read, */6/87/9877*, which corresponded to no online translation I have since been able to discover. Its diagnostic columns came under four headings: Protozoa, Helminths, Others, and Blood parasites. Under each was printed a list of causal elements, but none seemed in any way linked to my diagnosis. The first protozoa type marked, however, was "Eut (sic) histolyt", a poorly written abbreviation of Entamoeba histolytica, a cause of hepatitis with distinct liver abscesses.

The alert to blood parasites may have had validity, if only for the susceptibility of hepatitis sufferers to such nasties. "Others" applied to things like occult (faecel) blood, pus, mucous, fat and food; "helminths" or "helminthic infections" were infections from worms, but also viral. None of this was a help to me as, once again, I walked the long miles home. I was absolutely spent, exhausted, and at the end of my tether. With no one to talk to, I made what seemed to be the only possible decision – to fly home.

Spat on in Sydney

Without the wherewithal from Kabul to phone or cable, I was alert enough to my jaundice and smart – or silly – enough to struggle to the Chicken Street market to purchase a pair of dark sunglasses. I did not want to be refused access to an aeroplane because of the tell-tale signs of my eyes. I cannot remember buying a ticket, but I do remember the terrible price for 1974 – more than NZ$800! Russian airline Aeroflot did not question my appearance; they did accept my money. I was booked, Kabul-Sydney-Christchurch.

I think I flew out on the morning of the 5th, possibly late on the 4th. It was certainly October, and certainly 1974. I have the day's date from a very faded date stamp on an international telegram I sent from Sydney International Airport. To read the "5" required uncertain online polishing. I have no recollection of the flight. My memory of Sydney is slightly clearer: of a packed transit lounge, huddled on the floor in my Indian pyjamas, clutching my life's possessions close to me in my Nepalese shoulder bag. I know I managed to send that telegram, for it is in my possession. It reads:

"RETURNING TIRED OF TRAVELLING SYD CHC QF326 TONITE".

I have one other enduring memory of Sydney or, at least, its airport's transit lounge: I was spat on. I caught just a glimpse of the noble gentleman as he expectorated, the wet blob catching me on the side of my face. My reaction was to huddle, foetal position, which would have reinforced all his dearly-held prejudices. I had no energy to respond. No one came to my aid.

At Christchurch, I was met by my mother and brother. The memories grow stronger here: they tiptoeing about me as if scared to upset me; back at our Brooklands home, brother Ken going through my minimalistic bag and extracting my solitary towel, a small rag with a huge hole in the centre; and, for the first time in aeons, a comfortable bed! I had progressively divested myself of possessions, to the point where I had only the Indian pyjamas I was dressed in and one change of underpants. Anything not worn was contained in my Nepalese shoulder bag. Which wasn't much. In Asian heat, it had become possible to wash my clothes and wear them as they dried.

Over the next few days, I was channelled to a good doctor and the result was a proper diagnosis – and six-months' quarantine at my mother's Brooklands' home, 18kms north of Christchurch. She tied twine around the handles of the cutlery to ensure they were never shared, and my plates were similarly kept separate. But I can't remember getting visitors.

And me now

Looking back after nearly 50 years, I marvel how almost everywhere I visited on the trail was in the throes of momentous change. Wars were being fought, new countries being formed, and new power blocs arising, all within the sight of a new, anti-war generation that was hungry to be heard and to make its stamp. To young eyes, it seemed as if the world was emerging from a dark chrysalis. The perception was, as books like Reich's *Greening of America* rather too-hastily affirmed, positive change was just around the corner.

But despite its avidity for mind-improving drugs and spiritual searching, the nobility of the "hippie generation", let's face it, was a myth. As with every other labelled group of humans, the "beautiful people" still stole, still looked for perks, still behaved selfishly, at least in similar ratios to the others. The most extreme of them were very familiar on the trail: starry-eyed young women and men leading puppies on leashes, before ditching them, religion-trippers looking noble beneath blankets or in pyjamas or saffron robes. Some matted their hair in the manner of holy men. Of course, as in any grouping, many too were wonderful people, with wonderful ideals and idealism. But no better world has emerged since, no utopian path begun, no end to nonsensical wars and nonsensical politicking achieved.

There were some good outcomes emerging from my sphere of travel, not the least being that Angkor Wat emerged from the Khmer war unscathed. And despite continuing skirmishes, outright war has not broken out again between India and Pakistan, or with China. But the continuing tragedy that is Burma, now Myanmar – the cruelties inflicted on the Rohingya people – provides an unpleasant counter. So too, do the excesses of fundamentalist Islam, and of the West's excessive and dishonest responses. Not to mention the West's burgeoning white supremacy movements. Along with a cult of authoritarianism, religious intolerance, it seems, is everywhere thriving.

As far as individual OEs go, the experiences of this particular Kay One Double-U One, were superbly worth it, at the very least cementing a worldview that humans are pretty much the same everywhere, from good to bad, with a range between of every other extreme of human nature, regardless of ethnicity. It is hard to understand how anyone who has travelled deeply, with eyes open and a willingness to listen could be racist or intolerant of other beliefs.

It could be argued that the hippie invasion portrayed in literature, film and the news media, if with a basis at all, represented at least a positive outpouring of idealism or, at worst, was a harmless blip in history. Back in New Zealand, as I struggled with my hepatitis, my meditation practice became patchy and, for long periods, forgotten. When my isolation ended, I briefly took drugs again, but minimally, and nothing stronger than marijuana. I still adhere to a Buddhist *philosophy* that emphasises good living in *this* life over faith and idolatry, and sporadically enjoy the calm its meditative practice provides.

Very slowly, my health improved and life achieved some sort of normality. When my jaundice and sickness subsided, I belatedly turned my thoughts to making a living. I spotted an advert for a librarian at the Canterbury Public Library and was hired to work as a cataloguer. It wasn't really me, but I absorbed the requisite research skills and nobody minded a year down the track when I quit to begin study at Canterbury University, for a Bachelor of Arts majoring in English and Sociology and, subsequently, a Graduate Diploma in Journalism. My constant writing throughout Asia had at last found some practical use!

My first journalism job — given to me after I broke nationally the details of how the first halal kills would be performed in New Zealand freezing works — was with the *Christchurch Press*. I met and married then occupational therapist, Sally Tye, and moved with her to Wellington, beginning agency work with the now defunct *New Zealand Press Association* where I helped shore up a stretched newsroom at the time of the tumultuous 1981 — apartheid — Springbok rugby tour. And at the end of 1981, with company this time, I began a second big OE — through Europe and the Americas.

Sally and I bussed and hitchhiked through South America, the United States, and the home counties before finding work in London, she as an Occupational Therapist, I as editor of a specialist management magazine, *Catering and Hotel Management*. This was hardly *The New York Times*, but I learned new skills and, when the magazine went bust, I had impressed enough to be headhunted by its competitor, *Catering Management*. When that publication too folded, we resumed our travels, around Europe, this time with a new-born in tow — Alastair Matthew. Unsurprisingly, this was a very different sort of OE than previously: we had a car and a tent, and drugs were not on the horizon. At the start of our trip, Alastair was not yet potty trained.

I kept writing my diary, covering events of intense interest to us but of no wider interest than those experienced by thousands of other New Zealanders and Australians. Eventually, the family of three returned to Wellington, where Sally forged a new career in communications and I knuckled down with the then *Dominion* newspaper.

Among many journalism highlights, I covered the 1987 Fiji coup, the 1990 Aramoana serial killings, the long-lasting Peter Ellis child abuse saga, and the coinciding "satanic abuse" social panic that, like much of the Western world, infected Aotearoa. In Fiji I was arrested twice, once when my cameraman Simon Townsley and I surreptitiously recorded troop movements, and again when I was spotted on the roadside interviewing some Indian children. Back in Wellington, I was assaulted by a soldier who caught me rummaging through classified Defence documents prematurely revealing New Zealand Defence's withdrawal from Singapore that had been mistakenly thrown out with the rubbish. For a time, I had the health beat, then crime, before tackling a suddenly-significant environment and science. I was the only print journalist to cover the world-leading Royal Commission on Genetic Modification (*RNZ's* Veronika Meduna had broadcast covered).

When *The Dominion* was shut down (or *merged*, depending on one's perspective), I worked briefly freelance, before accepting a lectureship with Massey University's post-graduate journalism programme where I taught and researched for another 13 years, along the way earning a post-graduate diploma in business administration, and a Masters of Management (Communication). My thesis for the latter was on news media plagiarism.

For eight years, I exalted in the challenging role of being the journalists' (Engineering, Printing and Manufacturing Union, now E Tū) representative on the NZ Press Council (now Media Council) overseeing industry ethical standards. With executive director Mary Major I rewrote the council's Statement of Principles to encompass an emerging online news arena. I was responsible for it being given a Māori name: "Te Kaunihera Perehi o Aotearoa", though the move from "Press" to "Media" Council has seen this subsequently change to "Te kaunihera ao pāpāho o Aotearoa".

I continue to take a great deal of vicarious pride in the achievements of my son Alastair, a film and television online editor whose work has extended well beyond New Zealand shores. Now with his own company, his lengthy IMDb page highlights range from the *Lord of the Rings* to arguably New Zealand's most highly rated television drama, *Outrageous Fortune*. He has produced a full-length feature film, *Jake*, and been a regular achiever at the film industry's annual 48-hour challenges. He has all the qualities I could wish for in a son, fiercely opposing racism, sexism, homophobia et al, evidence that travel per se is not the only path towards self-betterment.

In my senior years, I have endeavoured to keep the adventures going, albeit more sedately. Courtesy of Asia New Zealand, I had a spell teaching journalism in Shanghai; and courtesy of Antarctica New Zealand, was privileged to visit the southernmost continent. With my brother Ken, I rode the Trans-Mongolian railway, climbed Mt Kilimanjaro, visited the great game reserves of Tanzania (Serengeti, Ngorongoro), and travelled extensively through Egypt and China.

I have also grown older. In 2015, after being diagnosed with prostate cancer I had a radical prostatectomy that ended with a scare when I collapsed post-surgery in the shower. I returned to health with a regime of walking, spurring myself on with an obsession for picking up litter, which continues. The *Dominion Post* called me "Wellington's first litter crusader". It was an obsession that added to my woes, however, when, reaching among a patch of rough grass, I stabbed myself in my right eye, tearing a cornea. Two surgeries and several years later, it still required treatment. It was also a tipping point. I retired from lecturing at age 67 and, a couple of years later, moved to Auckland to be close to family.

Nearly 50 years after my trail adventure, without quite understanding how it has happened, I am teetotal, vegetarian and don't use drugs. I still meditate sporadically, however, and, without labelling myself, still hold to the precepts of the Buddhism I imbibed on my travels. And to maintain a sense of purpose and self-worth post-journalism? Well, I continue to pick up litter! A 2020 article in community rag *The Hobson* refers to my "wonderful obsession" …

Made in the USA
Columbia, SC
08 September 2021

44833697R00163